D1447362

THE SASANIAN EMPIRE AT WAR

THE
SASANIAN
EMPIRE
AT WAR

*Persia, Rome,
and the
Rise of Islam,
224–651*

MICHAEL J. DECKER

WESTHOLME
Yardley

Facing title page: Unidentified Sasanian ruler depicted on horseback. Note the panoply typical of Persian heavy cavalry, with the long lance, quiver at his side, and armored front of the horse. The prominence of the shield carried on the left hand is important, as it is often assumed that these were rarely used by Sasanian cavalry. (*Philippe Chavin*)

©2022 Michael J. Decker
Maps by Tracy Dungan ©2022 Westholme Publishing

All rights reserved under International and Pan-American Copyright Conventions. No part of this book may be reproduced in any form or by any electronic or mechanical means, including information storage and retrieval systems, without permission in writing from the publisher, except by a reviewer who may quote brief passages in a review.

Westholme Publishing, LLC
904 Edgewood Road
Yardley, Pennsylvania 19067
Visit our Web site at www.westholmepublishing.com

ISBN: 978-1-59416-369-2
Also available as an eBook.

Printed in the United States of America.

Contents

Contents

Illustrations

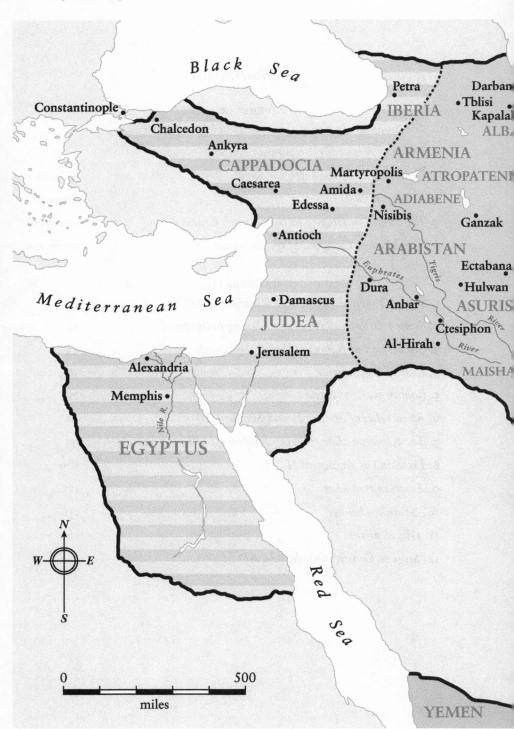

Black Sea

Constantinople

Chalcedon

Ankyra

CAPPADOCIA

Caesarea

Edessa

Antioch

Mediterranean   Sea

Damascus

JUDEA

Jerusalem

Alexandria

Memphis

EGYPTUS

Petra

IBERIA

Darban

Tblisi

Kapala

ALBA

ARMENIA

Martyropolis   ATROPATENI

Amida

ADIABENE

Nisibis

Ganzak

ARABISTAN

Euphrates

Tigris

Ectabana

Dura

Hulwan

Anbar

ASURIS

Ctesiphon

River

Al-Hirah

River

MAISHA

Nile R.

N

W — E

S

Red Sea

0   500

miles

YEMEN

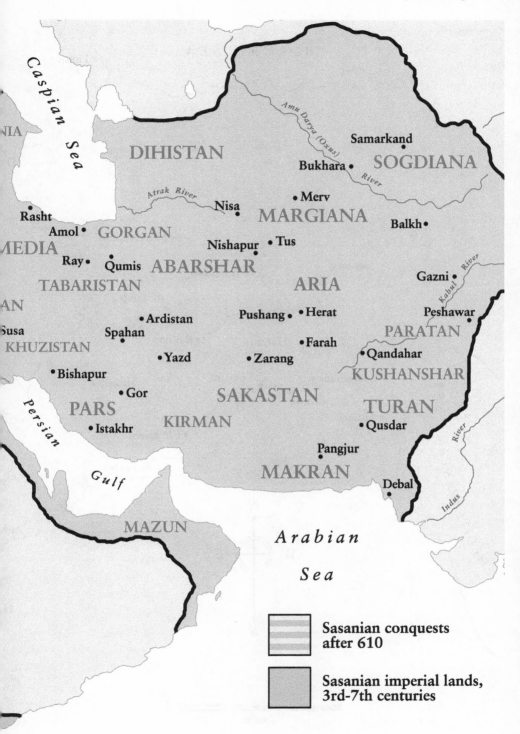

Caspian Sea

NIA

DIHISTAN

Amu Darya (Oxus)

Samarkand

Bukhara •

SOGDIANA

River

Atrak River

Nisa •

• Merv

MARGIANA

Balkh •

Rasht

Amol •

GORGAN

Nishapur • • Tus

MEDIA

Ray •

Qumis •

ABARSHAR

ARIA

Gazni •

Kabul River

TABARISTAN

Peshawar •

AN

• Ardistan

Pushang • • Herat

PARATAN

Susa

Spahan •

KHUZISTAN

• Farah

• Qandahar

KUSHANSHAR

• Bishapur

• Yazd

• Zarang

• Gor

SAKASTAN

TURAN

PARS

KIRMAN

• Qusdar

• Istakhr

River

Pangjur •

Persian

MAKRAN

• Debal

Gulf

Indus

MAZUN

Arabian

Sea

Sasanian conquests
after 610

Sasanian imperial lands,
3rd-7th centuries

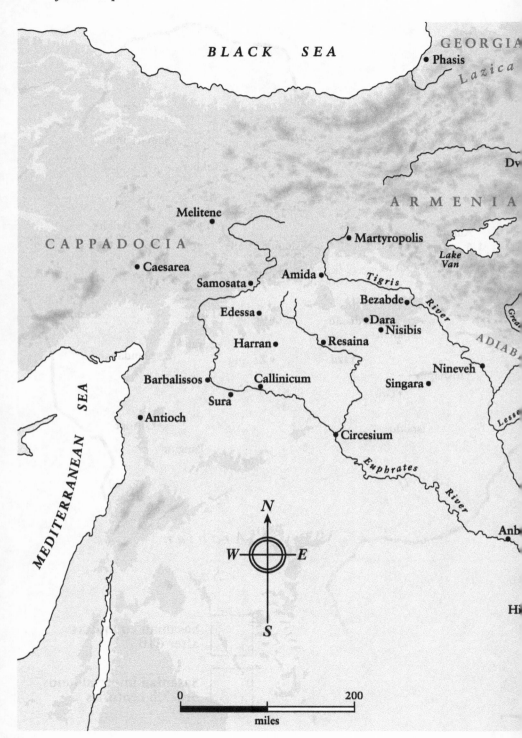

BLACK   SEA

GEORGIA

• Phasis

Lazica

Dv

ARMENIA

Melitene

• Martyropolis

Lake Van

CAPPADOCIA

• Caesarea

Samosata •

Amida •

Tigris

River

Bezabde •

Edessa •

• Dara

• Nisibis

ADIAB

Harran •

• Resaina

Barbalissos •

Callinicum

Nineveh •

Sura •

Singara •

Lesse

• Antioch

Circesium •

Euphrates

River

Anb

MEDITERRANEAN SEA

N

W ⊕ E

S

Hi

0   200

miles

Tiflis

Wall of
Barband

Darband

Lake
Gukcha

ALBANIA

Araxes River

CASPIAN

SEA

AZARBAIJAN

Lake
Urmiya

Ganzak

rbela

Ray

Ecbatana

Diyala R.

Dastagerd

Nihavand

Ctesiphon

ELYMAIS

KHUZISTAN

Kirman

Gundeshapur

Tigris River

Szahan

MESENE

Mesene

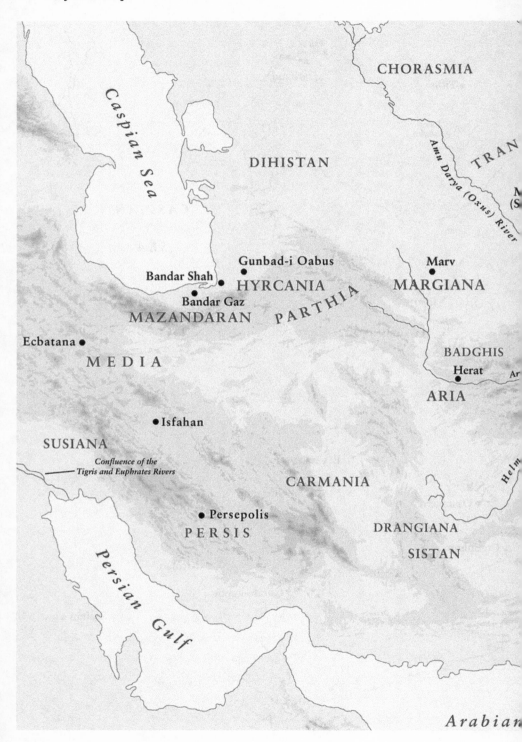

CHORASMIA

Caspian Sea

DIHISTAN

Amu Darya (Oxus) River

TRAN

M
(S

Gunbad-i Oabus

Marv

Bandar Shah

HYRCANIA

MARGIANA

Bandar Gaz

PARTHIA

MAZANDARAN

Ecbatana

MEDIA

BADGHIS

Herat

Ar

ARIA

Isfahan

SUSIANA

*Confluence of the
Tigris and Euphrates Rivers*

CARMANIA

Helm

Persepolis

PERSIS

DRANGIANA

SISTAN

Persian Gulf

Arabian

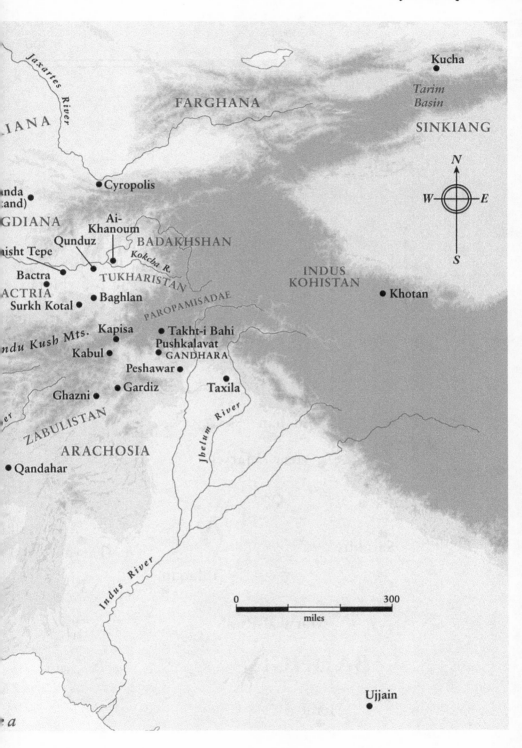

Kucha

Tarim Basin

SINKIANG

FARGHANA

Jaxartes River

...IANA

N
W ─⊕─ E
S

Cyropolis

...nda (...and)

...GDIANA

Ai-Khanoum

BADAKHSHAN

Qunduz

Kokcha R.

...isht Tepe

TUKHARISTAN

INDUS KOHISTAN

Bactra

...ACTRIA

Surkh Kotal

Baghlan

Khotan

...ndu Kush Mts.

PAROPAMISADAE

Kapisa

Takht-i Bahi

Pushkalavat

Kabul

GANDHARA

Peshawar

Ghazni

Gardiz

Taxila

Jhelum River

ZABULISTAN

ARACHOSIA

Qandahar

Indus River

0 ▬▬▬▬▬ 300
miles

Ujjain

...e a

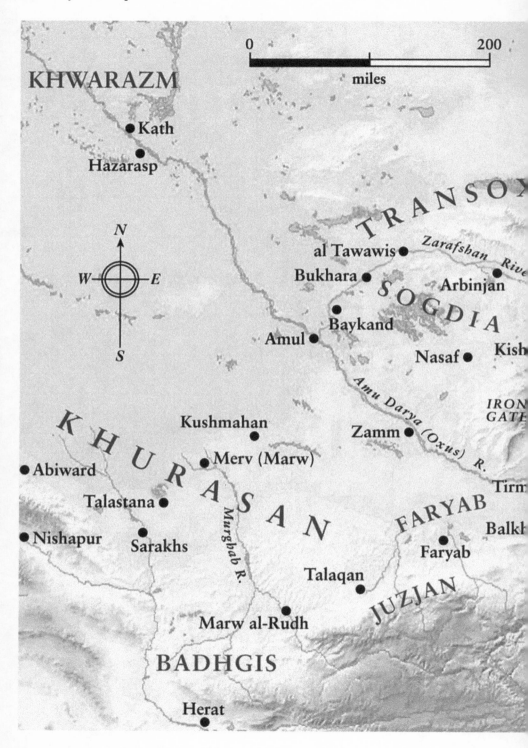

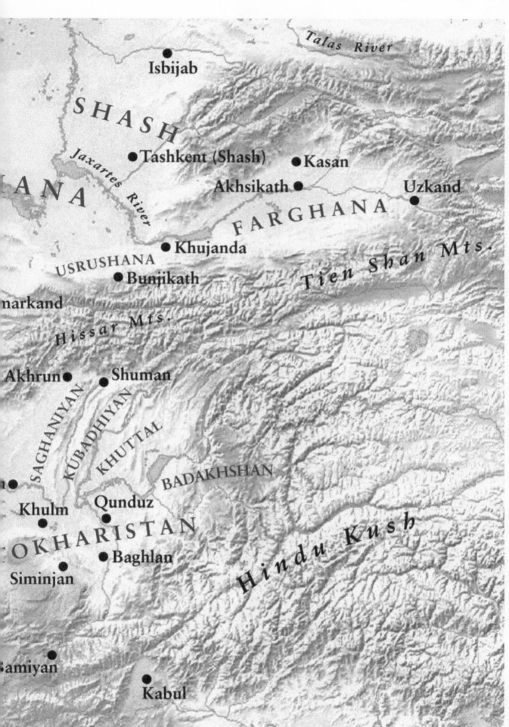

Avars

Black Sea

BYZANTINE

Constantinople

Phasis

Trapezus

ARMENIA

ANATILIA

Caesarea

Nisibis

ME

Ephesus

Edessa

Antioch

Mediterranean

SYRIA

EMPIRE

Damascus

Circesium

Tyre

Ctesip

Sea

LAKHMIDS

Barca

Gaza

CYRENAICA

Alexandria

Aila

Babylon

Tabuk

EGYPT

HIJAZ

N

Medina

W — E

Mecca

YA

S

Red

SARAT

Sea

0   1000

Himyar

miles

M

YEM

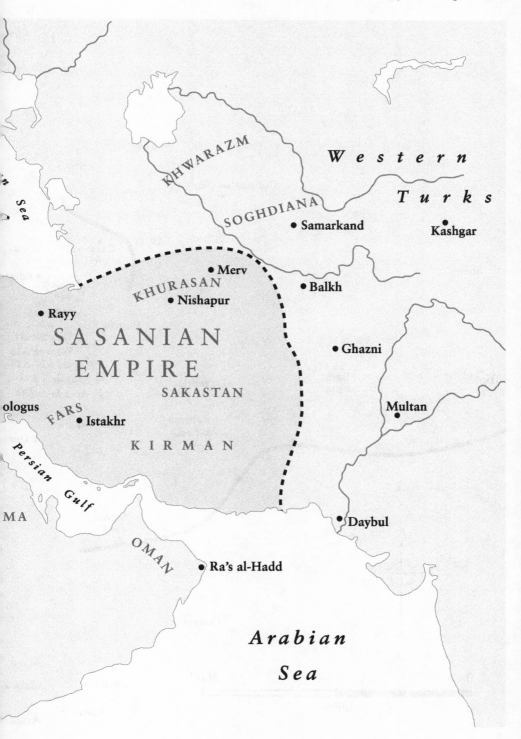

KHWARAZM

W e s t e r n

SOGHDIANA

T u r k s

• Samarkand

• Kashgar

• Merv

KHURASAN

• Balkh

• Nishapur

• Rayy

SASANIAN
EMPIRE

• Ghazni

SAKASTAN

ologus

FARS

• Istakhr

• Multan

KIRMAN

Persian

MA

Gulf

OMAN

• Daybul

• Ra's al-Hadd

Arabian

Sea

Sea

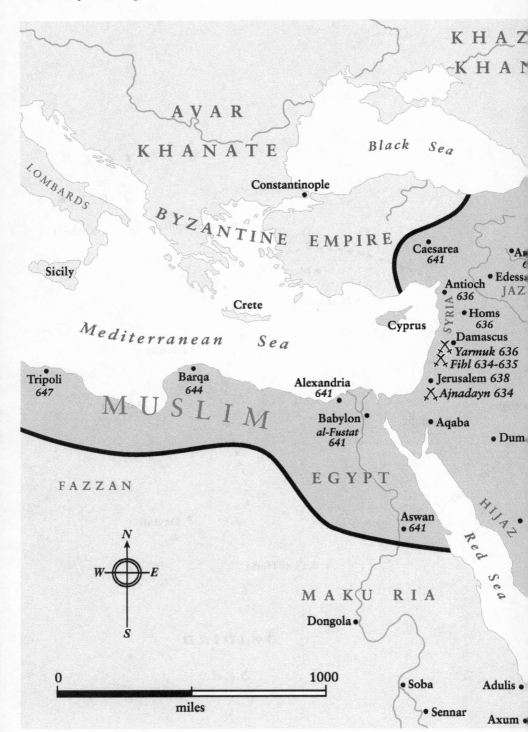

KHAZ

KHAN

AVAR

KHANATE

Black Sea

Constantinople

BYZANTINE EMPIRE

Caesarea
641

A
6

Edess

JAZ

Antioch
636

SYRIA

Homs
636

Sicily

Crete

Cyprus

Mediterranean   Sea

Damascus

Yarmuk 636

Fihl 634-635

Jerusalem 638

Ajnadayn 634

Tripoli
647

Barqa
644

Alexandria
641

MUSLIM

Babylon
al-Fustat
641

Aqaba

Dum

FAZZAN

EGYPT

HIJAZ

N

W—E

S

Aswan
641

Red Sea

MAKU RIA

Dongola

0   1000

miles

Soba

Adulis

Sennar

Axum

Turks

Caspian Sea

KHWARAZM

Bab al-Abwab
642

Bukhara   TRANSOXANIA
• Samarkand

MENIA

Ardabil •
642
AZERBAIJAN

Nishapur
•

Merv
650

Balkh •

Mosul
•

Nihavand
638

Rayy
643

Herat •
650

Kabul •

Jalula
638
✕

Hamadhan
✕ •

Ctesiphon
•

Isfahan
•

Sistan

Kufa
•

disiyya
636
✕

Ahwaz
•

Istakhr
•

Kerman
•

KIRMAN

andal

Basra •

Sirjan •

MAKRAN

SIND

Ator •

CALIPHATE

Persian Gulf

Daybul •

• Yamama
633

OMAN

na

cca
0

Arabian
Sea

• Najran

• Sana
YEMEN
Adan

Introduction

Despite the longevity and success of the Sasanian Empire over the course of its existence from the third through seventh centuries AD, there has not been a great deal written about the empire or its armies. The present volume grew out of my more than twenty years of teaching ancient and medieval military history at universities around the world. With it I aim to fill this gap and to make more accessible the history of an enigmatic and challenging period. Certainly, the success of the Sasanians through most of their history in the face of great challenges to their hegemony, from settled and nomadic powers alike, demands our attention and much further study beyond that possible in an introductory volume like this one.

The Sasanians are named after an obscure figure named Sasan who was probably the father-in-law of Papak, whose son Ardashir (224–242) united the Iranian peoples under his banner and established the Sasanian dynasty. It is possible that Sasan was a mythical figure or even a minor god worshipped during the Parthian era of Iranian history (247 BC–AD 224). Whatever the nature of Sasan, the dynasty named for him would prove to be one of the most important in world history, as the state dominated much of the Middle East for well over four centuries.

Sasanian ideology imbued the House of Sasan with a divine aura of kingship that provided legitimacy in the face of many challengers. Despite being surrounded by numerous rival families whose pedigrees were held more ancient and illustrious than their own, the Sasanian kings managed to craft ideologies and execute propaganda that served them through nearly a half millennium of tumult. The effectiveness with which the Sasanian family had cast themselves as the cement which kept the foundation blocks of the state in place can be viewed in the infrequency of challengers to royal rule from outside the family. Most non-Sasanian claimants to the throne enjoyed only brief success until the nobility and, in later times, the gentry class known as the *dehqans* once more rallied to a Sasanian candidate.

Despite their success in statecraft, which in those days relied heavily on the necessity of military force, the armies of the empire are relatively poorly known. In large part this is due to a lack of surviving documents. Extraordinarily little textual evidence in the language in which Sasanian-era people spoke, Pahlavi, also known as Middle Persian, regarding the dynasty survive. A small corpus of (mostly later) religious, judicial, and miscellaneous texts survive in the form of documents, seals, and inscriptions. Most of our information comes from later sources, predominantly Armenian, Syriac, Latin, Greek, and Arabic. In many instances the authors of these histories are only tangentially informed of the nature and inner workings of Sasanian society, and in more than a few cases, they are openly hostile and prone to suppression, distortion, and other manifestations of cultural bias. These facts make it difficult to separate the wheat from the chaff, and in the cases where valid historical information is transmitted, we often have frustratingly little detail, particularly of the kinds that military historians crave. For example, the numbers of troops, their tactical movements, and precise description of strategy and weapons are treated only anecdotally and are rare.

So why attempt to write a history of the Sasanian great king at war? The Sasanian Persians were one of the great powers of antiquity. Their empire occupied a crucial place in world history and was home to a splendid culture. The Sasanians were the last of the Persian dynasties of antiquity and one that played a significant and vital role in the history of Eurasia for well over a millennium, beginning with the Achaemenid Empire that comprised the largest land empire in history when it peaked under King Darius I (522–486 BC), an era that ended with the fall of the Sasanians in 651 AD. While the Sasanians apparently only had faint knowledge of the Achaemenid kings, they did draw links between their own kings and those of the Achaemenids as well as the remote, mythical realm of Iranian prehistory and mythology. Since the great western rival of the Sasanians was the Roman Empire, we are informed enough from Greek and Roman authors to discern the shape of conflict, at least at the campaign level. As noted, we also possess some information from eastern sources which is vital and allows us to talk further about the military successes and failures of the Sasanians.

In part, this book offers a corrective to what has traditionally been a subject approached from a Western perspective, usually by people whose interests lay principally in the Roman world. While I share in this tradition of Mediterranean studies, my training as an historian and archaeologist in the broader history of the Levant and Middle East has made me more agnostic to many of the readings currently in place within the Western tradition. As will be seen throughout the chapters which follow, whereas some historians have rather blindly accepted the word of Graeco-Roman authors at face value, I am at the least more skeptical of these claims. In the main, a careful reading of history impels us to take an ax to cherished props of ancient history: namely that the Sasanians were a second-rate power to Rome, that their army was unprofessional or even "feudal," a mass of barbarians who came together for war in some ancient violent antecedent to Burning Man, and then dispersed just as quickly.

THE SASANIAN ARMY

Little is known about small units, but the Persians likely organized themselves in a decimal system. The *drafsh* was a commander of a unit with its own identity and banner, apparently a thousand strong. The title *hazarbed* (chief of a thousand), probably commanded a thousand-man brigade. Like other great power militaries that existed over a long span of time, the army of the Shahs underwent changes. Our sources do not permit us a view into all these changes, but the most important, those of Kavad I (488–531) and Khusrow I (531–79) over the course of the sixth century transformed many structures of the military apparatus. These are discussed in more detail in Chapter 7. In summary, after these reforms, the Sasanian army proved even more capable than previously, especially in conducting long-haul, international campaigns which required rapid movement and sustaining forces over broad fronts for considerable lengths of time.

Among the major features of the reforms was the creation of four major commands. Each one of these areas was under the leadership of a marshal known as the *spahbed*, literally "army commander." The spahbed's aid or lieutenant was the *paygosban*, or infantry commander. The *sardar* was chief of the savaran cavalry.

In the quarters system, the northern command focused on the region north of Rayy (near modern Tehran) and stretched across the southwest flank of the Caspian to the Caucasus. Here the Persians fronted both the mountain passes and steppe lands that allowed easy access to Iran to the nomadic tribes that grazed their herds around the Eurasian plains. This territory also braced the northern frontier with Rome in Armenia. In the main the Armenians tended to favor Persian overlordship, as they shared many cultural elements in common with the Persians and traced many of their leading clans back to some common ancestors. However, the rise of Christianity in Armenia from the fourth century onward complicated affairs there, and Rome repeatedly tried to draw the Armenian lords into their orbit, offering as they did strategic territory at the headwaters of the Tigris and Euphrates and access down these into the fertile alluvium of Mesopotamia. The Armenian highlands opened, too, to the grazing lands of Azerbaijan through which ancient Media and the Iranian highlands could be reached.

The eastern command ran astride the northern sector in parallel with the east-west lying Elburz Mountains that form the spine of northern Iran. The western rump of the eastern sector comprised the regions of Tabaristan, amidst the rugged heights south of the Caspian and its eastern neighbor, Gurgan, where the steppe opened north of the mountains. The great oasis city of Merv in the north, Nishapur in the south, and Herat and Balkh in the east anchored the Iranian presence in their territory called Khorasan ("whence the sun arrives"). Khorasan encompassed the southern flank of the Eurasian central steppe that ran from the low mountains of the Chinese borderlands to the Caspian and from the Tien Shan Mountains of the south to the Siberian forests of the north. This is the land of the pastoral nomad; only a handful of oases with fertile soil and water allowed cities to grow up in this belt of land.

Nomadic elements were far from homogenous, but by late antiquity Turkic groups in the main dominated this sea of pasturage through which they moved their herds and flocks. Since they live in the saddle, raised from birth to be expert riders with every fit male capable of military action, nomad armies could quickly swell to a number that could overwhelm the conventional forces of sedentary societies. Armed mainly with composite short bows, nomadic cavalry presented a double advantage of long-range missile fire and extreme mobility. They used swarm attacks, sudden advances and equally rapid retreats, to confuse and harass the enemy. A favorite steppe nomad tactic was the feigned retreat in which nomad cavalry would give way before a strong enemy advance and then suddenly wheel about to confront and envelop the surprised attackers. Against this tactic, the Persians would prove vulnerable time and again.

The spahbed in charge of the western quarter watched over the granary of the empire—Mesopotamia, "the land between the rivers," as the ancient Greeks called it, the two rivers being the great watercourses of the Tigris and Euphrates, thought by many ancient people to have been among the rivers that watered the paradise of the Garden of Eden. Things were less pacific when the Sasanians held sway there. Not far from the great capital of Ctesiphon (which today lies in a suburb of Baghdad) lay the sands of Arabia, inhabited by fractious, independent tribes of Arabic speakers and others. These people, especially the nomadic Bedouin, recognized no authority beyond those of custom and, to a lesser degree, their chieftains. Most of the time, the Arabs of this hot, desolate periphery grazed their flocks among the stubble—sheep and goats offered fertilizer in exchange for grazing—and traded milk, wool, leather, and meat to the settled peoples who generally lacked these things. Like a hive of bees, though, the Arabs could become agitated for reasons that seemed utterly inexplicable to the settled people whose territory they bordered, and then they would unleash holy hell on their neighbors, raiding, kidnapping, and burning paths of destruction where their camels and fine horses would carry them. The Sasanians took steps to secure the soft underbelly of their empire—in the fifth century they built a long series of moats, fortresses, watchtowers, and military waystations to secure this frontier. They also added the dynamic component of allied Arab tribesmen in the form of the Nasrid families of the Lakhmid confederation. This delicate system, carefully tended and maintained, functioned effectively into the seventh century.

By the end of the fifth or the beginning of the sixth century, the Persian army held numerical, or near parity, with its major settled rival to the west, the so-called East Roman or "Byzantine" Empire, with its capital at the great city of Constantinople (today Istanbul). Prior to the rise of the House of Sasan, the Romans had accustomed themselves to invading at will the lands of the Parthians, as evidenced by campaigns of emperors like Trajan (98–117) who led western forces all the way to the head of the Persian Gulf. The Sasanians would prove an altogether tougher nut to crack and, as will be demonstrated, prove at least the equal of Rome on the battlefield. Among the later Sasanians of the fifth and sixth centuries, during times of conflict troop numbers can safely be placed around 300,000—give or take 10 percent—when one considers the long linear defenses to north and south to be garrisoned and requiring about 150,000 men.[1] To this number should probably be added a number of elite guard units stationed at Ctesiphon and attached to the person of the Great King, charged with defense of the city and the royal palaces.

Although our historians provide us frustratingly few figures, when they do provide numbers, campaign armies of twenty to thirty thousand are most frequently seen. When needed, the armies of the shah could be brigaded into (by ancient standards) truly large armies of sixty thousand. These facts of such large forces, as well as their standardization and professionalism, have recently been reinforced by the discovery of large Persian campaign bases or marching camps from throughout the empire. Those along the Gurgan Wall, such as that called "Fort 4," probably built in the fifth or sixth centuries, are impressive in their size and organization, connoting the presence of a professional force with great capabilities. Fort 4 covered 5.5 hectares (13.5 acres) and was protected by a wall and thirty-two towers. Internally it was divided into regular rectangular barracks blocks with spaces for supply and storage. At Qaleh Kharabeh a marching camp of forty-one hectares (101 acres) could have easily accommodated ten thousand troops on the move.

Sasanian recruits were not only drawn from the noble families and the gentry of Iranian ethnicity. Iranians provided the infantry, pages, and work details that supported the logistics and siege capabilities of the army. The Medes, comprised of Iranian tribal groupings who migrated into the region of what is today western Iran, Iraq, and Azerbaijan around 1000 BCE, had challenged the Assyrian Empire in the eighth century and become an integral part of the Achaemenid Empire. Median peoples were fully integrated into the empire and provided all manner of troops, but their main contribution was apparently in the domain of infantry and foot archers. Along the southern shores of the Caspian, Iranian-speaking Daylamite tribesmen provided heavy infantry units during the later years of the empire and, while close in language and culture, these regions were only loosely under Sasanian control.

The Sasanians also recruited peoples from the Caucasus, especially among the Laz and Albanians in the west. Most prominent, however, were the Armenians who provided valued horse archers and heavy cavalry to the armies of the Great King. At most times, at least fifteen thousand Armenian cavalry were available to the Sasanians. The Sasanians also recruited troops from among their eastern neighbors, including the Turkic Kushans and Hephthalites and these, too, would have been predominantly horsemen. Along the southern desert frontiers of Arabia, the Sasanians employed Arab infantry and cavalry contingents.

The primary offensive arm of the Sasanian era was the cavalry. Being trained as expert horsemen from boyhood, the Persians fielded superb horse soldiers. Aside from the cultural markers of wealth horses offered to those who bred and trained them—like nineteenth-century European arms—the expense of maintaining and equipping a cavalrymen marked the individual trooper from his lower-class comrades. Pragmatically, too, the Sasanians were people with a deeply ingrained love of horses that arose from their own days, deep in the recesses of history, when Iranian tribes roamed the central steppes of Asia as nomadic herders. The Sasanians might have been many generations removed from this nomadic life, but it nested within their DNA nonetheless.

Sasanian heavy cavalry, the cataphracts or clibanarii in the Roman sources, were called *savaran* in Middle Persian (Pahlavi). Heavily protected with a full body covering of armor, they were armed with a long, two-handed lance as their primary weapon. Arms and legs were protected by laminated armor, overlapping bands of iron fixed on leather backing or by small, overlapping iron plates sewn on a leather backing. This scale armor could also be used to cover the chest. The Persians also used lamellar armor in which small, hardened leather or iron plates were rigidly locked to one another using a system of leather knots that made a strong defensive covering. They wore helmets mostly of spangenhelm type, common over considerable portions of Eurasia. The spangenhelm was a multi-piece helmet riveted together and often with cheek guards. The most elaborate of these headpieces included face coverings of sheet metal or mail.

Although the lance was their main weapon with which they brought home devastating massed charges, contemporary accounts also indicate that the savaran carried secondary weapons, including sabres or broadswords and bows. Swords of just over one meter long were common, and the quality of steel in these blades could be extremely high, with archaeological evidence for the production of high-carbon crucible steel at Merv.

In the early years of the empire, at least, the savaran were drawn from among the seven elite families of the empire, foremost among whom were the Sasanians. These *wuzurgan* (noble families) had Aryan roots, and aside from the Sasanians, most traced their origins deep into the Parthian era as true-blooded Aryans. These families held power as regional lords in different areas of the empire; their support to the House of Sasan was vital to the survival of the regime. After the reforms of Khusrow I, discussed in Chapter 7, the gentry classes of the *dehqans* were admitted into the savarans for which they were provided land allotments sufficient to support their requirements for quality mounts and equipment. This move on the part of the shah permitted the expansion of Sasanian heavy cavalry.

We have scant information about the elite units of later Persian cavalry. We do hear of a unit called the Immortals, said to have numbered ten thousand men, whose existence is debated. If true, this unit's existence was inspired by Sasanian knowledge and reverence for the ancient Achaemenid Persian Empire, once the largest in the world, that ruled the Middle East for two centuries (553–330 BC). Other elite guard units were raised by Khusrow II (590–628), one called Khusrow's Own (*Khusrowgetae*) and The Victorious Ones (*Pirozetae*). Neither of these units were likely to number more than a thousand combatants.

Like their neighbors on the steppe and to the west, most Persian mounted soldiers were horse archers first and foremost. The mobile platform afforded by a well-trained horse gave these soldiers considerable advantages: speed of movement, the ability to strike the enemy from a distance, and, if pressed, the chance to escape. As the years wore on, medium cavalry, probably armored but reliant mainly on the bow, were never supplanted. Indeed, it is difficult to know what to make of the description offered of the late Sasanian army in the late sixth-century Byzantine military manual called the *Strategikon*, where certain characteristics ascribed to the Persians are puzzling. Since the *Strategikon* is attributed to the emperor Maurice (580–602) who spent a good deal of his career campaigning against the Persians, it is difficult to question the more puzzling assertions in the text, which remains one of our few detailed discussions of Sasanian arms.

Book XI is dedicated to meeting the Persians in battle. They are described as formidable when laying siege but even more formidable when besieged. They hid injuries and admirably endured the hardships of war. Skilled at using conditions to their advantage, in summertime the Persians tended to attack in the heat of the day. Like the Romans, the Sasanians drew up their armies into three equal bodies, center, right, and left, with a stronger center reinforced by four or five hundred select troops.

> They wear body armor and mail and are armed with bows and swords. They are more practiced in rapid, although not powerful archery, than all other warlike nations. Going to war, they encamp within fortifications. When the time of battle draws near they surround themselves with a ditch and a sharpened palisade.[2]

This description can be corroborated by other sources. The sixth-century historian Procopius asserted that Persian archery was rapid but not as powerful as that practiced by the Romans. During the Arab conquests, the use of fortified positions was a standard part of Sasanian warfare, and the discovery of large fortified marching camps also indicates such practices were standard. More difficult to reconcile with what we know from other sources are the assertions that the author of the Strategikon makes regarding the composition of Persian cavalry in which they are disturbed by:

> ... very carefully drawn-up formations of infantry, by an even field with no obstacles to the charge of lancers, by hand to hand combat and fighting because volleys of arrows are ineffective at close quarters, and *because they themselves do not make use of lances and shields.*[3]

As noted and known from illustrations, especially the monumental carvings of Sasanian kings described in the chapters that follow, the two-handed lance wielded by a heavily armored warrior was a staple of the savaran heavy cavalry. The lack of shields is corroborated by the visual evidence; while late Sasanian horsemen may have used bucklers attached to their shoulders, there was no easy way to cope with a shield alongside the use of the long and heavy two-handed lance. Whatever the reason, Maurice's emphasis on Persian tactics as relying almost exclusively on volleys of arrows delivered from organized and disciplined lines of cavalry seems out of place. It may well reflect developments of the later Sasanian Empire, or it could reflect the unique experiences of the emperor in confronting the Persians. This question must remain unanswered for the moment, but if the testimony of the *Strategikon* is accurate, then perhaps the foundations of the late Sasanian army had fundamentally transformed.

As time progressed, the Sasanians fielded heavy infantry elements, especially from the Daylamites, although the quality of Persian foot soldiers varied widely through time. Our clearest window into the equipment and manner of fighting of Sasanian foot soldiers comes only in the later period when Daylamite mountaineers formed a conspicuous element in Persian armies. That they were singled out for comment likely indicates that these infantry were exceptional, and we should not consider that the bulk of infantry cohorts resembled them. Likely, the foot soldiers of the line remained lightly armed, as they had been for centuries, with large goat-hide shields and armed only with spears.

The story of Sasanian martial success spans more than four hundred years and is replete with great victories and catastrophic defeats. In the pages that follow, we shall see how the armies of the King of Kings, as the head of the Sasanian state was named, used his armies to forge and unite his vast domains.

CHAPTER ONE

The Rise of the Sasanian Empire

B y the third century of our era the Parthian Empire had held sway over much of the Middle East for more than three centuries, having risen in the wake of the conquests of Alexander the Great. A confederation of Iranian-speaking tribal groups from the region of Parthia in the northern regions of Iran and spearheaded by the tribe of Parni, this Iranian confederation dwelled in the region between the Oxus and Jaxartes Rivers but soon moved south to challenge the successors of Alexander. Alexander had, by conquest of arms, opened up the whole of Mesopotamia and southern central Asia to Macedonian settlement, and the two great rivers would ever after resonate in history as the frontiers of Hellenic culture in Asia. Less than a century after his death, however, the dynasty founded by Alexander's great general Seleucus I Nicator ("the Victor," 305–281 BC) had lost its grip on the eastern quarters of their empire. Powerful governors (satraps) rebelled in Parthia, in northeastern Iran, and in Bactria anchored on the valley of the Oxus. The Parni, now led by King Arsaces I (247–211 BC), wrested the region of Parthia from the local Seleucid authorities and there established their kingdom. The Seleucid counterattack was late in coming and ineffectual; thus, under Arsaces, the seeds of the Parthian Empire found fertile ground. Rallying first the Iranian-speaking peoples who then dominated the regions from the Caspian to Afghanistan, and then a host of non-Aryan (Iranian) peoples, the Parthians continued to grow their power and influence. Under the energetic

Mithridates I (ca. 171–132 BC), the Parthians extended their authority in the east, against the Macedonian successors in Bactria and nomadic groups, as well as in the west, against the Seleucids and local princes. Through a series of successful campaigns, Mithridates carried the Parthian banner to the shores of the Persian Gulf and had himself crowned king in Seleucia, which itself had replaced Babylon as the political center of Macedonian rule. Succeeding generations of Parthian kings pushed the boundaries further afield to both east and west, where they clashed with new arrivals in the region, the mighty Romans.

In 53 BC, in the dusty plains of Carrhae, where centuries later the Islamist forces of ISIS installed themselves in a reign of terror, the Parthians met a Roman invasion led by the richest man in Rome, the notorious plutocrat Marcus Licinius Crassus. Crassus, who along with Julius Caesar and Pompey formed a junta of strong men known as the First Triumvirate, thirsted for a conquest that would put him on equal footing to his two colleagues; although Crassus had defeated the great slave revolt of Spartacus in 71 BC, his laurels did not shine so brightly as those of Caesar or Pompey. In 55 BC, Crassus left Rome under a storm of acrimony. Led by the famous lawyer and orator Cicero, Crassus's political enemies thwarted his attempts to gain the approval of the Roman Senate for the campaign. Rather than receiving the blessing of the people, Crassus marched out of the city only to find one of his enemies, Ateius Capito, calling down the most horrific of curses on him in the ritual of public execration. In light of what was to follow, Capito's imprecations would loom large in the popular imagination.

As governor of Syria, Crassus had access to one of the wealthiest provinces of the Republic, and he promptly raised troops from throughout the Mediterranean world and Armenia. The Roman move was well timed. The Parthians were in turmoil, roiled by civil war that had raged since 57 BC. Following an inconsequential campaign in 54 BC, Crassus mounted a drive into Parthian territory with a powerful army at his back. Seven legions formed the heart of the Roman host, upward of thirty-five thousand heavy infantrymen, most of whom were seasoned veterans. Alongside him marched a host of allies, including four thousand light infantry, four thousand light cavalry, and six thousand Armenian heavy cavalry sent by the Armenian King Artavasdes (55–34 BC). Artavasdes allegedly offered a much larger force to Crassus if the Roman would agree to mount the invasion through Armenia, where the troops could be more easily supplied and where the Parthians would be at a disadvantage in the mountainous terrain. Crassus refused. He preferred the direct route, through the desert country of eastern Syria and across the Euphrates into Parthian territory, lands in which the Romans had campaigned the prior year and with which they were thus somewhat familiar.

While the Roman host pushed eastward, the new Parthian king, Orodes, marched northwest to attack Artavasdes and cut off support from that quarter. Meanwhile his general, Suren (a member of the noble house of the same name, called "Surena" in the Latin sources), victorious over Orodes's rival the prior year, moved to confront Crassus. At Carrhae, the armies clashed. Despite being outnumbered four to one, the Parthians, who were all cavalry, used their mobility to devastating effect. Their horse archers peppered the Roman ranks with arrows and kept them from closing to engage. Surrounded by the enemy and suffering heavy casualties from the deadly Parthian missile fire, the Romans formed a testudo, in which the infantrymen locked their large shields together. While protecting them from the hail of projectiles, the infantry testudo made the Romans virtually immobile, and Surena ordered repeated charges by his cataphracts. These troops were Parthian heavy cavalry, encased in armor, equipped with lances and bows, and able to drive home a powerful charge. The Parthians charged repeatedly, rending portions of the Roman line and demoralizing the fading men, who, exposed to the intense heat and under constant attack, were unable to decisively engage the foe.

Crassus's son, Publius, was sent with his loyal elite Gallic cavalry troops to attempt to drive off the Parthian horse archers, but the Romans suffered the fate of many enemies of the Parthians, who employed the ages-old steppe tactic of the fighting retreat, in which the horseman was able to cover his withdrawal by shooting behind his horse; this is the famous "Parthian shot." By nightfall, his son dead and his army incapacitated, Crassus withdrew. On the next day, during a parlay, a skirmish erupted that led to the deaths of the Roman commanders, and the bulk of the Roman troopers were captured as they attempted to retreat.

Though it has been told many times, the story of the Battle of Carrhae illustrates several key points. While it is not proof-positive for the superiority of cavalry over infantry, the Parthian victory shattered the myth of Roman invincibility and demonstrated that expert and well-led cavalry could neutralize excellent Roman foot troops. Until that day, the Roman legions, with their close order and superb discipline, had carried the eagle over the Near East with near impunity. Over time, the Romans would adapt their armies to the realities of conflict that required mobility and shock from professional heavy horsemen. Certainly Crassus was outmatched by his Parthian opponent; when Crassus hoped his soldiers could endure the hail of arrows until his enemy ran out of missiles, the invaders' hearts sank on the realization that Surena had prepared a camel caravan to supply his men with fresh darts. Though they would fail to press their advantage by invading Roman Syria on several occasions on the heels of their staggering victory, the Parthians would never be able to oust the Romans from Syria and realize their dream of extending their empire to the shores of the Mediterranean. The sensational victory in the desert marked the eastern empire as a foe with which to be reckoned.

In the intervening centuries, Parthian political fractures plagued their empire. The powerful noble families and non-Iranian local princes maintained among themselves and vigorously opposed efforts of the kings of kings to centralize authority over the eighteen kingdoms of the empire. Despite pressing needs to war frequently in both the east against nomadic incursions or local settled powers and in the west against the Roman Empire, the nobility remained fickle and self-interested. War was for their personal enrichment or the defense of local interests, seldom for the profit of king or country. These structural weaknesses manifested on numerous occasions, especially in the listless response of Parthian armies to Roman invasions of Mesopotamia, the heartland in which was moored the wealth of the empire in the form of irrigated agriculture and populous cities.

Beginning in the second century, Roman aggression against the Parthians intensified. In 114/15 AD the Roman emperor Trajan (98–117 AD) fired his opening salvo by plunging into the heart of Armenia, long in the Persian cultural orbit and a crucial ally of the Parthians. For centuries Armenia had been ruled by a line of Arsacid princes descended from Arsaces, the founder of the Parthian kingdom. Trajan annexed Armenia and put to the sword the Armenian king. In 116, having settled affairs in Armenia, Trajan turned the Roman juggernaut on northern Mesopotamia and swooped south on the Parthian capital at Ctesiphon on the Tigris, today about thirty-five kilometers southeast of Baghdad. The Romans invested and sacked the city. The old emperor advanced at the head of his troops all the way to the head of the Persian Gulf.

Parthian power was hardly broken by the invasion, but the Roman incursion proved costly for both sides. Trajan decided to return home with hopes for another expedition to consolidate the Roman hold. On his return to Syria, Trajan lay siege to Hatra, an Aramaic-speaking oasis kingdom in what is today northern Iraq. Here, the Romans suffered their first failure of the campaign. The Hatrenes resisted stubbornly and, aided by the harsh desert climate, warded off the assault. By then, the emperor was facing rebellions within the newly conquered territories as well as the Second Jewish Revolt, which swept the eastern Mediterranean from Palestine to Cyrenaica and stretched Roman resources to their limits. Trajan would not live to see his eastern hopes realized. After suffering a stroke while sailing back to Rome, the old warrior died in August 117.

Hadrian (117–138), Trajan's successor, abandoned the recently won territories in Armenia and Mesopotamia, and peace prevailed between the empires. Yet the Romans refused to yield their ambitions in Armenia and the Parthians refused to give ground; Armenia maintained strong cultural and economic ties and looked naturally eastward. The wars between the great powers engaged in a tug of war over Armenia, with the Romans mostly having the upper hand. Parthian infighting generally played a role in the weakened position of the empire. In campaigns under Marcus Aurelius (161–180 AD), the Roman advance was contained, and in 217, during the reign of Caracalla, a large Parthian army inflicted a serious defeat on the Romans at Nisibis in Upper Mesopotamia. To buy peace, the Romans had to agree to pay a huge indemnity of fifty million dinars.

Scarcely had peace been achieved with the Parthians when internal tremors again shook the empire. The seismic event began in the south of the realm, in Fars, the sun-baked province then under the rule of a local prince named Ardashir, scion of a family who, one tradition holds, owed its fortunes to Ardashir's grandfather, Sasan. While the sources are contradictory, it seems that Papak, Sasan's son or son-in-law (it is not clear), served as a regional lord under the Parthians and likely exercised considerable autonomy.

The first Sasanian kings inherited potent cultural tools that they deftly employed in levering power. Fars had for centuries been a stronghold of Zoroastrian religion, an ancient faith and a key part of Aryan (Persian) identity. Among the basic components of the faith were a belief in the god, Ahura Mazda, who was also the supreme deity of a pantheon of gods. The religion incorporated a strong dualism, indicated in liturgical books known as the *Gathas*, at least some of which were written around the tenth century BC. Individuals must make a choice between service to the spirits of good and evil, which embodied concepts of the truth (*asha*, good/order) and the lie (*druj*, evil/chaos). These ideas had at least some currency in the Achaemenid period (550–330 BC); the Greek Herodotus, the father of history, wrote of the Persians of his day:

> They educate their boys from five to twenty years old, and teach them only three things, to ride the horse, shoot the bow, and speak the truth.[1]

Zoroastrians also venerated fire in their rituals, which symbolized not only the spiritual binary of light as opposed to darkness but light of the mind, of thinking as opposed to blind action of animal instinct, and of the revealing power of truth that destroyed the murksomeness of deception. The adoration of light and fire grew out of ancient conceptions of a divine spark in humans and the family hearth, the source of warmth, comfort, and protection. Each Persian male started a new hearth fire when he established his new household, and the fire was kept burning until his life ended.

Ardashir and his successors also inherited Zoroastrian religious beliefs about kingship, which also can be seen among the dynasties of their Achaeamenid and Arsacid predecessors. Kingly families were chosen by Ahura Mazda who gifted them with royal glory (*farrah* or *khvarenah*), a mystical aura that made one worthy of kingship. Ardashir thus possessed a ready-made ideology through which to claim legitimacy as a divinely ordained successor to the Arsacids. He simply needed to conquer them to prove it.

Ardashir's career likely began as lord of the fort at Darabgerd, a circular city whose formidable mud brick walls stand silent today in the south of Fars. The stronghold lay in a well-favored region, with fertile agricultural land and sufficient water. The provincial city of Jarhom was later famous for its fabrics and carpets, and cotton was probably already grown there in the time of the early Sasanians. Ardashir's rise to power is recorded in later sources and remains hazy, but around 220 he rebelled against the Arsacid king of kings, Artavan IV (sometimes reckoned as Artavan V). Artavan was hardly invertebrate, having first fought and defeated his brother in a civil war in 216.

A year later the king of kings fought a bloody three-day battle against a Roman onslaught at the northern Mesopotamian city of Nisibis. The emperor Severus (193–211) had recently raised Nisibis and nearby Harran (Carrhae) to colonial status, a special privilege afforded to citizens of these settlements, who were recognized as fully integrated within the empire. Normally such changes of status involved large-scale local and imperial investment in architecture and infrastructure. Both cities likely housed substantial Roman garrisons; possibly one served as the base for the recently recruited III Parthica ("Parthian Conquering") legion. After the Roman defeat, the Praetorian prefect and commander of the II Parthica legion, Macrinus, a Berber from North Africa whose portraits show him wearing a large earring, arranged the murder of the emperor Caracalla. Backed by the army, Macrinus claimed the imperial throne. He was the first man not to have attained the rank of senator to hold the reins of the Roman state. His hold on power weak, the army beaten down and restless, and his coffers empty, Macrinus parlayed and, in order to extricate himself from the conflict, agreed to pay hefty tribute to the Parthian shah.

By the time he pressed on to confront the Ardavan, Ardashir had marshaled sturdy forces, mostly ethnic Persians from Fars. Crucially, Ardashir had won the backing of the powerful house of Suren. This noble family's powerbase lay in the far east, in the Helmand River valley of what is now Afghanistan. Others also flocked to the banner of the House of Sasan, including men from Kirkuk (today in Iraqi Kurdistan), Kerman (today the borderlands of Iraq), and the territory of Isfahan. Among the allies of the Sasanians also numbered warriors of the powerful Iranian Mokri tribe whose territory stretched from the valley of the Jagatu River, ninety kilometers east of Erbil, as far east as the city of Mahabad (south of modern Tabriz). The upstart prince had thus extended his sway over a great swathe of the empire, enlisting ethnic Persians ripe for breaking free of Parthian rule. It was probably around these engagements that Ardashir slaughtered considerable numbers of the Karin family, one of the noble clans who buttressed the Parthian dynasty and who would play an important role in the history of Sasanian Iran.

In a battle near Istakhr, close to the ancient Achaemenid capital of Persepolis in Iran, Ardashir defeated the Parthian governor, who some sources say was one of the sons of Artavan. The Sasanids went on to seize Isfahan, a key city in central Iran, where Ardashir slew the local Parthian lord. These victories left the House of Sasan with mastery over a considerable portion of the empire and sent a message that Artavan could not ignore. The Parthian king mustered his army and prepared to meet his rival.

Near the small hamlet of Ram-Hormoz in southwestern Iran, the armies of the Parthian great king and Ardashir clashed. That the rebel's march had carried him westward from his home base reveals that he had designs on the twin-cities of Seleucia-Ctesiphon, the economic heart of Parthian Mesopotamia and the winter capital of the king of kings. With the Persian noble households of the south at his side, Ardashir believed he possessed the might to contest it. Ardashir's force comprised ten thousand heavy cavalry, shieldless and armed with bows and lances. The Parthian enemy was nearly identically equipped. While the Parthians appear to have outnumbered Ardashir's troops from Fars and other easterners, the rebels carried the day. During the battle, Artavan was struck dead; later sources claim that Ardashir himself had struck the fatal blow.

The entirety of the Parthian army was not present that fateful day, but Parthian pretenders to the Arsacid throne sprang forth like mushrooms until a sufficient portion of the noble clans tasted Ardashir's steel. The king from Fars moved against Parthian loyalists in northern Mesopotamia around Nisibis. Ardashir failed to take the great caravan city of Hatra but recovered to score a modest victory sufficient to quench the fires of rebellion for the moment. Finally, in 227, Ardashir forced the Parthian capital of Seleucia-Ctesiphon to surrender to his rule. Aged forty-seven, the rebel ascended the throne and was crowned with the diadem of the empire, claiming for the first time the title of king of kings. Parthian nobles and stragglers loyal to the cause fled to their Arsacid brethren in Armenia or Bactria as Ardashir moved briskly to consolidate his position. The Sasanian era had dawned.

"They use the bow and the horse in war, as the Romans do, but the barbarians are reared with these from childhood, and live by hunting; they never lay aside their quivers or dismount from their horses, but employ them constantly for war and the chase."[2] This opinion of the Persians held by the Roman historian Herodian (ca. 170–240) misses the mark, for while certainly the Persian troops the westerners faced were expert horsemen and equally skilled in the use of the bow, the Sasanians certainly did not make their living as hunters, however important it was in their pursuit of leisure and training for war. Herodian, not one to give too much credit to the barbarians—and all non-Romans were lumped in the same basket—probably exaggerated what was certainly a Persian mania for hunting. The great nobles maintained vast preserves and well-stocked hunting grounds. These enclosures were managed by wardens and often walled. These manicured parks with their abundant game, water, and trees within were called *paridaida* in Old Persian, and through the Greeks, gave us our word paradise.

While Ardashir enjoyed the hunt as much as any of his princes, in the year 232, the shahanshah had different quarry on his mind. The Romans had invaded his empire, led by the young emperor Severus Alexander, who had risen to power as a boy of seventeen and never managed to slip from under the thumb of his domineering mother. While Alexander was in the west, the king of kings led a raid in force into the highlands of the eastern empire, striking at Cappadocia in what is today central Turkey.[3] On its return, the Persian pack sieged the city of Nisibis, the bedrock of Roman defenses in Roman Mesopotamia. Here the great king failed and was turned away but not before he had done considerable damage to Roman property and honor. It was about this time that Ardashir sent messengers to the Roman emperor, laying claim to the lands of his forefathers, the Achaemenids. Memory of the ancient Persian Empire was very much alive. The biblical book of Daniel (2:4-49) related the famous dream of Nebuchadnezzar, which the Hebrew prophet Daniel was summoned to interpret:

31 Your Majesty looked, and there before you stood a large statue—an enormous, dazzling statue, awesome in appearance. 32 The head of the statue was made of pure gold, its chest and arms of silver, its belly and thighs of bronze, 33 its legs of iron, its feet partly of iron and partly of baked clay. 34 While you were watching, a rock was cut out, but not by human hands. It struck the statue on its feet of iron and clay and smashed them. 35 Then the iron, the clay, the bronze, the silver and the gold were all broken to pieces and became like chaff on a threshing floor in the summer. The wind swept them away without leaving a trace. But the rock that struck the statue became a huge mountain and filled the whole earth.

The vision of Daniel, the inspiration for the apocalyptically minded and televangelists till this day, was likely composed from 167–164 BC, very near the time of the desecration of the Jewish Temple in Jerusalem during the reign of the Seleucid king Antiochus IV Epiphanes (175–164 BC). In traditional Christian thought as far back as St. Jerome (c. 347–420), Christians had generally interpreted the four kingdoms as follows: the head of gold was the Neo-Babylonian Empire of Nebuchadnezzar (626–539 BC); the chest and arms of silver symbolized the Achaemenid Persian Empire (550–330 BC). The thighs and legs were thought to represent the Hellenistic kingdoms following the death of Alexander the Great, while the feet were often thought to symbolize the Roman Empire. The strength of the historical memory of the greatness of Persian rule, which had challenged the powers of the West for dominance, was enshrined in the cultures of the Mediterranean and Near East, however hazed in mist and garbled in the memory. The potent image of Achaemenid power and claims to their former lands Ardashir requisitioned as his own. The Roman Herodian put the following words into the mouths of the great king's emissaries to Rome:

> the great king Ardashir commanded the Romans and their emperor to withdraw from all Syria and from that part of Asia opposite Europe; they were to permit the Persians to rule as far as Ionia and Caria and to govern all the nations separated by the Aegean Sea and the Propontic Gulf, inasmuch as these were the Persians' by right of inheritance.[4]

Even if fundamentally wrong, as some have claimed, Herodian knew his audience. The menace that the great king posed to the Roman state in the east was not taken lightly, as events were to prove. In any case, the broad territorial claims allegedly made by Ardashir differed very little from those lodged in Rome centuries before by his Parthian predecessors.[5]

In 228, again threatened with fracture in the north, where the Armenians remained loyal to the Arsacid Parthian line and backed rebels against the Sasanian king, and where elements of the old order resisted, Ardashir went on the attack, marching northeast to northern Mesopotamia. There the shahanshah suffered defeat at the hands of a coalition of Armenians, Georgians, and steppe nomads marshaled by the Armenian King Tiridates II (217–252).[6] The reverse in the north forced Ardashir to withdraw and gather fresh soldiers from Fars and the eastern provinces. With his reinforcements, Ardashir traversed the Armenian region of Arzanene, southwest of the Taurus Mountains, and menaced the major garrison at Bezabde (Eki Hendek), where the beleaguered Romans were powerless to halt his advance into central Asia Minor and the highland region of Cappadocia. The Persians plundered freely over Cappadocia and perhaps into the fertile lowland plains of Cilicia.[7]

The following year, Ardashir returned to the offensive and took aim at the Roman defenses in Upper Mesopotamia. By virtue of their commanding positions on the edge of the highlands overlooking the plains of the Euphrates and Tigris, these fortified cities offered the Romans a bridgehead into Persia and were a menace to the fertile lowlands and the capital, Ctesiphon. Ardashir attacked the desert principality of Hatra and invested the Roman frontier cities of Nisibis and Edessa, although we do not know if these centers fell at this time. For the second time in as many years, the great king dispatched flying columns of cavalry to raid as far as Roman Cappadocia. Like the later chevauchees of the English in the Hundred Years' War, the Sasanians used their superior mobility to undermine a more powerful but static enemy. Once their enemy bypassed the garrisons, the dispersed Roman infantry could not hope to catch their mounted foe. The speed of maneuver of the Sasanians and their surprise appearance behind Roman lines spread fear, even as the shahanshah's troops gathered spoils in the form of money, livestock, and slaves. While on paper, their shocked soldiery cantoned in the eastern provinces were sufficient to confront the Sasanians, in all likelihood Roman arms had run down through a combination of neglect, corruption, and indiscipline. After the failed Parthian campaign of Caracalla, the emperors took scant note of the region. The chaos sparked by the Persian advance fanned across the provinces, attesting to poor communications and overwhelming fear. Corruption, always a scourge among the provincial troops, led to abuses like plundering of civilians and doctored muster rolls, so that officers could pocket the pay packets for nonexistent troops. A fractured Roman high command further weakened their response to the crisis.

In the pandemonium wrought by Ardashir's breach of the frontiers, panicked by the arrival of Sasanian raiders in the rear of the curtain of Roman defenses, the pressed Romans in Mesopotamia mutinied and murdered their commander, Flavius Heracleo. Soon afterward, the Roman soldiery declared an otherwise unknown figure, Tarinus (or Taurinius), emperor. Even worse, numerous Roman troopers deserted to the enemy and joined Ardashir's pillage of the civilians they had pledged to protect. The emergency deepened further. Before the arrival of the emperor in Syria, the soldiers at Edessa in Mesopotamia declared a certain Uranius (perhaps Taurinius, sources are not clear) emperor. News of the crisis quickly spread to Syria and thence to Rome, where the young emperor Severus Alexander received the news with grave concern. He recruited a large army and, despite Alexander's bluster, the large bonuses the emperor paid out prior to departure speaks to both the risks the enemy posed and Roman consternation at having to meet them.

Our sources are silent on the numbers and other details, but the Romans gathered an exceptionally large force. Enlistment, training, and logistical support took time to organize. Only in 231 did Alexander move eastward, where he established his headquarters at the illustrious city of Antioch, the pearl of Syria on the Orontes River. There, in preparing his battle plan, Alexander demonstrated strategic ambition beyond all skill. The emperor and his generals conceived of a division of the army to prosecute an elaborate, three-pronged attack. Given that any one of these forces could be expected to encounter the full weight of Ardashir's Sasanian troops, it is unlikely each numbered Roman contingent numbered fewer than ten thousand men. Upon the arrival of the emperor and his campaign army at Antioch, the Sasanian raiders withdrew from Cappadocia, and Ardashir broke off his attack on Nisibis.

Alexander's counterstroke, as unlikely to succeed as it was bold, might have been devised by Wile E. Coyote. The strategy called for each of the three armies to advance independently into different parts of Ardashir's realm. The first, marching north from Antioch, would descend from the rugged highlands of Armenia into the lands of Media, today northwestern Iran, a land which was then divided among a number of petty princes under Parthian suzerainty. Into this country, the Romans plunged, raping and reaving over a broad area. Hearing of the Roman slash into the torso of his realm, the king of kings mustered his field army and moved to intercept them.

The middle Roman army forged through the Tigris-Euphrates corridor into the dusty desert plains of northern Mesopotamia, the region where Ardashir had recently attacked in force. There many Roman units had previously been ineffective or in revolt. The open wound of these disorders had not been staunched until the appearance of the emperor in the east.

Alexander himself, under the watchful eye of his domineering mother, led the southern group through Mesopotamia, probably to strike through Syria from the Roman frontier fortress-city of Dura Europos. In any case, the southern attack never materialized due, we are told, to a combination of an overwrought mother and fever. Like many of his soldiers, Alexander succumbed to sickness that physically drained him, most probably malaria which plagued the length of the Tigris and Euphrates. As with so many unseasoned troops throughout history, mighty Rome was cut down by the bite of the tiny *anopheles* mosquito.

Ardashir, apparently still campaigning in the Upper Mesopotamia against Nisibis or Hatra, first responded to the northern prong of the Romans into Media. The ruggedness of the terrain prevented the Sasanian king from engaging the raiders, who, considering the lateness of the season and their unfamiliarity with the country, withdrew loaded with spoils. The king could do nothing but leave behind a strong garrison in anticipation of the renewal of the war with the arrival of the spring thaw that would make the mountains passable.

The great king learned of the central Roman thrust into the lands along the Upper Euphrates and Tigris and swung the remainder of his army south to fall upon the central invasion force. The Romans advancing across the Euphrates and onto the plains of Upper Mesopotamia could not believe their luck. Instead of a hard-fought slog and an onslaught under a thunder of cavalry, the Roman infantry marched mile upon mile unopposed, firing villages as they fanned out across the countryside and seized cattle, food, and slaves from the unfortunate villagers too slow to make their escape. The invaders ascribed their good fortune to the success of their comrades to the north in Armenia or south under the emperor's direct command. The great king must have been forced to confront their armies elsewhere; perhaps he had been defeated or even killed? Loaded with human and animal chattel, silver and pilfered food, the Romans' murderous amble continued. Scorched fields and hollowed-out settlements coughed a curtain of smoke into the incandescent Mesopotamian sky, and clouds of carrion fowl marked the enemy passage. Whatever precautions the western invaders took failed to warn them of the danger that stalked them as silently as the raptors gliding overhead. One can only imagine the shouts of the legionnaires, choked on dust and sweat as they first apprehended the dread sight of lines of riders, moving at the trot, bows and lances ready. Whatever cavalry the Romans fielded, if any, it mattered not a jot. As centuries before and not far away, at Carrhae, the Roman infantry proved helpless against the cavalry onslaught. Herodian provides our only story of the encounter:

> The king attacked it unexpectedly with his entire force and trapped the Romans like fish in a net; firing their arrows from all sides at the encircled soldiers, the Persians massacred the whole army. The outnumbered Romans were unable to stem the attack of the Persian horde; they used their shields to protect those parts of their bodies exposed to the Persian arrows. Content merely to protect themselves, they offered no resistance. As a result, all the Romans were driven into one spot, where they made a wall of their shields and fought like an army under siege. Hit and wounded from every side, they held out bravely as long as they could, but in the end all were killed. The Romans suffered a staggering disaster; it is not easy to recall another like it, one in which a great army was destroyed, an army inferior in strength and determination to none of the armies of old. The successful outcome of these important events encouraged the Persian king to anticipate better things in the future.[8]

If the Persians massacred the central army like carp caught in a weir, the Roman northern force withdrew unopposed and in good order. But it was late in the marching season and the Romans had tarried too long in enemy country, no doubt tempted by the choice pickings on offer in Media. Their route home took them through the highlands of Armenia. There, where no Persians stood to oppose them, the ancient Latin god Aquilo, lord of the north wind, intervened:

> This army, in its advance, was almost totally destroyed in the mountains; a great many soldiers suffered mutilation in the frigid country, and only a handful of the large number of troops who started the march managed to reach Antioch.[9]

While his invasion to the north suffered from frostbite and hypothermia, Alexander's host in the south of the theater fared no better. Many in the emperor's field army soldiers hailed from the mountains of Illyricum, in the cooler western regions of the Balkans. They quickly succumbed to heat and perished from tropical illnesses. Having survived his ordeal, Alexander returned to Rome where he held a triumph. Imperial propagandists proclaimed a great victory over the Persian barbarians and reminded the populace that they could rest easy.

Ardashir spent the rest of his reign consolidating his grip and bringing to heel the Parthian clans who continued to resist. He conquered Merv, one of the most important cities on the northern frontier, a flourishing center of agriculture and trade, and a melting pot of the cultures of Iran and Central Asia. In 240, after multiple sieges, the great king and his son and coregent Shapur, finally captured the rose of Hatra, whose thorns had dug into the flesh of the empire. Once a vibrant hub of culture and commerce, Hatra, Rome's easternmost bulwark against the Sasanians, withered to a ghost town, the impressive ruins of which remain today. The same year, in the wake of their defeat at Hatra, the Persians swept aside demoralized Roman defenders and bagged the prizes of Nisibis and Harran (Carrhae). The Romans could not brook the loss of these key fortress cities, which, like canines in a wolf's maw, they so needed to strike at the body of their prey.

A Roman counterattack was not long in coming. In 242, Roman imperial forces, reinforced with western legions, recaptured Nisibis and Carrhae. With his work of welding together the lands of the former Parthian Empire under his dominion still unfinished and the reins of state in the grasp of his fiery, bellicose son, Shapur I, the great king Ardashir, the first of the Sasanian kings, breathed his last.

CHAPTER TWO

The Great King

"When at first we had become established in the empire, Gordian Caesar raised in all of the Roman Empire a force from the Goth and German realms and marched on Babylonia [Assyria] against the Empire of Iran and against us. On the border of Babylonia at Misikhe, a great 'frontal' battle occurred. Gordian Caesar was killed and the Roman force was destroyed. And the Romans made Philip Caesar. Then Philip Caesar came to us for terms, and to ransom their lives, gave us 500,000 *denars*, and became tributary to us."[1]

If the king of kings Ardashir could be likened to a fox, using a combination of tact, diplomacy, and a firm bite to extend his interests, then his son, Shapur I (240–270), was a wolf, constantly on the move and always on the hunt. A later source says that Ardashir judged his favorite son, "the gentlest, wisest, bravest and ablest of all his children."[2] At least these last two traits Shapur was to prove in dread fashion. The stylized colossal statue of the great king, finely drawn in 1876 by George Rawlinson shows a handsome, well-proportioned man with a tight beard and strong nose, but it would be wrong to read this image of perfection as according too closely to reality. Whatever Shapur's physical appearance, he was one of the most active and martial of all Sasanian kings and strove to keep his enemies at bay and to expand the empire over his entire thirty-year reign.

Shapur ascended to corulership with his father on Sunday, April 12, 240. Shapur was an experienced soldier and administrator; likely he served at his father's side from the beginning of the Sasanian revolution. The young king of kings faced a crisis. Roman honor had been tainted by the loss of their eastern bulwark cities of Nisibis, Harran, and Hatra. The Sasanian conquest of these outposts exposed the eastern flank of Rome to attack and, with it, the richest cities of Syria. But the Romans were in turmoil. Following the murder of Alexander Severus in 235, the last scion of the Severan dynasty that had ruled since 193, the empire sank gradually into a quagmire of anarchy. Disorder seeped across the Roman provinces like ink spilled across parchment, as soldiers vied for power and civil wars exploded in every quarter. This period, known to history as the Military Anarchy, or less colorfully as the Third Century Crisis, touched the lives of all Roman citizens and weakened the once-great empire. Across the Rhine and Danube barbarian tribesmen grew increasingly bellicose. In Africa and elsewhere, one rebellion nipped the heels of the next. The mega rich of Rome and the provinces held as much private wealth as the emperor could command and sometimes more. As the screws turned, the army buckled; the old legionary culture and structures threatened to shatter.

Well informed by his spies, Shapur knew full well how to take advantage of a calamity. To him, Roman discomfiture must have seemed like Ahura Mazda smiled on his reign. But Rome, even in its weakened state, remained a tiger to be tamed, and the great king readied for the hunt. Only in 243 did the Romans appear in Mesopotamia. Their leader was the youngest ruler ever to ascend to the throne of the empire of the eagle. When a rampaging Praetorian guard unit thrust the purple of empire upon him, Gordian was a child of thirteen. He would be the third emperor of his name, following the short-lived reigns of his father Gordian I (238) and brother, Gordian II (238). It is hard to imagine that the boy, even at his age, could have welcomed his prospects when he donned the imperial diadem. With the empire in tumult and competing factions at seditious work with daggers drawn, Gordian's ascent to office assured him the Hobbsian fate of his kinfolk, a struggle that promised to be nasty, brutish, and short. Gordian III would not play the part of the mouse. Probably he—or far more likely his political handlers—knew that the only security for the lad and for themselves was something that everyone craved, a shattering military victory over a worthy foe. Only the barbarians, broken-backed or on bended knee, the armies sated by blood and spoils, would suffice. Then—and only then—could the brain trust and the sychophants, the magnates and kingmakers of the Roman elites, get a restful night's sleep. Thus, this King Tut of the Romans, with the same sort of tragic resolve and destined to share the same fate as the pharaoh of old, headed in

Sketch of a colossal statue of Shapur I, "The Great," drawn by George Rawlison in 1876.

the direction where the twin maws of the mighty Tigris and Euphrates waited to snap shut, plunging him into the belly of the Mesopotamian badlands where bleached the bones of thousands of his countrymen.

In his Mesopotamia adventure, Gordian was at least partly impelled by his able Praetorian prefect who hailed from the Greek east, Timesitheus, who had married his daughter to the youthful emperor. A man of vast experience and capabilities, Timesitheus had survived the tempests of his age through acumen and talent. As the officer who essentially served as the chief administrator of the empire, the lot fell to Timesitheus to organize and supply the campaign in the east that would restore Roman greatness. Given the storms that lashed the political shores of the empire, the Roman response is impressive and shows that, despite a heavy coat of rust, the old state and legionary cogs still maintained some iron. Gordian threw open the gates of the Temple of Janus Geminus in Rome, the traditional signal that the Eternal City was at war. Janus, the two-faced deity, was the god of passages, of coming and going, and his two faces reflect not only the outward journey and return home but the peril of such forays in which fortune might smile upon, or destroy, the emperor who marched to war.

In 242 Gordian III appeared at Antioch with "a huge army and a great quantity of gold."[3] Around the time of the campaign, Timesitheus oversaw the appointment of a fellow easterner, Priscus, as joint office holder of the Praetorian prefecture. At least one source credits Timesitheus with much of the success of the early part of the campaign. Considering Roman performance after his death in 243, there is likely truth in this. But Priscus also basked in the triumph of the opening salvo of the war, executed ably by Timesitheus. Unfortunately for the Romans, the able Praetorian prefect succumbed to dysentery after the Persians had been driven from Nisibis and Harran. After Timesitheus's passing, Priscus ensured that his brother, Marcus Philippus (Philip), shared the Praetorian prefecture. Philip had been born to local notables in the black basalt village of Shahba in the Roman province of Arabia, "a wicked country" according to the sour claims of the sixth-century historian Zosimus. In Shahba, about ninety kilometers south of Damascus in what today are the lava lands of the Jebel Druze, few could have predicted the evanescent career of the man known to history as Philip "the Arab."

As is so often the case, details of the Roman-Persian war are scant and contradictory. The official Roman version is filled with Gordian's resounding victories:

> he fought and won repeated battles, and drove out Shapur, the Persian king. After this he recovered . . . Antioch, Carrhae, and Nisibis, all of which had been included in the Persian empire. Indeed, the king of the Persians became so fearful of the Emperor Gordian, that, though he was provided with forces both from his own lands and from ours, he nevertheless evacuated the cities and restored them unharmed to their citizens . . . the Roman power occupied the whole of the East.[4]

In an alleged letter to the Roman senate, the young, would-be Alexander wrote that he had put the Persian foe to flight and that "if it be pleasing to the gods, we shall even get to Ctesiphon."[5] If Gordian cherished the idea of marching on Babylonia and, like Trajan and Alexander before him, conquering southern Mesopotamia, events were to prove the notion a chimera.

Historians have mostly bought the Roman line without much reservation. It does seem that in the first year of the conflict, Shapur gave way in the face of Roman arms. After a clash around the likely base of the Third Parthicus legion at Resaina (later Theodosiopolis, today Tel Fakhariya in southeastern Turkey), the Sasanians evacuated their recently hard-won cities. There is some support of this in the overly triumphant records of Roman historians, like that of Eutropius, who notes of Gordian, "He did, indeed, manage this war successfully and humiliated the Persians in momentous battles."[6]

According to the western accounts, the Roman juggernaut was brought to heel not by the Persians but by dissenting forces within. Philip the Arab intrigued against his master, contrived his murder, and thus engineered his own ascent to the throne. The internecine bloodletting paralyzed the army and broke the tip of the Roman spear. Unwilling to continue the fight, and in his haste to extricate himself, Philip concluded a "a most shameful treaty."[7] If the Romans had dealt such a hammering to the Sasanians, why the need for such an unfavorable peace? Philip signed the treaty then marched back to Rome to consolidate his grip on power and claim the title "Parthicus," conqueror of Persia.

If, as most Roman sources state, Philip machinated to overthrow his former master, why did he permit his soldiers to build a tomb for the corpse of the young Gordian, tragically felled at the age of nineteen? Writing around 370, the historian Eutropius, who accompanied the star-crossed expedition of the emperor Julian alongside another eminent historian, Ammianus Marcellinus, wrote of the final resting place of Gordian III. They precisely noted the tomb's location—at the twentieth milestone from Circesium (today al-Busayra, Syria), a Roman fortress overlooking the Euphrates near the junction with the Khabur River. There, before taking his remains back to Rome, the army accorded Gordian full honors and worshipped the fallen boy hero as a god. As a usurper, it is unlikely that Philip would have lionized the memory of his murdered predecessor in such fashion. Whatever the case, Roman historians bequeathed a somewhat muddled picture of a campaign that, despite its poor ending, was, in the final reckoning, an imperial triumph.

Such was the accepted line until the German archaeologist and émigré to America, Erich Schmidt, put his spade to earth in the heartland of Persia. Following the path blazed by another erudite German orientalist, Ernst Herzfeld, Schmidt dug at the ancient site of Persepolis, sixty kilometers north of modern Shiraz. Persepolis, seat of the Achaemenids, held special significance for the Sasanians, who appropriated the vast terraced spaces of their ancient forebears to claim their place as heirs to the great Persian past. The site, whose ruins rested impressively on a gigantic terrace, were partly delved out of living rock of a mountainside. Nearby, at Naqsh-e Rostam, lie a cluster of Achaemenid and Sasanian monuments, and Schmidt's workmen scraped and troweled their way to an astonishing find. In June 1939, with the storm clouds of a world war roiling, Schmidt unearthed the final carvings of a monumental inscription. Known to posterity as the "Deeds of Shapur," the proclamation etched in three languages—Pahlavi (Middle Persian), Parthian, and Greek—dates to 262, when the old king looked back on his reign and left for posterity his genealogy, a record of his wars, and works rendered for the Zoroastrian religion.

The heading of this chapter contains a portion of the royal decree and answers the riddle of why, if Philip led a victorious army, he felt so pressed to conclude an unfavorable treaty with Shapur. According to the great king's inscription at Persepolis, the Sasanians had met the large Roman invasion, which included great numbers of Goths and other Germanic-speaking tribesmen, at Misike, where the Tigris and Euphrates flow close together, in early 244. The Sasanian king led his army in a:

> great frontal battle. And Gordianus Caesar (Gordian III) perished, and we destroyed the Roman army. And the Romans proclaimed Philip emperor. And Philip Caesar came to us for terms, and paid us 50,000 dinars as ransom for his life and became tributary to us.[8]

Both the Roman and Persian accounts appear to contain truth but also critical omissions. In his recollection of events, Shapur failed to mention the initial Roman victory at Theodosiopolis, which forced him to withdraw from the northern cities deemed vital to Sasanian strategic interests. The Roman side cloaked, behind a mask of triumphalism, Shapur's smashing of Gordian's force and perhaps even the unprecedented fact that Gordian III may well have been the first Roman emperor ever to die on the field of battle. The truth, it seems, was too awful to digest, and thus Philip, given the unkind moniker "the Arab," was cast in the role of Judas, who betrayed his master, and, with it, the final victory that lay within the grasp of the young prince. It did not help matters that, in a largely pagan Roman Empire, Philip is said to have embraced an upstart religion whose practitioners worshipped a Jewish carpenter and crucified rebel against Rome: he was a Christian.[9]

While Shapur's inscription at Persepolis is certainly propaganda, there is little reason to doubt its basic accuracy. The great "frontal battle" that the Sasanians memorialized in the rock face for as close to eternity as humans can come, likely remembers a charge by the great king's kataphraktoi, heavily armored lancers, the weight of whose charge crushed the legionary infantry and broke the cohesion of the Roman infantry. The prominence of thousands of Goths and other Germanic auxiliaries is noteworthy, as it is one of the earlier instances of the barbarian peoples to the north of the Danube whose fate was increasingly tied to their Roman foes. From the northern tribes along the Rhine and Danube, the Romans would increasingly draw their recruits, until the army became in large part ethnically Germanic.

Equally intriguing is the claim in the *Historia Augusta* (a work whose weaknesses are well known) that Shapur's army numbered in its ranks "forces both from his own lands and from ours." Armenians and Arab auxiliaries are possibly meant; both would be mainstays in later Sasanian armies, and the Romans claimed sovereignty over both peoples. However, there is a strong likelihood that, as in Ardashir's campaigns against Severus Alexander, sizable numbers of Roman troopers along the frontier had deserted to the great king.

More doubtful is the manner of Gordian's passing. It is unwise to disregard the voices of the Latin and Greek historians, who uniformly allege that Philip acted treacherously. A rather garbled, much later account of the Byzantine historian John Zonaras asserts that Gordian recklessly spurred his mount into the thick of the fray to rouse his troops, but his mount stumbled and the emperor suffered a broken thigh from which he died.[10] A plausible reconstruction of events is that, stripped of his ablest protector, Timesitheus, and exposed to a demoralized army and officer corps in the wake of the miserable defeat at Misike, Gordian succumbed to severe injuries and Philip then engineered his own elevation to the throne.

Whatever the precise manner of Gordian's death, the Romans faced annihilation at the hands of the Persians, and Philip had to parley for his own life and the lives of his soldiers. In exchange for peace, Philip ceded much of Roman Mesopotamia and Armenia to Shapur.[11] This, much more than the heavy indemnity of five hundred thousand *dinars* (silver *denarii* presumably and not Roman gold *aurei*) wounded Roman pride and established the Sasanians as a serious rival to Roman pretensions in the east, particularly in Armenia, where both empires maintained strong interests.

The Parthians had maintained close bonds with many Armenian noble families and viewed the region as circling within their cultural orbit. An Arsacid prince, Tiridates II, related to the Parthian dynasty whom Shapur's father Ardashir had extinguished, continued to rule in Armenia. Since the first century, the Romans had laid claim to the key border region, where the cold highlands and bellicose inhabitants provided a buttress to Roman power in the east. The Sasanians could not reconcile themselves to this state of affairs, and the treaty with Philip bolstered their pretensions. Closer to the Iranians than the Romans in language and customs, the Armenians maintained ties with the Sasanians that would only grow through time, and the shahanshah eyed the rugged land as a strategic opportunity, a plum ripe to fall from the Roman tree. From Armenia, the Persians could shield with one hand the Mesopotamian lowlands, while with the other they could wield the club over Roman Asia Minor, with its hundreds of cities ripe for conquest. Little could Shapur and his court have dreamt that the fruit would prove so hard to digest. As the Sasanians cast their envious eyes on the vast uplands, they could not have foreseen that their ambitions would, as the tides of history pitched and rolled, lead them into conflict with mighty Rome for more than three centuries.

Philip the Arab had appointed his brother as *rector* of the Roman east, and Priscus ruled with an iron hand and imposed heavy taxes, no doubt in response to the attrition suffered by the army and the need to shoulder the expense of rearmament and the payment of tribute to Persia. Priscus's oppressive policies bred dissension, and he soon faced a revolt led by a local aristocrat named Iotapianus. This rebellion occurred near the end of the reign of Philip, who was killed in battle in 249 fighting the rebel senator and general Decius. Facing Gothic, Carpi, and Gepid incursions along the Danube, and with Priscus apparently removed from the scene in the east, it is highly doubtful that Rome had fully replenished her legionary strength along the Euphrates and in the northern garrisons. Shapur knew of the internal anarchy that shook Rome to its foundations, and he ruthlessly sought to advantage himself.

In his decree carved into the walls at Persepolis, Shapur offered this laconic preamble to the next phase of the war: "And Caesar lied again and did wrong to Armenia." While the Roman sources are silent on the reason for the strife over Armenia, later Armenian sources are clear: Philip the Arab provided military assistance to Khosrov II, king of Armenia (252–258). Khosrov was a prince of the house of the Arsacids and thus related to the Parthian dynasty and its noble families. He received aid from some of the noble clans inside Persia. In 252, with a largely mercenary army collected from Roman territory and beyond, Khosrov defeated and drove out Hormozd Ardashir, the Persian great king of Armenia who had been installed on the throne by his father Shapur I.[12] This act provided the Sasanians with a casus belli, and a just one at that. Persian wrath was not long in coming, and when the great king descended on Roman lands, his coming was like a hurricane. The great king's first foray came in 250, but Shapur aborted the expedition to deal with trouble in Khurasan, on the empire's northern frontier. In 252, having quenched the fires of trouble in the north, Shapur unleashed his forces on the Roman east and conquered Armenia.

The same year the great king led his army into Syria, marching upriver toward the Syrian heartland. In his inscription at Persepolis, Shapur claims that a Roman army of sixty thousand opposed him. This is an extraordinary number. Is it likely or even possible? Reconstructing the Roman order of battle in the east, especially amidst the tumult that plagued the empire in the middle of the third century, is difficult.

In Cappadocia, legionary bases at Melitene and Satala guarded the eastern end of the main route crossing Anatolia as well as the civilian population. The Twelfth Legion, *Legio XII Fulminata*, or "Thunderbolt," an army group that had won numerous commendations over its long history, had its legionary fortress (castrum) at Melitene, where a sizeable civilian settlement soon grew. Astride the northern reaches of the Euphrates, in a mountain valley where the road from the Black Sea port of Trebizond ran to Samosata, the Fifteenth Legion, *Legio XV Apollinaris*, watched over the vital route at its place of permanent garrison called Satala.

In the Syrian north, the *I* and *III Parthica* legions, raised by Septimius Severus for his Parthian campaign, garrisoned key fortresses. *I Parthica* commanded the basalt upland salient at Singara (Sinjar in present-day Iraq) and *III Parthica* was cantoned at Resaina (Theodosiopolis). The fate of the *II Parthica* is less certain. The legion was marched west by Severus Alexander before his murder and was known to have operated in Italy in the following years, but it may have returned to Syria prior to the attack of Shapur or in the train of the emperor Valerian in 260. The Scythian Fourth Legion (*Legio IV Scythica*) protected the vital bridge crossing at the city of Zeugma or had been redeployed behind Antioch to the mountainous terrain of Cyrrhus. Further upriver, the *XVI Flavia* made its home at the storied city of Samosata, which lay on a patch in the narrow but fertile valley of the Euphrates River. In one of the sadder tales of blatant modern disregard of ancient world heritage, the city is now completely submerged beneath the waters of the Atatürk Dam.

Severus Alexander reconstituted the *Legio III Gallica*, raised by Julius Caesar during the waning days of the Republic and disbanded in the early third century by the emperor Elagabalus after it rebelled against him, and stationed it in or near Emesa (Homs). Near the ancient Israelite city of Megiddo was the base of the Sixth Legion, *Legio VI Ferrata*, or "Iron Clad." The unit lent its name to an area called Legio (which in more recent times became Arabic "Lajjun"), a station astride a strategic portion of the major north-south coastal road artery of the eastern Mediterranean, the Via Maris. Jerusalem hosted the likely headquarters of the *Legio X Fretensis*, famous (or infamous, depending on one's perspective) for its role in the great Jewish revolt, AD 66–73, in which the Romans destroyed the Temple of Herod. The Tenth Legion rooted out the last of the Jewish resistors at Herodium and at Masada, where their siege works can still be seen today. At peak strength and efficiency, these nine legions would have numbered around fifty-four thousand fighters, but in all likelihood, the numerous insurrections and border wars that marked the third century had siphoned off many of the best soldiers from these units and displaced them; doubtless many did not return to their old bases.

Alongside the legionary forces fought numerous auxiliary troops. In Cappadocia, four cavalry wings, or *alae*, each in the third century numbering five hundred horsemen divided into twenty-four troops. Such cavalry reminds were usually recruited from the indigenous population amongst whom they served. Cappadocia also supported fifteen additional cohorts. At maximum strength—something rarely achieved except during wartime when recruitment intensified—the auxiliary forces in Cappadocia matched legionary strength, notionally some 11,500 men. The rest of the cavalry and infantry auxiliaries, including mounted and infantry archers, provided, on paper at least, strength to match those of the legions. In other words, the Cappadocia region in the north could have offered about twenty-three thousand men for a campaign army. Adding to this the army detachments in Mesopotamia and Syria, a Roman expeditionary force of sixty thousand is not out of the question, but the muster of such a host would have left the remaining garrison forces woefully understrength, and given the constant wars plaguing the Romans it is difficult to imagine the legions were anywhere near peak efficiency.

In 252 a weakened Roman Empire, staggering from multiple wounds, steadied itself. To cripple Shapur, the Romans determined to make a herculean push. Despite the claims of some, the empire cannot be thought to have taken the eastern king lightly; the state poured resources into the east and prepared tremendous military force. After their heavy bloodletting at Misike only a few years prior, morale among the westerners was low. Unfortunately, we know nothing of who commanded the guard action aimed at shielding the wealth of Syria from the Persian hunters. Priscus had likely been purged, and many commanders and veterans of Gordian III's campaign had probably been moved to Germany or the Danube.

The little that remains of Barbalissos, where Shapur's inscription records the battle took place, can be found today on the waters of Lake Assad, formed by another Euphrates dam. The strong fortifications at Barbalissos faced the desert; the only available water in the midst of a parched world was the Euphrates that rushed at its back. On the flatlands, probably within site of the towered walls, the Romans and Persians fought the Battle of Barbalissos. No Roman sources mention the battle nor its awful consequences for the empire: they forced themselves to forget the second body blow dealt them by the great king. His overwhelming victory punched open enemy defenses. The whole of the Roman northeast lay to Sasanian predation. "Syria and the environs of Syria we burned, ruined and pillaged all," said Shapur.[13]

Following their victory at Barbalissos, Shapur's men raged over northern Syria. The Shahanshah's cavalry erupted into Armenia where the Sasanians installed Shapur's son, Hormozd-Ardashir, as king. The Georgians also fell under Shapur's sway. By taking the kingdoms of Armenia and Georgia, the great king had secured the passes over the Caucasus Mountains through which funneled nomadic tribes from the steppes of south Russia, frequently with disastrous results for the settled peoples of the south. The second Sasanian king ushered in an era where the dynasty involved itself heavily on protecting and policing its interests against the predations of swift, powerful nomad armies whose manpower, mobility, and unpredictability made them the bogeymen of kings.

Shapur divided his army in two. His son, Hormozd-Ardashir (whose first name is a variant of the supreme Zoroarastrian deity Ahura Mazda), led one prong of a thrust to the north into Armenia. The great king himself led the second prong into the fertile coastlands dominated by the city of Antioch the Great on the Orontes River. Second only to Alexandria in population, riches, and prominence, Antioch was home to many of the elites of Syria, a hub of trade, manufacture, and farming. The great king encamped against the city, plundered and burned its suburbs, and sacked the town. Antioch was only the most prosperous and renowned to be submitted to pillage; in his inscription at Persepolis, Shapur had carefully catalogued thirty-six other fortresses and settlements through which his men rampaged, wolves let loose in the sheepfold.

The Roman sources on which historians have relied to reconstruct these events are as chaotic as the politics of the mid-third-century empire, and the Sasanian account, bare as it is, is to be preferred. At his leisure, Shapur smote Syria as far south as the minor city of Arethousa (al-Rastan) upstream from Antioch on the Orontes, south of Epiphaneia (Hama), another smaller city that the great king robbed and fired. Absent from his list of conquests is Emesa (Homs), the next major urban center to the south which lay on the major trunk road to Damascus and which had traditionally hosted a strong Roman military presence. It may be that troops from the south and from the belt of bases from southern Syria to Palestine—if they had not been wiped out at the Battle of Barbalissos the year prior—barred his progress. It is equally likely that Shapur simply ran out of time in the campaigning season. Satisfied with the enormous quantity of plunder, his troops returned home well rewarded for their faith in the monarch and motivated to follow him onward to what promised to be more rich pickings and glory.

It is likely that Hormozd-Ardashir's column served as the Persian wrecking ball against the now crumbling northern bulwark of Rome's eastern limits. The shah's son apparently faced no resistance from the XII Thunderbolt legion anchored at Melitene—though importantly this fort is not listed in the catalog of devastated places. But Satala, the base of the Legio XV Apollinaris did fall prey to the Sasanians, and from this one can surmise that the legion was among those defeated at Barbalissos. The thrust of the Persian spear struck as far west as Soandos (Soganli) in central Cappadocia. There they encountered the rock-cut communities delved out of the soft volcanic tuff, relics of an ancient explosion of the volcano Mount Argeaus (Erciyes) that created a landscape akin to mountains on the moon. In times of trouble the inhabitants of the region disappeared into elaborate caves and tunnels and waited out the predators above ground. The western end of the swath of flame the Persian worshippers of fire had visited on the prostrate Romans stretched along a path from Barbalissos to the rugged highlands of Asia Minor, a trail of devastation and misery that stretched some six hundred kilometers.

To this middle chapter of the war belongs one of the most extraordinary archaeological finds. Today, Dura Europus is a large ruinfield of an ancient city lying on the banks of the Euphrates in the Syrian Desert, about thirty-five kilometers west of the Iraqi border. After the conquests of Alexander the Great, his Macedonian successors, the Seleucids, had founded the site as a colony. Like all cities, Dura was to serve as a bastion of Seleucid·power. Following the collapse of the dynasty, the town fell into Parthian hands, where it remained for many years until they, in turn, were driven out by the Romans in 165 AD. Under Roman control, Dura flourished, in part due to its place as a way station on the east-west trade routes that ran through Syria and into Iran and farthest Asia.

Archaeology has managed to capture some of the flavor of this melting pot of a city where mingled the descendants of the original Macedonian, Greek-speaking military colonists, local Aramaic-speaking peasants, and their Palmyrene trading brethren from the magnificent commercial oasis farther to the west, as well as Parthian, Persian, and Jewish communities. The aridity of the landscape permitted preservation of many buildings and even paintings and archival documents on papyrus. Impressive ruins of Graeco-Roman temples, with decided Syrian and other eastern influences, Parthian architecture, a Jewish synagogue, and the earliest Christian church ever discovered survived until the horror of the Syrian Civil War and ISIS. Militants and radical Islamists, in acts of barbarism that are the hallmarks of war, wrecked the site and destroyed nearly the whole of its priceless remnants.

To Shapur's army, however, the world owed the archaeological gem that Dura briefly became. After the Battle of Barbalissos, the Romans set about a frantic program of strengthening the defenses of what was their easternmost bastion. Roman military engineers strengthened the city walls with the construction of a massive mudbrick glacis along the exposed western perimeter to blunt attacks there by artillery and other siege engines.[14]

Over decades of archaeological exploration by French, Syrian, and American teams, researchers discovered evidence of a large, sustained Persian assault now dated to the year 256. Among traces of the Sasanian investment was a huge earthen siege ramp, a focal point of Sasanian efforts to throw an earthwork to the top of the Roman walls and thereby allow their troops to assault the fortifications. Of course, the Romans, who employed such combat engineering themselves, were all too familiar with these techniques; they were part of the primary tactics of western siege warfare. But of all the foes that gnawed on the bones of the Roman Empire in the third century, only the Persians had the technical knowledge and logistical skills to mount such operations. Compared with the Rhine and Danube frontiers, warfare on the eastern frontier was, for the legionaries and auxiliaries involved, an entirely different animal. In the case of the defenders of Dura, that animal was about to swallow them whole.

Evidence came to light of frenetic action on the part of both besiegers and besieged that focused on the ramp, including extensive sapping operations, Roman countermines aimed at collapsing the ramp, and Persian efforts to mine underneath the city defenses. At the main western entrance to the city, the Palmyrene Gate on which the road led to the desert city, researchers determined that the Persians had made a number of vicious, but ultimately failed, efforts to gain egress into the city.

On the western curtain wall immediately north of the Palmyrene Gate, two defensive towers flanked one another, named by the excavators Tower 19 and Tower 18. From this section of the defenses emerged evidence of another Sasanian effort to destroy Roman linear defenses and enter the town. Probably at the same time the opposing forces fought viciously over the siege ramp, the Persians undertook a major sapping operation, whose aim was to undermine a fifteen-meter stretch of curtain wall and bring it down. If their sappers could succeed, the collapse of such a length of wall would allow the Persians to rush the city in force and overwhelm the defenders.

To mine, the Persians required basic surveying, earthmoving, and tunneling skills. To keep the work moving efficiently and to conceal its progress required planning and organization. None of these were in short supply among the Sasanian troops, many of whom were drawn from the semi-arid and arid regions of the Iranian plateau, where for centuries their ancestors had irrigated the landscape via *qanats*. Qanats are essentially covered underground aqueducts. Once they located a water source, builders surveyed the route through which to cut the qanat, and then a tunnel was dug to lead the water mined from the aquifer along a predetermined course, with a steady slope that would gradually bring the water to the surface or to shallow wells where the precious water could be easily accessed. Qanat builders would have therefore made perfect army sappers.

More than forty meters from the curtain wall, on the flat, parched plain, the Persians swung their picks against the thick, hard surface crust. They had to punch through more than three feet of solid, iron-tough limestone. Underneath the stone cladding of the desert, they found much more friable and easier to work gypsoid substrata, through which they could cut with considerable haste. As the works advanced, from their perch on the city walls, alert Roman lookouts spotted the growing spoil heap that betrayed the Persian mine but not before the Sasanians had made significant progress on their approach to the wall.

The defenders adopted the textbook response: they began their own mining operations. So as to not weaken their own wall, the Romans were forced to tunnel beneath their own massive mudbrick glacis on a course to intercept the Persian miners. As they excavated their own tunnel, just to the north of Tower 19, which they thereby hoped to avoid weakening by their own actions, the Romans advanced their tunnel and shored up the walls and ceiling at intervals with lintels and timber reinforcement. The Romans aimed to intercept the vertical access shaft through which the Sasanian sappers ascended to make their horizontal cut; capturing and destroying the access shaft would end the enemy works but reveal fears that the Persians would fire their own wooden structural braces in the event of a Roman breakthrough and thereby trap and suffocate the attackers.

Things did not go as the defenders had planned. Instead, the Persians detected the enemy countermine as it neared their own work. Beneath the city wall, where the attacking Persians mined and where the desperate Romans feverishly labored to cut them off before their defenses collapsed, archaeologists made an incredible discovery. Near the curtain at Tower 19, among the finds of the 1930s excavations, was a pile of corpses, the skeletons of Roman soldiers complete with their arms and kit, still reeking of decay with at least one man's desiccated brain still intact. During a fight, the original interpretation went, the Romans fell where they died, as many as nineteen of them. In fact, the full story is as fascinating as it is grisly.

When the Roman countermine approached the Persian tunnel, the Sasanians detected the enemy's presence. The Persians rushed with bitumen, a sticky form of petroleum. To this they added sulphur and ignited them together, pouring clouds of noxious fumes over the Roman chain gang and its vanguard of soldiers. They died in minutes. Terror spread inside the town, and the garrison rushed a ballista or other heavy projectile thrower from the walls above to fire blindly into the darkness of the tunnel, heedless of whether they killed friend or foe. To counter this, the Sasanians collected the nineteen or more dead Roman troopers and piled them in the narrow tunnel, human sandbags to defend them from the barrage of bodkin bolts.

Still fearful of an enemy attack through the breach, the frantic Romans choked the entrance to their mine with earth and a huge stone. Unknown to them, the Persians had no intention of entering the enemy countermine: they only wished to destroy it. Their workers hurried forward, carrying large amphorae filled with bitumen and sulphur. As the timbers turned to ash, the tunnel collapsed. The murderous chemical attack by the Persians was not without cost. Near the piled-up Romans archaeologists discovered the corpse of another soldier, dressed in chainmail and with a pointed iron helmet nearby. The remnants of his sword included a pommel worked from jade—a valuable green mineral that in this case likely came from India or farther east but certainly not from the Roman Empire. The dead trooper had one arm still frozen near his midsection, testament to the feverish moments when he made a futile effort to free himself of his mail cuirass. The dead man was a Sasanian, likely an officer, who had ordered his men to the rear while he started the fire that would destroy the Roman mine but would take his own life in the process.

It is an irony of history that, despite their efforts, the Persian undermining of the walls caused the curtain of Dura to crumple and sag—damage that can still be viewed today, but the wall, buttressed by the heavy mudbrick reinforcement, did not give way. However the Persians entered the city during their capture of it, it was not through their sapping of the wall at Tower 19. But take Dura the Sasanians did. After the Persian sack, the city was abandoned forever.

While the drama of a bitter siege unfolded at Dura Europos, the Romans had not been idle elsewhere. The rattled elites briefly lay aside their internal murder and intrigue to see to the appointment of a new emperor, the aged senator Valerian. Despite his age, Valerian enjoyed a sterling reputation, in no small part because he came from an ancient Roman family of senatorial rank and thus represented a refreshing departure, in the eyes of the elites of the Eternal City at least, from the succession of rough and ready generals who enjoyed bloody careers and brief reigns. The later, not terribly reliable,

Byzantine chronicler John Malalas painted the following portrait of the star-crossed emperor: "He was short, slender, with straight gray hair, a slightly up-turned nose, a bushy beard, black pupils and large eyes; he was timorous and mean."[15]

When, a few years prior, as Shapur mauled the eastern forces of the empire at Barbalissos, the emperor Decius, who had overthrown the great king's old nemesis Philip the Arab, rushed north along the Black Sea coast in an effort to intercept an army of Goths who had killed the emperor's son. While Decius finally caught the Gothic troop, for him and his men it would have been better if he had not. Trapped in marshy ground and surrounded, the emperor and his men were cut to ribbons. The Danube frontier now burned near the ferocity of the deserts in the east.

Appreciating the burdens with which he had been laden and mindful of his advanced years for the time—he was about fifty-four at the date of his investiture—Valerian immediately elevated his son Gallienus to rule jointly with him. Valerian would deal with eastern affairs and Gallienus would command the troubled west. Regrouping and rebuilding his forces took time, but Valerian recruited a mass of new forces from throughout the provinces. By 257 Valerian was in Antioch where the grateful citizens received respite from the menace of Shapur, but the Persians were not the only people drawn to feast on the body of the eastern provinces; an attack by a large force of Goths across the Black Sea ran riot across Asia Minor and required Valerian to divert forces to meet and drive them away but not before the Goths had made a deep cut into the flesh of Roman Asia.

In 260, Shapur, not one to sit idle, busied himself with the siege of the cities of Harran and Edessa. Valerian pursued the great king with an impressive host; in the inscription at Persepolis, Shapur provides details about the provinces which provided troops, an extraordinary catalog from as far afield as Spain. Among the legions marched large contingents of Goths and other Germanic tribesmen. The Roman train included the emperor and the whole of his high command and upper administration, including the Praetorian prefect and various senatorial notables who would have been well advised to stay home. The Persian king claims that the Roman forces tallied seventy thousand men. While this makes for good propaganda, such a huge number is suspicious—an even ten thousand more men than Shapur had beaten at Barbalissos.

Under Valerian, the miserable record of Roman arms eight years prior on the Euphrates would not be repeated. It would be exceeded. The emperor led his great host into Upper Mesopotamia and relieved the key, thriving city of

The surrender of the emperor Valerian to the Persian king Shapur I, rock relief, 260 CE. (*Carole Raddato*)

Edessa and drove the Persians to retreat. Soon the triumphant entry of the Roman army was marred by the stink of death and the groans of soldiers in agony who dropped by the hundreds to deadly illness, probably malaria and dysentery. Not to be deterred by the ravages of pestilence, Valerian forged ahead. The emperor was made of stern stuff. The gods favored him, he was certain, especially after he had moved to persecute the insidious cult of the "Galileans," as Christianity was known. In a wave of persecution that led to the deaths of such notables as Cyprian, famous bishop of Carthage, Valerian sought to appease the old gods, whose wrath had clearly been inflamed against the state. Steel willed, the emperor led his thunderous host to confront Shapur, hoping to bring his great foe to battle and destroy him.

In 260, the two armies clashed somewhere in Upper Mesopotamia near Harran. While the sources are silent on the details, the Sasanians dealt another sharp defeat to the Romans and, during the battle, captured the emperor himself. In his inscription, the great king memorialized the day when, "we with our own hands took Valerian Caesar prisoner and the rest who were the commanders of his army, the Praetorian Prefect, and the senators, and the officers all of these we took prisoners and we led them away into Persis (Fars)."[16] Shapur memorialized his feat in a rock carving, vividly depicting the victorious shah on horseback with two figures before him. One stands, holding out tribute to Shapur: this is Philip the Arab whom he first defeated. The second figure, kneeling before the bridled mount of the great king, is Valerian, the humiliated emperor, the first Roman emperor ever held captive by a "barbarian" people.

Christian commentators were quick to ascribe Valerian's capture to the wrath of God, just punishment for the persecution unleashed against their coreligionists. An apocryphal story circulated widely and often repeated was mistaken for fact by ancient and modern historians alike. The colorful tale held that the Persian monarch used the unfortunate Valerian as a mounting block: on his rides from the palace, the Sasanian stepped on the unfortunate captive to get astride his horse.

Freed from the menace of Roman troops, like hornets in July, Shapur's men swarmed over the Roman east. The great king boasted, "And Syria, Cilicia and Cappadocia we burned, ruined and pillaged."[17] Along the upper waters of the Euphrates they thronged against the castrum of the Sixteenth Legion at Samosata. Doubtless, like so many comrades, the blood of the Sixteenth had drained into the cracked chalky plains in the service of Valerian. Stripped of its shield, the proud city was home of the famous Greek writer of the prior century, Lucian, a sharp-witted commentator and satirist whose scathing critique of those who believed in the supernatural preserves the earliest extant version of "The Sorcerer's Apprentice." Had Lucian lived to provide an account of the Persian sack, we could have expected a masterwork of thick description and heaps of blame on those who deserved it. How, after all, could things have come to this?

Shapur's iron-clad columns clattered across the Taurus Mountains in search of more victims. In the upland rolling country of Cappadocia, amber under the summer sun on dry grass and tawny wheat fields, they found cattle, horses, and slaves aplenty. Centuries before, during the Achaemenid period, Cappadocia had witnessed significant Iranian settlement and the spread of Persian culture. In the Hellenistic and Roman periods, local elites had Hellenized, not on account of being swamped by outside settlers or other measures of force, only slowly and of their own volition. In the third century, these cultural strains continued to be heard, expressed in countermelodies still audible beneath the refrain of Greek and Roman life. The Iranian notes to this tune aired in the form of great temple estates where citizens worshiped the old Persian gods, in a rural, landed aristocracy that prided itself in its equestrian prowess and cherished the breeding of both horses and men of pedigree. The vast upland marches of the plateau were ideal country for roving bands of Sasanian horsemen, who plundered at will. Roman resistance had all but collapsed. The capital of the province, the important city of Caesarea, best known as the future birthplace of its famous Christian bishop, St. Basil, was stormed and its inhabitants deported. In all, the Persians sacked and looted thirty-six cities and fortresses.

Meanwhile, Hormozd-Ardashir, the Sasanian viceroy of Armenia, invaded the regions of that country still outside of his authority, and, as one later ancient Armenian historian colorfully described it, the Persians "freely invaded us and, putting the Greek [i.e. Roman] army to flight, took captive the major part of the country and turned it into a wilderness." The Romans raised two forces to confront the son of Shapur. The two armies clashed in Pontus, just south of the Black Sea. The Persians won the day and, as had become their custom, the defeated Roman soldiers mutinied and murdered their general. Hormozd-Ardashir then swung south. Eighty days later, at Tarsus, birthplace of Paul the Apostle, the Persians defeated the second Roman force and killed its commander.[18]

The new emperor, Gallienus, the son of Valerian, attempted to free his father from captivity, but Shapur rebuffed his efforts. He had grown fond of his new pet and kept the unfortunate former emperor in the gilded cage of his palace confines, on display to the awe of his sub-kings and neighbors. The great king was no longer the inferior of the emperor of Rome; he had repeatedly bested him in trial by combat and had taken his rightful place as the premier power in southwest Asia.

Gallienus cherished no immediate aspirations to avenge Roman losses in the east. Smoke from the wildfires from myriad conflagrations on the Rhine and Danube cast a pall over the empire of the eagle. His forces were spread like a glaze of butter over bread, and the loss of an entire expeditionary army left the pantry empty. In the summer of 260, while his father was on his way to captivity, Gallienus intercepted and defeated Alemanni raiders near Milan. Farther west, he faced the rebellion of Marcus Cassianus Latinius Postumus, who prized the western provinces of Germany and Gaul from Rome and established himself as a rival emperor.

In the wreckage of Valerian's expedition, the wealthy Roman quartermaster Macrianus asserted himself in Syria. To restore order in the snake-bitten provinces, Macrianus assumed authority in the east from his headquarters at Emesa (Homs), a strong indication that the city hosted a significant Roman military presence unscathed by Shapur's nearby operations. While he did not himself seize the purple, claiming old age and poor health, Macrianus raised his sons Macrianus and Quietus to the rank of *Augusti* (the imperial title), establishing them as rivals to the emperor in Rome. Macrianus rallied to his banner those stragglers who had escaped Shapur's hands and appointed as his Praetorian prefect a certain officer with the evocative name (likely a nickname) Ballista, who, late in 260, moved against the withdrawing Sasanian raiders. In Lykaonia, just south of Cappadocia, Ballista fell upon the Sasanian rear guard. The Romans finally claimed a modest victory and recovered considerable plunder and captured Shapur's harem. However, this was hardly the major reversal of fortunes that the Romans needed to shore up their position in Syria.

Despite his weakness, Macrianus unwisely marched off with a portion of his troops and his son of the same name to wrest the throne from the beleaguered and unpopular Gallienus. Ballista and Macrianus's son Quietus remained in Emesa. In early 261 in Illyricum in the western Balkans, the imperial cavalry commander, Domitianus or Aureolous, intercepted and defeated Macrianus, father and son, whose own troops murdered them. Ballista and Quietus continued the struggle from their power base in Emesa.

By the beginning of 261, the Persians had mostly withdrawn. Shapur was apparently dealing with matters farther afield more pressing than the knackered Romans. The Persians who remained in Roman territory were probably loose companies of freebooters led by Sasanian noblemen and not the king of kings. Fighting throughout Syria was likely low intensity and sporadic. The defeat of Valerian and subsequent impotence of Gallienus drew additional eastern challengers. Most formidable of the lot was the king of Palmyra, Odenathus.

Palmyra lay in an oasis in the Syrian Desert, 250 kilometers northeast of Damascus and 150 kilometers east of Emesa. From its earliest days, the arable land of the settlement was insufficient to support much of a population, the climate and soil being best suited for dates and not the extensive cultivation of cereals, grapes, and other basic foodstuffs. Despite its desert location, Palmyra was not terribly far removed from the major cities of Syria, nor to the Euphrates. Merchants from Syria, especially the center and south, preferred the cross-desert route to the much longer coastal route which hit the Euphrates only east of Antioch. Palmyra capitalized on its position astride the desert trade routes that crossed the desert from the coast of Syria and leveraged its possession of the most precious commodity in the desert: water.

With control of the local springs and wells, the only real water for many miles, Palmyra levied tax on the merchant caravans which traversed their lands. The Palmyrenes also provided protection to caravans through escorts, guard posts, and desert patrols to keep at bay bandits and frisky Bedouin. The citizen's language, the Palmyrene dialect of Aramaic, allowed them to communicate freely over much of the Near East. Along with the city's position and early alliance with Rome, these aided the Palmyrenes in expanding their business interests. Since Achaemenid times, Aramaic had served as a lingua franca over the Fertile Crescent. Palmyrene merchants traded far and wide, especially in Mesopotamia, and established a trade network throughout the Roman east and Parthia. The backbone of their trade was likely exotics like silks and spices, but they also carried more workaday goods, such as wine and dates that filled out their camel trains. One of their merchant quarters was based at Dura Europos. They also had established a trading presence farther south and east, where their citizens had local ties and clout, in places like the metropolis of Seleucia-on-Tigris in Parthia, until it was destroyed in 115 AD. They were prominent among a garland of emporia in places like the Charax, a river port in southernmost Mesopotamia at the confluence of the rivers Tigris and Karun, not far from the head of the Persian Gulf. Charax owed its prosperity to far-flung eastern commerce in silk and other luxuries. The Palmyrenes were also conspicuous at nearby Forat, about twenty kilometers down the Tigris, as well as into the Persian Gulf at Tylos (Bahrain). Crucially, Palmyrene trade in the gulf declined at the end of the second or early third century. With the defeat of Valerian in 260, a local distinguished Palmyrene, Odenathus, seized the opportunity to restore the city's fortunes.

Around Odenathus has accreted a sizeable body of lore, some of it ancient. Scholars have been fascinated by the figure of the wife and successor of Odenathus, Zenobia, and their son, Vaballathus, and the tragic, romantic tale that unfolded at Palmyra. Given the state of our sources, weasel words are most appropriate in characterizing the man and his career. Born around 220, Odenathus was one of only two of the city's citizens who were of senatorial rank, an honor first attested in the 250s.[19] In Roman eyes, he was thus among the elite strata of imperial society. In the caste hyperconscious world of late Roman society, senatorial rank certainly helped shape favorable literary views of the man.

It is likely that the emperor Philip the Arab, a fellow Syrian, bestowed the senatorial rank on Odenathus. In the wake of the defeat of Gordian III, Philip understood better than most the importance of the city as a friendly power and buttress of Roman power along the desert frontier. Up till now, Roman and Palmyrene interests usually intersected. With the dismal Roman record in the east from the time of Severus Alexander onward, the aura of Rome had corroded in the acid bath of defeat. He knew what all the citizens of a merchant city facing hard times knew: war was bad for business. Lately there had been far too many wars, and worse than fighting them was fighting and losing them.

Historians have been too ready to accept claims of Roman writers of the spectacular feats of arms of Odenathus. Given that these are either ill informed or much later, one should take with a grain of salt at least significant portions of these reports, which salve western pride by lionizing the "king" of Palmyra. On Palmyrene inscriptions, his senatorial credentials are noted, as is his position as *ras*, "chief" of Palmyra: a good equivalent to this would be the later Arabic "amir" or "sheikh." The Greek equivalent is *exarch*. While the later Arab confederation of Ghassan who patrolled the identical stretch of desert for the Byzantines held the same title, their chief was eventually given the title of "king" of the Arabs. It is something of a stretch to use this title for Odenathus, especially as contemporary evidence does not attest to his use of the title. Far from splitting hairs on academic matters, these distinctions are important if we are to understand the Palmyrene leader's self-perceptions and the truth of the actual power he wielded. More crucially, by 257/8, Odenathus seems to have achieved the rank of consul, a holdover title from the Republic, which in theory, at least, gave the Palmyrene lord a rank superior to the legionary commanders operating in the east, as well as the ability to govern in civilian affairs. Odenathus may also have served as the governor of Syria Phoenice, but this, as with most of his career, is disputed.[20]

That Palmyra had its own armed force is certain. Like all client principalities, the city was expected to keep the peace and to support Roman military efforts in the field. At Dura Europos, the *Cohors XX Palmyrenorum*, named after the city, included mailed heavy cavalry, cataphracts (kataphraktoi in the Greek east). These horsemen were heavily armed and armored lancers like their Sasanian counterparts, although it is doubtful that they carried bows. These heavy horsemen the Romans wryly dubbed *clibanarii*, "ovens," in which the troopers baked like the local Syrian flatbread under the withering rays of the desert sun. Added to this unknown number of Palmyrene clibanarii, the desert dwellers recruited light Arab Bedouin horsemen, dromedary troops who fought as mounted infantry, and their own infantry forces. Like the pretender Macrianus, Odenathus also drew to his standard remnants of the Roman garrisons from Syria and survivors from Valerian's eastern field army.

On learning of the defeat and death of the two Macriani in Illyrium, Odenathus struck the remnants of the rebellion, Ballista and Macrianus's son Quietus, at Emesa, the immediate neighbor of Palmyra to the west. The sixth-century Byzantine historian Zosimus, who relied heavily on the work

of the third-century historian Dexippus, reports that Gallienus charged Odenathus with restoring order in the whole of the east, which suffered under
the twin yoke of Persian carnage and the outbreak of a deadly plague that
took a severe toll. Quietus, seeing the writing on the wall, extended the olive
branch to Odenathus. For this, Ballista promptly had him murdered. Says
Zosimus:

> Gallienus . . . ordered Odenathus, the Palmyrene, to assist the East
> where the situation was desperate. The latter joined the largest possible
> force of his own men to the legions which remained in the East and vig-
> orously attacked Shapur, recapturing the cities already possessed by the
> Persians. Nisibis, which had been taken by Shapur and was pro-Persian,
> he overwhelmed and razed to the ground. Then pursuing them as far as
> Ctesiphon, not once but twice he shut the Persians up in their own city
> so that they were glad to save their children, wives and selves, while he
> restored order in the lands already as far as he could.[21]

One can hardly blame the desperation of the Romans who had been hard
done by the gods of war. If real victories of substance could not be won, then
literary trifles would have to suffice. Unfortunately, Roman-admiring modern
historians, however, have been quick to seize and elaborate upon many details.
A balanced reconstruction is less exciting than the Palmyrene "empire." Upon
their retreat from their victorious campaigning at the end of the season in
260, Odenathus attacked part of the Persian army near the Euphrates and
apparently scored some success. The *Historia Augusta* states that Odenathus
recaptured Nisibis and Harran and that the Palmyrene leader sent the satraps
(an archaic word for Persian governors) to Gallienus. These cities apparently
revolted against Sasanian rule.

We can exclude a major Palmyrene defeat of the Persians, as well as the
oft-made claim that Odenathus drove the Persians out of Syria. The Sasanian
shah had just defeated two exceptional Roman field armies, apparently with
relative ease, and yet we are to accept that the leader of a city, a patchwork of
legionnaires and auxiliaries and peasants, defeated the Persians? After Odenathus was assassinated at Emesa, his wife, the famous Zenobia of romance
who captured the imaginations of both ancient and moderns alike, and her
son took power. They could do nothing to prevent the Danubian legions of
the new emperor Aurelian from crushing Zenobia's ephemeral empire in 272.
The Palmyrenes were certainly locally effective and militarily important but
no match for either the Roman emperor or the great king.

If, as Zosimus claims, Odenathus had led his troops as far as the walls of

Ctesiphon, he could not hope to capture the vast, well-guarded city, nor did he ever face Shapur in battle. Elsewhere, the *Historia Augusta* asserts that Odenathus pursued Shapur to Ctesiphon and captured his harem. One wonders how many harems Shapur had, since, as previously noted, Ballista is also said to have captured the Sasanian ladies.

Roman motives to lionize the lord of Palmyrene were varied, but the historians who survive are universally hostile to Gallienus to a point that verges on hysteria. Odenathus provided an appropriate foil to the emperor, and doubly so, since Odenathus was a senator and a man of action, essentially their perceived antithesis of Gallienus, under whose unfortunate watch the empire began to disintegrate into regional states as the locals turned to strongmen who would protect them when the central government fell far short. Amidst all of his failures, though, it is easy to miss an important reform that Gallienus imparted to the legions. No doubt in large part due to their bitter experiences against the Persians and his need to fight conflicts over wide distances, the emperor vastly increased their cavalry strength. Legions which normally possessed 120 mounted men now counted sixfold more, 726 horse in total. These emergency measures seemed to have influenced later Roman military thinking, but it is uncertain to what extent they were institutionalized.

As hostile as the historians are to Gallienus, they are much more favorable to his successor, the soldier emperor Aurelian (270–75). Glorifying the Palmyrenes, whom Aurelian defeated with scarcely an effort, served to underscore the valor and firm hand of a man on whom the shaken Roman elites could finally invest their hope.

Roman pride had been cut to the quick, and their historians fumed at the indolence of Gallienus and his impotence in the face of grave challenges. But they need not have feared the loss of their eastern provinces. Apart from a few strategic strongholds along the borderlands, such as Harran and Nisibis, Shapur had no intention of permanently seizing Roman territory. After he broke Valerian, the focus of the campaign turned to gathering the fruits of his labors. The king of king's operations in the west were the ancient equivalent of economic stimulus, satiating the desires of the noble families for prestige and gold to fuel their passion for display, feasting, and patronage. The shah himself benefitted too from the haul of free goods, labor, and expertise, vine cuttings from which to grow his own vineyards. In this, Shapur behaved like all good potentates for centuries before and after, uprooting the source of his enemy's prosperity and transplanting it in the marshy silt of Mesopotamia. The great king's inscription at Persepolis boasts of, and Roman sources confirm, the taking of thousands of captives, physical symbols of the discomfiture of the enemy, their misery the tangible results of Caesar's lie. While the Romans claimed their face-saving but hollow victories in Mesopotamia, Shapur was likely long gone. The Sasanian lord had, it seemed, pivoted to march east, into the rising sun to which he made obeisance.

Shapur's eastern campaigns in the east are poorly understood, their timing disputed and largely unknown, but his turn to the east after the Roman menace had been decisively dealt with through the capture of Valerian seems most probable. Another support for this date is the appearance of the title *Kushanshah* given to Arsdashir, son of Shapur, which appears only after 262.[22] While Shapur's father Ardashir had reduced some of his budding dynasty's rivals in the eastern marches, there was unfinished business. Likely knowing the great king was distracted by the Roman menace thousands of kilometers away, his eastern foes made mischief. Most prominent among his antagonists was the Kushan Empire.

From the first century, the Kushans, a Central Asian great power, had dominated a vast swath of territory from the Oxus (Amu Darya) Valley to the Indus. Shapur's father Ardashir had campaigned against the Kushans, whose founders were Indo-European Yuezhi, nomads likely descended from those the Greeks called the Tochari people of the Tarim Basin, a region dominated by the vast Taklamakhan Desert, today in northwestern China. Driven westward from China in the second century BC by the expansion of the Xiong-nu tribal confederation, the Kushans migrated into the territory of the Sakas, Scythian peoples known from Achaemenid times, and into Afghanistan where they encountered the Indo-Greeks in Bactria.

In Bactria, north of the towering Hindu Kush and south of the Oxus, flourished a kingdom founded by the Macedonian, Greek-speaking Demetrius I the Invincible (ca. 220–180 BC) and held amidst land which Iranian speakers had long dominated. Under Alexander and his immediate successors, Macedonian colonists in large numbers had planted their spears in Bactria and determined to make a new life. Demetrius established his capital at Bactra (today Balkh in modern Afghanistan), and his Greek Bactrians represent the farthest east the Hellenic tide washed onto Asia's shores.

In 222 BC, outside the walls of his capital, a young Demetrius skillfully parried the sword thrust of the armies of the Seleucid monarch Antiochus III. Demetrius later ruled his kingdom from Taxila in the Punjab, today northern Pakistan. Near the end of his life, Demetrius campaigned south of the Hindu Kush and his hybrid Greco-Bactrian kingdom, striking through Kuliab (in today's Tajikistan), campaigning as far as Patna (ancient Paliputra), capital of the fallen Mauryan Empire in eastern India. Not only a cultural melting pot of Hellenic and ancient Central Asian polytheisms but of Hinduism, Zoroastrianism, and Buddhism as well, the Greco-Bactrians fused societies from west and east. The Kushans, whose language resembles more closely Greek or Celtic rather than Iranian, undertook long-distance trade, which helped generate prosperity: spices, silks, and aromatics from China and Arabia and nard and pepper from India flowed through their cities and turned into copper and gold in the hands of Jewish, Central Asian, and Hellenic merchants.[23] Not only these, but the Kushans exported far and wide skillfully blown glass and the precious local Afghan bright blue mineral, lapis lazuli, alongside "nice-looking girls for concubinage."[24] The Kushans sent frequent embassies to China, where the imperial annals record their arrival and tribute they brought, some of it paid in their spectacular gold coinage.

Ardashir's campaigns further chiseled away the foundations of the Kushan Empire, the western portions of which paid him tribute. Shapur appeared with his army at Bagram, which the Kushans called Kapisa. Today a dusty city in northern Afghanistan, the town played host to the largest US military base during the two-decade fight against the Taliban. As the crow flies, more than 2,500 kilometers separates the mudbrick walls of the settlement where the great king's host tightened their cordon at Bagram and Mesopotamia, where lay rotting piles of Roman dead. The Sasanian's epic trek ended with the sack of Bagram and its incorporation into the rising edifice of Persian power.

In May 270, Shapur died in a city he refounded just four years prior, a new capital built on the labor of his Roman captives. Unlike any other city in Iran, Bishapur ("Shapur's city") had a rectangular, gridded plan, a new city for an old king. During his lifetime Shapur's ambitions, tactical abilities, and understanding of strategy had no parallel. His victories over the Romans enhanced Persian prestige and brought a flood of resources into his kingdom. Shapur founded or refounded numerous cities, many of them using captured Romans, including Gundeshapur in Khuzestan in southwest Iran. The city was destined to become a renowned center of higher and medical learning and is home to a famous library. It, like the victories of the great king in his hearty and hale days long past, would change the world.

CHAPTER THREE

The Challenge to Rome

The passing of Shapur left his third-born son Hormozd on the throne. Hormozd, the former viceroy of Armenia, reigned for only a little more than a year, from May 270 until June 271. Hormozd's successor, Bahram I, named after the old Persian god of victory and the eldest of Shapur's sons, assumed the throne as the fourth of the Sasanian line. During his father's lifetime Bahram was viceroy of Gilan (also called Daylam), on the southwestern coast of the Caspian Sea. Gilan is a mountainous belt girdling well-watered upland plains. Northerly winds pass over the Caspian and then strike the mountains which compresses the air so that they dump abundant rainfall on the Gilan plains, which receives as much rain each year as Florida. Daylam provided the finest Iranian infantry to the armies of the shahs.

Despite being the eldest, Bahram's powerful father had viewed him as the runt of the litter, and it was only through the intervention of the powerful, reforming Zoroastrian priest Karder that Bahram assumed the throne. The great king enjoyed the reputation as a king who loved to feast, to fight, and to hunt. After his coronation, he had to contend with his restless siblings, powerful lords over regions where their father had emplaced them: Shapur in Mesene (southern Mesopotamia), Hormozd-Ardashir in Armenia, and Narseh, king of the Sakastan, a vast region embracing eastern Iran and the border region of Sasanian India (Hind) and the mountains of Baluchistan known as Turan. After the death of Hormozd-Ardashir in 271, Narseh held the viceroyalty of Armenia, the most strategically vital area of the empire. In the new Sasanian protocol, the kingship of Armenia was the heir apparent to the throne. Narseh thus viewed himself as the rightful great king and his elder brother Bahram as a usurper and the tool of the Magian priestly class. Despite his powerful position, Narseh apparently did not openly resist.

In September 274, after a reign of only three years, Bahram I died. Bahram II, son of Bahram I, followed his father's path and established himself on the throne with the backing of the Zoroastrian priestly elite. While the reign began without incident, by around 282, Bahram faced the fires of rebellion blazing in the east. The shahanshah's brother, Hormozd, viceroy of Sakastan, raised the banner of revolt. To his standard flocked men from the province of Sakastan, no doubt some of the region's doughty tribal hillmen and Kushans. Fighters from Daylam, probably also some of the mountaineers for which the region was famous, also joined the insurrection. Bahram marched east to confront his brother, taking with him the bulk of Persian forces in the west, which left Sasanian Mesopotamia exposed to attack.

As the Sasanians had taken full advantage of the turmoil in the bowels of the empire, it was time for the Romans to repay their debts and cause the great king his own case of heartburn. In 283, the emperor Carus invaded through Armenia and made his descent into Mesopotamia. Without any sizeable army to oppose them, the Romans marched beyond the Persian capital of Ctesiphon. It is doubtful, historians' claims to the contrary, that Carus sacked the capital.

Bahram crushed the eastern rebels and swung his armies to the west. In Mesopotamia, probably at the hands of local Persian troops, the Romans suffered a defeat and Carus was forced to retreat. As so many promising leaders of the Roman world, Carus met an untimely death. Our sources largely repeat the outlandish claim that Carus, encamped along the mighty Tigris, was struck by a lightning bolt. In addition to the remote statistical odds of a literal bolt out of the blue, it bears mentioning that lightning was the favorite weapon of Jupiter, the king of the gods, who happened to be the patron deity of Diocles, the man who would emerge victorious from the scrum for power that followed. More plausible are the minority reports of Carus's death: according to one, the emperor succumbed to illness; according to another, the lightning bolt that felled the emperor was of the sort hammered from iron in a Roman forge.[1] Still another history claims that Carus fell in battle along the Euphrates, cut down by the Persian forces of the viceroy of Armenia, Narseh.[2]

Numerian, son of Carus, was acclaimed emperor and found himself in peril. As they recalled the days of Philip the Arab and a trapped Roman army

A 3rd Century AD relief at Naqsh-e Rostam depicting Bahram II's defeat of Roman Emperor Carus, top, and his victory over Hormozd, bottom. (*Diego Delso/CC BY-SA*)

not far from where they stood, a fire-breathing Sasanian host bearing down, hoary old Romans could be forgiven a sense of déjà vu. Unlike Philip, however, Numerian escaped the danger with his army intact and supposedly crowned in the laurels of victory, precious currency that kept many a soldier emperor alive in an era of intrigue and mutiny. There was no peace agreement and no negotiations. It seems that Numerian left open the possibility of another campaign to solve the Persian problem once and for all.

In March 284, as cold desert winter gave way to spring and the air was heavy with the scent of hyacinth in bloom, Numerian traveled to the Syrian city of Emesa. While journeying several months later, in November, the emperor fell ill. Suffering from an eye malady, Numerian was sequestered behind the heavy curtains of a litter, borne upon the shoulders of slaves as he made his slow, royal progress across the Syrian countryside. His Praetorian prefect Aper insisted that the emperor's eye ailment required his seclusion. When imperial bodyguards noticed the stench of decay, suspicious soldiers threw open the curtains of the litter to find the rotting royal corpse, already dead for days. The clumsy attempt to hide the fact of the emperor's untimely death calls to mind the farcical disappearance of dictators in the old Soviet Union. As with numerous other premature deaths of emperors, the troops once more eagerly seized the chance to play kingmaker. Chaos was certain to follow. This is precisely what Aper and his colleagues feared, and precisely this happened.

As a youth, Diocles, the now middle-aged Count of the Domestics, commander of the imperial guard cavalry, had enlisted in the army to escape the fate of millions of poor commoners like himself. A shrewd and lethal peasant from Dalmatia, Diocles rose through the ranks on grit and ability. Unlike the unwashed masses to which he belonged, the count from Dalmatia escaped their fate of dying in poverty and being forgotten. As part of the inner circle of the dead Numerian, Diocles seized his opportunity and accused Aper of murdering the young royal. In front of the assembled troops, Diocles dragged the unfortunate Praetorian prefect to the rostrum, denounced him, and ran him through with his sword. The cavalry commander received the accolades of the soldiers and donned the purple robe and diadem of empire and then assumed a new name: Diocletian. Few could have suspected that the rough, bearded, forty-year-old Dalmatian would end the anarchy that had throttled the state for fifty years. Along the way Diocletian would revolutionize politics and nearly every other aspect of Roman life. Among his ambitious projects was the creation of a college of emperors; there would be two senior coemperors, each holding the title of Augustus. One Augustus would manage the western, Latin-speaking half of the empire while another would manage the Greek east. Eventually, Diocletian found it necessary to raise to power two junior colleagues, called Caesars, who had broad authority in their spheres of action but who ultimately were subservient to the Augusti. The plan was bold, innovative, and a little desperate. The salty dog from Dalmatia understood that Rome's vast size and its sinuous, torturously long borders were painful to manage; internal resistance to the emperor made this colossal task impossible for one or even two powerful men.

Diocletian received overtures from the great king and arranged a truce. The emperor then busied himself overhauling the empire, but his eye was always on the east. He fortified the city of Circesium at the confluence of the Khabur and Euphrates Rivers and then moved south. He built several large legionary fortresses and reorganized the length of the frontier. Around the same time, Diocletian goaded the Persians by dispatching an army to back Tiridates III (287–ca. 330) as king in Armenia. Around 287, with Roman help, the Armenians pushed the Persians out of most of the land, and Tiridates firmed up his rule there as king of a Roman protectorate. Roman propagandists rightly crowed that Diocletian had brought Armenia back into the imperial fold.

Bahram was essentially a usurper and could not count on universal support. Despite occupying a low rung of the ladder in the eyes of his father and the nobility, he had attained power and therefore had to struggle to keep it. His brother, Narseh, was the senior son and the governor of Armenia and had therefore been the rightful heir to the throne. Successful military action against the Romans would only enhance Narseh's prestige and enrich his followers and further gnaw away at Bahram's authority. As later events would prove, Bahram could not risk foreign adventures while sizeable powers remained restless in his own realm. For his part, Diocletian took advantage of the grace afforded by the rare Sasanian lassitude. The emperor campaigned along the eastern frontier against fractious Arab tribesmen who had filled the vacuum left by the collapse of Palmyra twenty years before.

Bahram II died at the end of 293. A succession crisis loomed. Nobles led by Wahman, son of Tatrus, and Zoroastrian magi led a movement to enthrone Bahram's son, whom they crowned Bahram III. This was done without the knowledge of Narseh the son of Shapur, who, according to Persian protocol, should have ascended to the throne. Narseh received a group of Persian dignitaries from the aristocracy and the royal court who asked him to assume the throne. Narseh turned to the chief of one of the powerful families, the Andigans, whose power base likely resided in the far east of the empire, in the Ferghana Valley (in modern eastern Uzbekistan), where to this day a city bears the name Andijan. The lord of the Andigans led his followers to guard the borders of southern Mesopotamia and protect the eastern approaches to the capital, while Narseh himself made ready to march across Iran and rally his supporters before confronting his rival.

Hearing of Narseh's movements, Bahram and Wahman marched from Khuzestan, on the border with southern Mesopotamia, toward Armenia. The Sasanian sub-king of Messene then joined the rebellion. However, after a series of machinations, many rebel soldiers deserted to Narseh, who also captured Wahnam, whom he sent back, humiliated, to Bahram. The rebellion of the "King of the Lie," as he termed it, collapsed and Narseh assumed the throne as the seventh king of the Sasanian line. Narseh executed the rebel Wahnam, but the fate of his great-nephew is uncertain.

In the spring of 297, the Romans struck. Diocletian ordered his Caesar, the junior emperor Galerius, to attack the Sasanian Empire. Galerius was fresh off a successful campaign in Egypt, concluded in 295 when he was about forty-five years old. Like the Augustus, Diocletian, Galerius was an experienced military man, having served under Aurelian and Probus. Naturally, Roman historians blame Narseh for the start of the troubles, but it is far from certain that the great king had moved into the eastern Roman borderlands at any time prior to the outbreak of hostilities, and the Roman sources are suspect on this point. It is true, however, that the Roman establishment of their proxy king Tiridates there was a pebble in the Persian shoe, and Narseh may well have attempted to settle affairs in Armenia, whose partial loss was a particular affront, especially as it represented the royal province assigned to the crown prince of the line. If the shahanshah "gravely vexed the East," as one Roman claimed, he had followed the standard Sasanian regimen of seizing upon enemy discord to his advantage.[3] In the 290s, Diocletian's regime was hard pressed by rebellions in Britain, Egypt, and Africa.

Galerius advanced into Persian Mesopotamia, probably from the imperial city of Antioch, while Diocletian advanced on Egypt to smother the fires of rebellion there. Near Harran the forces of Narseh inflicted a serious defeat on Galerius, who retreated to Roman territory. Several versions of the story of the emperor's reception of the beaten Galerius survive; most involve the junior emperor being forced to run for more than a mile beside the imperial carriage before Diocletian could bother to stop and grant him an audience. Whatever the truth of the matter, Diocletian maintained faith in his underling and dispatched fresh forces from the Balkans to reinforce the eastern army, among them a large number of Gothic mercenaries who had just made merry plundering the coastlands of Roman Asia Minor.

Galerius marched his new troops through central Asia Minor via Cappadocia to the legionary fortress of Satala, which is the reason the subsequent battle is sometimes referred to as the Battle of Satala. We have no firm indication precisely where the battle was fought; a confused later account places the battle at Osha in the region of Basean (modern Pasinler in Turkey), forty kilometers east of the Armenian city of Karin (today Erzurum), and indicates that the Sasanian king encamped there in contested Armenian territory.[4] The Roman attack completely surprised the Sasanians. Narseh was wounded and barely escaped; he probably owed his delivery from danger only to the speed of his fine Persian charger and the courage of his picked bodyguard. In his flight, the great king abandoned precious possessions, the royal treasury and his wives, sisters, and children of the harem. Caesar Galerius returned to his master in Mesopotamia, driving the royal train of captive grandees in front of him, and delivered them as a cat drops a mouse at its owner's doorstep.

Not long afterward Narseh dispatched an embassy to Antioch to extend the olive branch. Before Galerius, the Persian ambassador Apharban is said to have claimed, "It is clear to the race of men that the Roman and Persian Empires are, as it were, two lamps; as with two eyes, each one should be adorned by brightness of the other and not for ever be angry seeking the destruction of the other."[5] This colorful, potent metaphor cast Rome and Persia as the "twin eyes of the world" and carried weighty symbolism. Persians claimed to be the bearers and protectors of light and civilization against the forces of darkness and barbarism, no less than equal to the Romans. Galerius fumed but referred the matter to his Augustus.

In 298/99 Diocletian sent his own diplomats to meet the great king. That the terms favored the Romans is telling and clearly indicates that the severity of the Persian defeat was no exaggeration: Narseh agreed to cede territories along the borderlands, allow the Romans to give the kings of Iberia their royal insignia, a symbolic act of fealty, and make his new western frontier the Upper Tigris valley.

The major points of the resulting Treaty of Nisibis of 299 are known from the sixth-century historian Peter the Patrician. Historians have tended to overplay the territorial concessions Narseh afforded Diocletian. They have taken the names of the provinces listed to imply that Roman control extended much farther to the east while disregarding the statement from Peter that "the river Tigris should be the boundary between each state."[6] This must mean that the old Hellenistic-era kingdoms, which formerly straddled the river and which were named earlier among the concessions, were partitioned. The treaty was humiliating for the Iranians, and, like the infamous Treaty of Versailles that ended World War I, sowed the seeds of the next war. The Peace of 299 was not devastating to Sasanian strategic interests, however, it did shift the balance of power in Upper Mesopotamia to the Romans.

The treaty terms were, for the moment, acceptable. While the great king had been humbled, the Roman victory was hardly a catastrophic blow. Persian acceptance hinged not on military weakness but the specific personal situation in which the great king found himself. Narseh, at least sixty upon his accession to the throne, was in no mood to quibble. Rather, the aged king looked inward, his gaze fixed upon the future of his dynasty and the domestic wounds that had slowly festered over the past thirty years and, with the brief and failed enthronement of Bahram III, erupted into open warfare. As part of the terms of the Treaty of 299, Narseh's family was returned to him and no doubt most of the other Persian noblemen as well. Narseh died in 303 and his son Hormozd II ascended to the throne.

Diocletian and Galerius returned and celebrated a triumph in Rome in 303 AD. As part of the gaudy, glitzy procession they put on a display of "a king of the Persians with all his people and placed their garments adorned with pearls to the number of thirty-three about the temples of their lord.

Thirteen elephants and six charioteers and two hundred and fifty horses were paraded in the city."[7] Who this "king of the Persians" was (if the chronicler is not mistaken) is unknown.

Hormozd faced tumult in the realm. Fractious nobles rose against him, and although we have no details of the rebellion, a rock relief at Naqsh-e Rostam in Fars depicts the mounted great king with a lance, striking his foe from the saddle. The later Muslim historian Tabari (839–923) records that, in 309, the Persian king invaded the Syrian desert fringe of the Roman Empire, allegedly to chastise the Arab tribal confederation of Ghassan (Ghassanids), which had migrated into the Roman desert *limes* (frontier) at an unknown date. The assertion of Tabari that the Arabs were Ghassanids is probably anachronistic: while Hormozd probably launched a raid into Syria, the story in Tabari is a literary device that aimed to put the great king in the desert in pursuit of his kingly passion for hunting. As with so many ancient and medieval kings, during the hunt the monarch became the quarry. However it transpired, Hormozd was murdered. He likely fell to a cabal of disgruntled nobles who wished to deprive his sons of the throne; Hormozd's chosen successor, his eldest son Adar Narseh, was particularly repellent to the coup leaders.[8] Upon the death of the great king, aristocrats and priests seized power from Adar Narseh, blinded another son, and a third, Hormozd, after a long imprisonment, fled to the Romans. Hormozd would appear many years later in the train of invading emperor Julian.

It is unclear why the ringleaders of the coup acted with such violence against Hormozd and his offspring, but they chose the late shah's infant son, Shapur, as monarch, the second of his name to rule the empire, and took good care of the impressive youth:

> When he came into the world, perfectly made, of noble race, shining with the mark of majesty and all the characteristic signs of royalty that vied on its behalf, we chose the most devoted nanny, the most suitable abode, and the most suitable food.[9]

Fortunately for the baby, the nobles in power behind the throne groomed him to rule, and thus he was not doomed to share the fate of so many child rulers who found themselves corrupted by ne'er-do-wells and favorites, dominated by powerful kingmakers, or murdered. After surviving the perils of the revolution, Shapur would hold the throne for seven decades, the longest of any Sasanian king. Rarely at peace, Shapur II faced challenges from every quarter of the empire, and his reign coincided with the rise of the powerful house of Constantine in the Roman Empire, the imperial family who embraced Christianity.

Christians had been present in Persia since apostolic times, and according to early tradition they spread to the lands of the east by the Apostle Thomas, the famous doubting disciple who refused to believe in the risen Christ until he had touched the wounds in Jesus's side. The deportations conducted by Shapur I had settled thousands of Christian prisoners of war within Sasanian domains and had the unforeseen result of spreading the faith even more deeply into the interior. The religion had thereby gained a firm footing and, alongside Judaism, Zoroastrianism, and Manichaeism, vied for converts. The Zoroastrian magi viewed Christianity with increasing fear and hostility, as it threatened the Persian national religion. As a foreign faith from the west, Christians fell under suspicion as forming a possible fifth column in support of Roman ambitions, and these tensions were only to rise throughout the fourth century as their numbers grew and hostilities between the empire once more broke into open warfare. In Armenia, too, Christianity had taken deep root, a direct consequence of Roman interference in the region. Under King Tiridates III, who assumed the Armenian throne with the backing of Diocletian, Armenia became the first land to adopt Christianity as the state religion. This was a serious blow to Sasanian pretensions there since the Zoroastrian religion was increasingly enmeshed with the Persian government and Iranian imperialism. The Christianization of Armenia, so physically and culturally close to the Sasanian Empire, presented a Gordian Knot to the great kings, and it is unsurprising that the wars to come were to take on an increasingly religious dimension.

Diocletian unleashed a wave of bitter persecution against the Christians of the Roman Empire, who in the east were conspicuous for their numbers and quite flagrant about their practicing an illicit religion. While far from the first time the followers of Jesus had suffered at the imperial whim, as with everything he undertook, Diocletian's steps were sweeping and decisive. Along with his imperial colleagues Maximian, Galerius, and Constantius, Diocletian promulgated a series of harsh measures against the "Galileans," stripping them of their legal rights and requiring them to sacrifice to the traditional gods. In 298–99, Diocletian purged the army of Christians: soldiers were ordered to sacrifice, and those who refused were discharged. Relative calm prevailed for five years when a claque of devoted polytheists, led by the Caesar Galerius and influential court advisors and intellectuals, pushed the conservative emperor to act. The coup de grâce belonged, however, to the god Apollo to whom the senior Augustus turned for counsel. The priests of Apollo maintained seers at the famous sanctuaries of Delphi, in Greece, at Didyma, near the renowned ancient city of Miletus and at Daphne, a suburb of Antioch. The statue of Apollo at Daphne answered the questions of worshippers, and it was there in 299 that Galerius heard the god tell him to strike down the Christians. It was Galerius who lobbied most vigorously for the legislation against Christians and who acted with the greatest relish on his orders; Christians fled in droves from the authorities throughout the east, and many crossed the frontier into Persia, where the Sasanians viewed them with a mixture of concern, suspicion, and puzzlement at the sudden turn in imperial policy.

In 305, Diocletian put to the test his bold idea of the college of emperors whose creation was aimed at ending the chaos that accompanied imperial succession. He and his fellow Augustus, Maximianus, stepped down and Galerius and Constantine Chlorus ascended from their ranks of Caesars to Augusti of the east and west, respectively. Galerius made Caesar another Illyrian, like Diocletian, a bullheaded, warlike peasant, Maximinus Daia. In 310, the Roman wolf scented the blood of the fawn on the Persian throne. With a baby on the throne of the great king, Maximinus went on the hunt, invading from his base at Antioch into Armenia. Despite claims to the contrary, the eastern portions of Armenia clearly remained under Persian control: the sixth-century chronicler Malalas notes that Maximinus Daia ranged throughout Armenia and conquered Persian territories there. Persian generals did not confront Daia. Instead the Sasanians invaded the Roman province of Osrhoene in the valley of the Upper Euphrates and sacked and razed a city called Maximinopoulis. Two cities, both far from Osrhoene, are known by this name. Malalas possibly meant Birtha, also known as Makedonoupolis, modern Birecik in eastern Turkey. The campaign ended inconclusively. Distracted by the death of his master Galerius, Maximinus turned his attentions to claiming his place in the sun. Forced to share power over the Roman east with Licinius, another of the college of emperors, tensions between the two erupted into civil war that left a defeated Maximinus to die, covered in failure, at Tarsus. The Persians were small beer for Licinius, who knew that sooner or later he would have to face his brother-in-law Constantine in a battle for supremacy over the Roman world. The bitter Roman infighting provided welcome breathing space as the boy Shapur grew to manhood.

The Persian Muslim historian Hamza al-Isfahani (893–ca. 961) described a painting from the lost Persian Book of Kings describing Shapur:

> His vest is rosy and embroidered, his trousers are red and embroidered and he is sitting on the throne with a battle-axe in his hand. His crown is sky-blue, colored gold around the edges and in its center two crests and a crescent of gold.[10]

When he came of age, the young monarch Shapur had to deal with a threat on the empire's southern flank. In 325 AD, aged sixteen and thus a man, Shapur campaigned against Arab tribesmen who menaced Mesopotamia. Arab semi-nomads in the region of what is today southeastern Iraq, Kuwait, and Bahrain had blazed across the empire. Like desert locusts, their passage brought turmoil to farming and trade. Arab raiders "seized the local people's herds of cattle, their cultivated lands, and their means of subsistence, and did a great deal of damage in those regions."[11] Of Shapur's expedition, Tabari continues:

> . . . he selected one thousand cavalrymen from among the stoutest and the most heroic of the troops. He commanded them to go forward and accomplish his design and forbade them to spare any of the Arabs they encountered or to turn aside in order to seize booty. Then he led them forth, and fell upon those Arabs who had treated Fars as their pasture ground while they were unaware, wrought great slaughter among them, reduced [others of] them to the harshest form of captivity, and put the remainder to flight.[12]

Shapur then crossed the Persian Gulf and attacked Arab settlements at al-Khatt (in the east of the modern United Arab Emirates), attacked the tribesmen there, and proceeded west to the island of Bahrain, where he spread carnage. The great king's march continued, back toward the east of the Arabian Peninsula, where he attacked three tribal groups in what Tabari's claims make tantamount to a campaign of extermination:

> He spread general slaughter among them, and shed so much of their blood that it flowed like a torrent swollen by a rainstorm. Those who were able to flee realized that no cave in a mountain nor any island in the sea was going to save them.[13]

Shapur was not finished. According to later Islamic tradition, where much of our information derives, the great king rained terror upon the lands of the tribe of 'Abd al-Qays (in modern Kuwait) and then turned inland, striking into the heart of Arabia, and fell upon al-Yamamah in the Najd region and continued his bloodletting. He stopped up the wells, took captives, and killed the Arabs wherever he found them, all the way to the marchlands of Syria and the Persian frontier of Fars, traversing the head of the gulf where Arab traders were involved in regional and long-distance trade with India. The shahanshah broke the established order by rearranging the settlement of Arabia. Having painfully chastised the Arabs, he moved the unfortunate deportees into newly founded cities in Mesopotamia. A Persian writer of the

Islamic period recalled Shapur as "Lord of the Shoulders" for his fondness of piercing the shoulders of his captives and stringing them together via rings.[14] More likely is Tabari's Arab captives would dwell under Sasanian hegemony, especially along the Tigris at Buzurg Shapur (Fayruz Shapur) at the ancient village of 'Ukbara. The Arab military colonists planted there, in a place later famous for its gardens and vineyards, served the empire as border auxiliaries guarding the approaches to Persian territory from Syria. Other Arab prisoners of war he settled in a new establishment at Susa, where the great king refounded the city and named it Khurrah Shapur.

Immediately after the bloody campaign in which Shapur pummeled into submission the tribes of the borderlands and Arabia, he began the construction of the so-called Wall of the Arabs (Persian *War-i-Tazigan*), which the Arabs called "Shapur's Ditch," dug from Hit on the Euphrates to Kazema (Kuwait) near Basra, a distance of over 650 kilometers. Behind the ditch, Sasanian engineers constructed watch posts and fortified garrisons in order to stop the desert tribesmen from entering the fertile lands of Persian Mesopotamia. The desert barrier was, in fact, a series of massive canals flooded with waters diverted from the Euphrates. Shapur's Ditch comprised a group of moats that provisioned water to a succession of Sasanian fortresses as well as farms that helped develop the agricultural potential of the region. Though it is uncertain, it seems that the Persian side included, at least for stretches, a fortified wall. Shapur installed a margrave, a warden of the march, over the length of the defenses and the troops who manned it.

The Roman frontier remained quiet during the reign of the emperor Constantine the Great (324–337), who nonetheless had rankled the Persians with a strange letter dispatched to Shapur in 324/5. Written in his own hand, from one sovereign to another, the emperor opened his missive by stating that he served the "most holy God." The power of this god as his ally had allowed Constantine eventually to come to rule the entire Roman world.

> The God to whom I accord my pre-eminent honor is the one whose sign my army, which is dedicated to God, carries on its shoulders and to whatever places the world of justice summons it, to them it makes its way directly. And, in return, I receive from the hands of my soldiers immediate recompense with splendid tokens of victory. This God I avow to honor with undying remembrance.[15]

Constantine goes on to detail the virtues of God, how he punishes and rewards, and how he destroyed the wicked men of Diocletian's imperial college, all of whom met bad ends. The Roman sovereign then waxes on in strange, ominous fashion:

With regard to this class of individuals, namely the Christians . . . you cannot imagine how delighted I am to hear that the most important parts of Persia too are . . . adorned far and wide [with their presence]. May the very greatest success attend you and them likewise, since they too are yours! For in doing so you shall keep the sovereign Lord of the universe gentle, propitious and benevolent. These, therefore, I commend to you because you are so great, entrusting these same persons to your care because you are famed for your piety. Love them as befits your humanity. By keeping your trust you will render both to yourself and to us an incalculable service.[16]

Shapur, a lad of fifteen, must have received this pious epistle with a mixture of befuddlement and outrage. Here the leader of the western Roman dogs deigned to reach his grasping, bloody palm into the body of the Persian Empire and claim to protect the Christians there! No amount of moral posturing could make the message less incendiary. One has the impression of a mob boss letting his underling in on the secret, sotto voce, and the secret was for the minion to make nice, or suffer the consequences at the hand of God, or Constantine, whomever was more available.

The emperor, a veteran of countless wars and the improbable victor in multiple civil wars, clearly attributed this rise to the god of the Christians. His pretensions to sovereignty over all Christians, not just those in the empire, reeked of hubris. Yet the cagey, condescending letter exposed a revolutionary thought: that communities transcended political boundaries and that community was forged in the crucible of faith. Constantine had just invented Christendom.

If the Xhi Rho, the two letters of the Greek alphabet which began the world *Christos*, Christ, adorned the tunics of Roman soldiers, this fanatic's letter could, to the mind of the young king and his wizened advisors, only mean trouble. Yet, however large loomed the contest between Christianity and Zoroastrianism, pragmatism, not religious zealotry, governed fourth-century politics. The terms of the Treaty of 299 gashed Persian pride and, worse, created a strategic disadvantage for the shahanshah. Armenia, wracked by anarchy as nobles competed with one another, was happy to play the great powers against one another in order to further their parochial interests. A young Shapur, untested save for his hammering of impoverished, loosely organized Arab tribesmen, needed to prove himself on the killing fields and restore the strategic balance along the western frontier. Only victory could solve his dilemma.

Having settled affairs inside Rome to his liking, Constantine prepared for war with Shapur. Hearing of the Roman preparations, Shapur sent envoys to his imperial counterpart, seeking peace. Constantine agreed, but it was a pact that neither side intended to keep. Both empires used the intervening year to prepare for war. Said one influential Roman rhetorician:

> They offered a peaceful appearance, but had the disposition of men at war . . . and continued indeed to acquit their obligations towards the treaty from that time onwards . . . but arranged everything towards that purpose. They equipped their own forces and brought their preparation to perfection in every form, cavalry, men-at-arms, archers and slingers. They trained to a consummate degree what methods had been their practice from the beginning . . . .[17]

In 335 or 336, the emperor made a curious but stunning move, marrying his daughter Constantina to his nephew, Hannibalianus. Constantine then named Hannibalianus "King of Kings" (Latin *rex regum*) and "ruler of the Pontic peoples" (Pontus is the region of the southeastern Black Sea) and dispatched him to Caesarea in Cappadocia. Had not Constantine already delivered the inflammatory letter proclaiming himself protector of the Christians and describing his career of conquest which had proceeded, under divine guidance, from the far west to the east? How far east would the emperor go? In his youth, Constantine had fought in the army of Galerius that had supposedly marched to the very walls of Ctesiphon, and nearby he had seen the ruins of the magnificent, mythical Babylon. Trajan was one of his heroes, a man whose propaganda and administration Constantine imitated.[18] Shapur, no idiot, clearly divined the cogs turning in the emperor's head: Constantine intended to install Hannibalianus in Armenia, and probably even more, to drive the great king from his throne and make the newly crowned Hannibalianus the Roman proxy king of Persia.[19]

The emperor sent his son, Constantius, to Antioch where preparations for an invasion of Persia began in earnest in 336. Constantine called upon the support of Christian bishops, who eagerly clamored to march with the army. The emperor had made a large tent in the shape of a church and made preparations to be baptized in the river Jordan before setting off on his invasion.

In the face of such aggression, Shapur preempted his rival. He sent agents to curry favor among pro-Persian noble families in Armenia, and there were more than a few who resented the turn to Christianity and watched with alarm as their countrymen made bedfellows with the Romans. The Persian governor of Atropatene, Waras, who managed to seize the Armenian king,

Tiran, and his family and deliver them into the hands of Narseh, brother of Shapur II who had made him king of Armenia. Shapur blinded Tiran and defeated an Armenian retaliatory expedition. The great king then assembled the Sasanian field army and gave command to Narseh, who marched on Armenia, intent on bringing the whole of the country into the Persian fold. Armenian sources confuse the two Narsehs and repeat the engagement at Basan decades before during the reign of the great king Narseh I.

By now Shapur had realized that the Armenian hound would continue to bay for blood unless he took decisive action. Although he hated the Arsacids, whence came the Armenian kings, only throwing a sop to these rowdy mountaineers would calm them. It was probably Narseh who installed Tiran's son, Arsaces, who became King Arsaces II and brought Armenia into Shapur's tent.[20]

Amida sat on top of a volcanic bluff overlooking the Tigris. Built entirely in black volcanic basalt stone, the city presented a mournful aspect. When the Austrian officer Armand von Scheiger-Lerchenfeld visited the place in the late nineteenth century he remarked, "In this cauldron formed by the basalt dark stones life in every aspect is stopping; the fountains are drying out."[21] The sinister aspect of the toothy battlement-encrusted walls, which at their foundation date to the late Roman era, is echoed in the Turkish proverb, "black are the walls and black are the hearts of black Amida." Here, Narseh's forces overran portions of Roman Mesopotamia and tried to claw their way through the fortified line. Their best chance for a breakthrough lay at this strategic point, well connected to the Anatolian hinterland. Subsequent Roman engineering efforts prove that in the opening phase of the war with Shapur, the black city was both a prize worth having and inadequately defended. Narseh captured the city, but in a battle that followed, he was defeated and killed at the battle of Narasara, probably the road station of Nararra, nine Roman miles (about twenty kilometers) east of Amida. Checked in his punitive expedition, Shapur braced for the Roman counterattack. The Roman intellectual and teacher Libanius of Antioch described a Persian embassy seeking to buy iron from the Romans, which Constantine apparently willingly sold them, even though he knew it would be forged into weapons to be used against the armies of his son.

> Indeed, darts, sabers, spears, swords and every warlike implement were forged in a wealth of material. When he [Shapur] examined every possibility and left nothing not investigated, he contrived to make his cavalry invulnerable, so to speak. For he did not limit their armor to helmet, breastplate, and greaves in the ancient manner nor even to place bronze plates before the brow and breast of the horse; but the result was that

the man was covered in chain mail from head to the end of his feet, and the horse from its crown to the tip of its hooves, but a space was left open only for the eyes to see what was happening and for breathing holes to avoid asphyxiation. . . . These men had to ride a horse which obeyed their voice instead of a bridle, and they carried a lance which needed both hands, and had as their only consideration that they should fall upon their enemies without a thought for their action, and they entrusted their body to the protection of iron mail.[22]

Sometime just after he eliminated all rivals and assumed rule over the whole of the empire, Constantine had completed the long process of military reforms begun under Diocletian. The border fortresses were manned by frontier guards who, despite their garrison duties and static nature, were not a militia but regular troops. Their job was to police the frontier and resist smaller-scale incursions. In the event of full-on onslaughts, the frontiersmen, called *limitanei* after the *limes* (limits), would link up and fight alongside the regular campaign army.

The *limes* in the east were largely the result of Diocletian's efforts, but other emperors certainly recognized the shambles that the region facing the Sasanians had become and lent their hand in the reforms. From the Red Sea to the Euphrates ran a military highway, called the Strata Diocletiana, studded with rectangular forts at intervals of a day's march. Major fortress cities were strengthened and given more robust garrisons, and large bases were constructed at strategic points behind the military road from which the legions could muster and coalesce into capable forces.

Constantine made permanent the practice of the imperial field army, the *comitatus praesentalis*, the escort or guard troops "of the emperor's presence." Under the command of the emperor and his top lieutenants, the *comitatenses* provided the crack, mobile forces required for hard campaigning and confronting the invasions in force along the frontiers that had become commonplace. Following the practices established by Gallienus, the mobile forces likely included a greater proportion of cavalry, which enhanced their speed of movement and striking power. In the stormy days of the fourth century, the capacity of the emperor's men to move quickly from one end of the empire to the other, along borders strung out along more than five thousand kilometers (three thousand miles) of territory, required tremendous logistical skill and the ability to move at speed to where duty called. Constantine and his successors continued to adapt their cavalry warfare to the new realities that beset them, including increasing use of heavy horse and mounted archers to counter the Persians and enemies from the steppe.

Constantine prepared his new model army and marched out of his new capital. Characteristic of his modesty, he had named the settlement after himself. Constantinople was to become the greatest city in medieval Europe, the jewel of Christendom, and capital of the East Roman Empire for the next thousand years. The old emperor, who knew his time was near, never made it past Nicomedia, Diocletian's old capital. There, on the Christian feast of Pentecost, May 22, 337, the old war dog and newly baptized Christian breathed his last. Keeping things all in the family, his sons Constantine II, Constantius II, and Constans divided the empire into thirds and ruled it as co-Augusti. Clearly the job was too big for one man, unless that man was Constantine the Great. Constantius tended to his father's funeral, ensuring that the deceased sovereign was, as he wished, buried in Constantinople in the Church of the Holy Apostles, his porphyry sarcophagus placed alongside those of the twelve apostles, which effectively made Constantine the thirteenth apostle.

Flavius Julius Constantius, known to posterity as Constantius II, was born on August 7, 317, in Illyricum. The second son of Constantine and his wife Fausta, Constantius had Syrian blood in his veins; his maternal grandmother, Eutropia, the wife of the emperor Maximian, was a native of the region. As a boy, Constantius lost his mother in the most horrific way imaginable—his father had her locked in a bathhouse which was then overheated so she died by heat exhaustion or asphyxiation. According to later sources hostile to the family, Fausta was involved in a dalliance with her stepson Crispus, Constantine's eldest son through an illegitimate relationship. Crispus soon followed Fausta to the grave, dispatched with the businesslike and unpitying manner that his father dealt with so many problems.

A bust presumed to represent Constantius portrays a man with a thin, long face, a strong aquiline nose, large eyes, and a pinched mouth. Among few good things the haughty Syrian historian from Antioch, Ammianus Marcellinus, has to say about Constantius was that he was chaste, dignified, a fine rider, and skilled with the bow and javelin. He was never seen to wipe his nose or spit in public.

He was rather dark, with bulging eyes and sharp sight; his hair was soft and his regularly shaven cheeks were neat and shining. From the meeting of neck and shoulders to the groin he was unusually long, and his legs were very short and bowed, for which reason he was good at running and leaping.[23]

The negative side of the balance sheet was extensive: he was dull of mind, henpecked, paranoid, and extremely cruel, and worse—in the eyes of Ammianus—a Christian. "And as sparks flying from a dry forest even with a light breeze of wind come with irresistible course and bring danger to rural villages, so he also from trivial causes roused up a mass of evils."[24] In his savagery, we are told, he surpassed Caligula, Domitian, and Commodus, infamous monsters of the early empire. "For it was in rivalry of the cruelty of those emperors that at the beginning of his reign he destroyed root and branch all who were related to him by blood and race."[25] It was probably Constantius who engineered the gory purge of his family after the death of Constantine. The cousin of Constantius, Julian, saw his father, uncle, and six cousins murdered. Among them were the Caesar Dalmatius, the late emperor's half-brother. Along with him assassins felled his son Hannibalianus, whose lofty title of king of kings could not save him from this Roman night of the long knives.

In the east, Constantius inherited fire and sword. His rival Shapur was in his prime, twenty-eight years old and had been king for as many years. Learning of the death of Constantine, the great king cast the die. The fifth-century church historian Theodoret remembered the Persian's opening salvo of the war, the ferocious attack on the border city of Nisibis:

> At this moment the king of the Persians, whose name was Shapur and who despised the sons of Constantine as being less capable than their father, marched against Nisibis at the head of a vast army comprising both cavalry and infantry, and also as many elephants as he could muster. He divided his army as for a siege and completely surrounded the city, setting up machines of war, commissioning towers, erecting palisades, the areas between strewn with branches placed crosswise, then he ordered his troops to raise embankments and build towers against the city towers. Then, while dispatching his archers to ascend the towers and direct their arrows at those defending the walls, at the same time he charged others with undermining the walls from below.[26]

When conventional measures failed, the Sasanians took more drastic steps. Nisibis lay on the Mygdonius River. Shapur's engineers set to work damming the river. Once the waters had accumulated behind the barrage, they unleashed it against the walls. The force of the foaming waters collapsed a whole stretch of the city wall. Deciding against an immediate assault of the waterlogged city, the Persians decided to wait for the flood to recede.

Within the city, Jacob, the graybeard firebrand Christian bishop, rallied the townsfolk to action. They piled up timbers, rocks, mud—whatever materials they could find—and built a makeshift rampart on the ruins of the washed-out wall. Their constant work throughout the night paid off—by the morning the barricade was of sufficient height to bar a cavalry charge or even

Bust of Constantius. (*Marie-Lan Nguyen/Creative Commons*)

scaling ladders. But Jacob delivered the finishing blow when, in answer to the supplications of the people, he ascended the ramshackle wall and prayed. The gnats of Nisibis, which had a nasty reputation, swarmed in dark clouds and drove men and beasts to madness. Faced with a plague of stinging insects of biblical proportions, Shapur cut his losses and skulked away. Whatever the reality of the encounter, the Persians' heroic efforts at Nisibis fell short. The city was spared.

Constantius was well prepared for war. Even his detractors, such as Ammianus and the emperor's cousin, the later emperor, Julian, praised Constantius for his care in military affairs. He was organized, assiduously attended to soldierly drill, and only promoted seasoned veteran fighters to positions of high command. The Romans had not only increased their cavalry numbers in response to fighting foes like the Persians and Sarmatians who fielded strong horsemen but had improved their panoply:

Your cavalry was almost unlimited in numbers and they all sat on their horses like statues, while their limbs were fitted with armor that followed closely the outline of the human form. It covers the arms from wrist to elbow and thence to the shoulder, while a coat of mail protects the shoulders, back and breast. The head and face are covered by a metal mask which makes its wearer look like a glittering statue, for not even the thighs and legs and the very ends of the feet lack this armor. It is attached to the cuirass by fine chain armor like a web, so that no part of the body is visible and uncovered, for this woven covering protects hands as well, and is so flexible that the wearers can bend even their fingers.[27]

But like the early Army of the Potomac in the American Civil War, Constantius's troops lacked one key ingredient: a bold leader, or at least one with lower regard for his own life and the lives of his troops. If the emperor is described as possessing a sociopathic streak, he did not carry it onto the battlefield. In response to Shapur's slap on the Roman face at Nisibis, the emperor waited out the cold months of winter and, with the coming of the spring lilies in northern Syria, drew to his side, like snowmelt gathering into a torrent, the flower of his rested, well-provisioned, and meticulously prepared troops. Constantius's idea was to meet the great king in the field and annihilate him. Like a dog trying to dislodge a flea, Constantius scratched the countryside in vain. Shapur had departed and refused the invitation to the dance. Unwilling to mount a real invasion, with its sieges, extended supply lines, and high probability of mishap, the emperor contented himself with a raid in force. While his caution meant his strong army remained intact, it did nothing to change the balance of power.

By 340 Constantius and his fine soldiery filed from Edessa and his skilled engineers threw a pontoon bridge across the Tigris. The emperor marauded across Persian Mesopotamia, where he probably sieged and captured the city of Nineveh. This settlement was likely a small, ramshackle town of mudbrick, its star long fallen from its days as the capital of the ferocious Assyrian Empire. Julian slightly later asserted that the Persians offered no resistance because they were afraid to fight the Romans. Was Shapur afraid of meeting his imperial rival in the field? It is certainly possible. Surely, Shapur's spies had informed him that Constantius led a spit and polish outfit and took every precaution to avoid the breakdowns in discipline and surprise that had undone his predecessor. If, in fact, Shapur was reluctant, he may have lacked confidence in his own generalship or that of his army. For more than forty years, Sasanian performance in the west had been uninspired, and the days of the smashing victories of his kingly namesake Shapur I belonged not to living memory but to distant tales kept alive in wine song and poetry.

The mount of Sinjar rises low and dark over the Syrian Desert, a finger of basaltic high ground cast up over the alluvium by volcanic eruption eons ago. The place briefly erupted onto screens around the globe in 2014 when ISIS unleashed its vicious bloodletting of the local Yazidi minority there. To the Sasanians the slender spit of land was a digit dismembered from their empire and made a trophy by the Romans. The arid fortress town lived off its scraps of arable land, wells, and its position on secondary routes of communication.

From the heights of the jebel, one held a vantage overlooking the expanse of flatlands beyond. High ground and water, Singara formed one of the salients of Roman territory overlooking the Iranian realm. For reasons of security, as with Nisibis, the great king could not let the Romans occupy it. Shapur was well prepared. His forces comprised Persian savaran heavy cavalry, with their barded mounts and heavily armored troopers, archers and a mix of light troops, boys conscripted from the wider population to serve as laborers and camp attendants, and even women serving as sutlers. Constantius moved with the praesental army to intercept Shapur.

The Sasanians moved against the black fortress. The Persians threw three bridges across the Euphrates and, by forced marches, came to Sinjar. The Persians established their own camp, ringed with an earthen wall and palisade, seventeen miles distant from that of the Romans. After a rest, they sent skirmishers ahead to draw the enemy to battle. As the Romans drew up their legions and tried to close on the men, the Persians employed a feigned retreat—a classic steppe nomad tactic for which their Parthian forebears had been justly famous. The legionnaires pursued them across the scorched plain at the foot of Jebel Sinjar, and the heat of the sun beat down and baked the flatlands and troopers, wearing them down. Constantius knew that his men suffered from heat exposure, fatigue, and lack of water. The emperor ordered a retreat, but his commands were either not received or disregarded. The Romans poured across the plain, dismantling the walls of the Persian camp. As night fell and offered some relief from the blazing day, the Persians regrouped and attacked. In the sharp struggle that ensued, the Roman infantry pressed their advantage; in a close-in fight the legionnaires had the advantage over the Persian horse and light skirmishing troops. Constantius's men snatched the victory and drove the easterners from the field. Along with the enemy camp and its spoils, the Romans seized the Sasanian crown prince, whom they later executed. While the Romans claimed a victory, in his account Julian acknowledged that there had been an engagement near Sinjar in which both sides suffered heavily. One interesting detail that he preserves is how the Romans effectively dealt with one of the Sasanian savaran heavy cavalry charges; this was to open their ranks and allow the enemy to penetrate the lines of heavy infantry, who then attacked the horsemen from the flank and bludgeoned them with maces, felling them and their mounts. While the Romans cast the encounters at Sinjar as a great victory, as with so many of Constantius's battles against Shapur, the campaign was nothing better than a draw. Clearly the Romans had suffered heavy casualties, and the outer defenses of Sinjar had been ruined.

The failure of Shapur to act with full vigor in defense of his son or to mount a rescue operation, or to even negotiate for the life of the prince, the heir to the throne, make it likely that the great king was not present at the first Battle of Sinjar. On at least one other occasion (discussed later), the Romans mistook one of the Sasanian sub-kings for the great king, an easy enough mistake to make for those unfamiliar with the distinctive crowns that each Sasanian monarch wore.

Not long after the Battle of Sinjar, the Roman sources hint at a defeat of Constantius by Shapur. Worsted in the field, the emperor fled to a small frontier outpost with a few companions. Whatever the reality of this engagement, it was likewise indecisive. Shapur, for his part, seized the initiative and for the second time laid siege to the frontier fortress city of Nisibis. In 346, the great king enveloped the city, but after a hundred-day investment, he decamped and returned home. Constantius remained active along the frontier, bringing his forces to Edessa where he could counter the next strokes of the shahanshah. The emperor refused, however, to bring Shapur to a decisive engagement, preferring to let the soldiers of the great king attrit themselves in a grueling siege. Contemporary Christian writers, present in the city during the war, offer only poetic accounts of what was clearly another bitter dose of siege warfare in which the Persians once more tried to throttle the key fortress into submission but ultimately failed. Shapur withdrew and Nisibis remained a bone in the Sasanian gullet that they could neither spit out nor swallow.

In 350, Shapur was forced to break off his war against Constantius. He had bloody business in the north and east. The desert ranges and steppe lands that belted the northern and eastern reaches of his kingdom stretched seemingly into an eternal inland sea, over which sailed nomadic hordes, their horses serving as ships would on the ocean. Khurasan, the region by the Caspian, was under attack. The Huns had arrived.

In the same year, having over the previous thirteen seasons fought several inconclusive engagements against his eastern foe, Constantius departed Syria. The emperor faced multiple rebellions across the empire, from Sicily to Anatolia, and Shapur's troubles offered welcome quiet along the eastern borderlands. The emperor saw to the ongoing Roman fortification of the limes, attested by inscriptions that show the refortification of the citadel at Bostra, in southern Syria, and the building of watch towers along the front. In addition, the emperor added to the garrisons of the cities of Syria and provisioned them with food, weapons, siege engines, and the other accoutrements of war.

Already in the year 325, when Christians met in the first ever ecumenical church council, called by the emperor Constantine and held in the city of

Nicaea, the King of Armenia, Tiridates III, begged off attending due to his anxiety over an alliance between Shapur II and the "king of the Indians and the Eastern Khagan."[28] The king of the Indians here likely means Chandragupta I, founder of the Gupta Empire that held sway over much of the northern Indian subcontinent. The Eastern Khagan is more mysterious. Most likely, the title, which is Turkic, refers to the leader of a confederation of recently arrived Huns, referred to in the Greek sources as "Chionites," whence derived the term "Hun."

Mention of the Huns usually evokes images of the fierce hordes of Attila and Mongolian or Turkic groups who migrated east. The origins of the Huns have perplexed scholars for more than a century, and while it was once thought that the tribal confederation bearing this name, who first appeared on the European steppes around 370 AD, were to be equated with the ancient Xiongnu, known from Chinese sources from the third century BC. But the first recorded appearance of "Huns" in Bactria comes from Ammianus Marcellinus who calls them Chionites and notes their presence in 356/57 at Shapur's siege of Amida. There are several other groups labeled as "Huns" by classical Greek and Latin authors, including peoples which were not Turkic or Mongolian but Iranian speakers as well. The Chionites were likely of Iranian origin and were recent migrants to the region of Transoxiana and Bactria. Genetic studies relying on recovered ancient DNA from archaeological excavation indicate that the "Huns" throughout the centuries were formed of an admixture of groups from among various eastern and western Eurasian groups. We must understand "Hun" and other nomadic steppe confederacies as polyglot, comprised of tribes of multiple ethnicities, fighting under the banner of dominant clans who gave these groups their name.

We can guess—and it is nothing better than an educated one—that tribal migrations pressed the Sasanian empire from the 320s onward and demanded the great king's attention in the north and east. Raids and battles along the empire's front from the Caspian eastward likely explain the absence of Shapur from the Roman scene for much of the first half of his reign. On at least one occasion, Shapur defeated a large incursion of northern tribesmen who threatened Armenia through the Caucasian passes.[29] What is certain is that, by the 350s, when the war with the Romans entered its next phase, Shapur seems to have gotten the better of his eastern foes, or at least fought them to a stalemate which allowed him to freely recruit mercenaries from among their numbers.

The Chronicle of Arbela, a later source written in Syriac, summarizes the deeds of Shapur II during the third siege of Nisibis:

And in this year (350/51) Shapur, the great king, collected all of his fighting strength and planned to besiege the cities of the Romans. And he killed many of their men. And he laid waste to many localities. And as he was incapable of taking Nisibis, he left it and strengthened his fighting forces and marched back to Nahrin [Persian northern Mesopotamia]. He, himself, however, returned to his land, that he free his own cities from barbarian peoples, which came against him from the Caspian Sea.[30]

Constantius, likely made aware of the threat Shapur faced from the reports of Silk Road merchants and spies, felt secure enough to evacuate the field army from the eastern provinces. Likely he hoped that the Sasanian king would be defeated or at least pinned down for years to come. In fact, this is what happened. Though we have no detailed information, there are echoes in the Roman sources of a protracted, hard-fought war between Shapur and his eastern foes. The great king's campaigns lasted seven years. Only in 358 was the shahanshah able to sign a favorable peace treaty from which we can glean that he was victorious. A Sassanian triumph, while not detailed in any surviving source, can be confidently concluded based on three important scraps of information. Firstly, the Chionite Huns appear in Sasanian service at the siege of Amida in 359. This is clearly not the case of the Persians simply hiring bands of Hunnic mercenaries; on the contrary, the Roman historian Ammianus is clear that the service of the Chionites arose from a treaty to which they had bound themselves. Secondly, after the end of the Chionite war in 358 and late in his long reign, Shapur II established Sasanian royal mints around Kabul, in Afghanistan, the former territory of the Kushans and their Kushano-Sasanian successors. Finally, on some Chionite coins, only the name of the ruling Sasanian shahanshah appears, a clear indicator of Persian hegemony over the lands in which they settled. Nonetheless, the Persian road to Central Asia ran in two directions, and the ambitions of the great kings would meet their doom in the bloody fields of the east.

In 356, when Constantius was fresh from quelling yet another revolt in the western provinces, he sent peace feelers to Shapur. At this point, Constantius must have realized that he was not strong enough to score a decisive victory over the Sasanians, weakened as he was by multiple revolts and still, despite two decades in power, not secure from his internal enemies. Unofficial Roman envoys approached the marzban, the marchwarden of Adiabene, in Persian Mesopotamia across the Tigris. Might his lord, Shapur, be inclined to peace? Intelligence gathering had raised their hopes, for the Romans:

Had certain knowledge from the unamimous reports of their scouts that Shapur, on the remotest frontiers of his realm, was with difficulty and with great bloodshed of his troops driving back hostile tribesmen . . . .[31]

Shapur, for his part, is said to have imagined that these peace overtures meant that Constantius was in dire straits, and he wrote a letter to his imperial counterpart demanding the return of Armenia and Mesopotamia, which, he added, "double-dealing had wrested from my grandfather."[32] For good measure, the great king added that if his demand was not met, he would undertake an invasion as soon as winter had passed. Constantius's reply, as one might expect, was less than enthusiastic. After all, he reminded Shapur, he was victorious over all comers who would have stripped him of the purple, and the Persian could expect the same treatment, "for we both know by experience and by reading that while in some battles, though rarely, the Roman cause has stumbled, yet in the main issue of our wars it has never succumbed to defeat."[33] The Roman position, his ambassadors conveyed to the great king, was an end to the war with no change in the borders. The ambassadors arrived in Ctesiphon and found Shapur in no mood to compromise, fresh as he was off his victories along the northern frontier.

Constantius, bogged down along the Danube frontier against the Sarmatians, did not wish to cast aside the possibility of a rapprochement. He dispatched a second embassy but with the same terms. Perhaps he hoped to buy time to allow his own arrival in the east. This mission, like its predecessor, failed. The emperor was still at Sirmium (today Sremska Mitrovica in Serbia) in the province of Pannonia, dealing with the disturbed situation in the Balkans, when he received word that the relative calm that had ruled in the east for the last nine years had been swept away. The great king was on the march. In the spring of 359, neither monarch could guess the remarkable turns in store for them, nor that Shapur's gambit had opened the decisive, final phase of the war that would leave one of the two empires beaten and humiliated.

CHAPTER FOUR

Clash of Empires

I n northern Mesopotamia in the city of Amida, a certain wealthy merchant named Antoninus had risen through the ranks of the Roman administration to become a *protector*, a bodyguard in the retinue of the governor, probably Euphronius, who in 359 held the office, according to Ammianus. Unfortunately for Antoninus, he had fallen deeply into debt, so deeply that he felt his situation unrecoverable. As his creditors pressed him and threatened his position daily, Antoninus hatched a plan. Fluent in both Greek and Latin, he used his position to acquire detailed information on the order of battle of Roman troops in the east, their pay schedules, and their logistical situation. At the same time, he acquired a farm across the Tigris River. Under the cover of managing his new estate, he made frequent trips there. In secret, he ordered skilled swimmers from among his attendants to make contact with Tamsapor, the Persian commander in the west. When the time arrived, likely in the autumn of 358, Antoninus defected to the Persians. Antoninus is alleged to have provided the impetus for Shapur to invade Roman territory, not at Nisibis where Persian armies had thrown themselves like a sea on a breakwater but into the territory of Amida, which he promised was ripe for the picking. Though the Romans would later lay the blame for the invasion that would follow at the feet of Antoninus, Shapur needed little persuading, and it is doubtful he needed to rely on a low-level Roman deserter to formulate his master strategy.

Fresh from his hard-won victory in the eastern lands of his empire, Shapur decided to launch an attack into Syria. His plan seemed to be a raid in force into northern Syria, away from the hardened defenses of Upper Mesopotamia. The shahanshah had drawn the king of Armenia, Arshak, to his side; the Armenians arrived on the borderlands of Roman Mesopotamia before the large Sasanian host had crossed the Tigris.

Knowing that the Romans expected attack in the quarter of Nisibis, the great king divided his army. Some twenty thousand Sasanian cavalry, the vanguard of his force, struck across the Tigris and over the plain of Nisibis, overrunning the Roman defenses at the end of the thirty-mile-long scrap of rocky heights known as Mount Izala, or Tur 'Abdin to the local Syriac speakers who called the mountain home. Tamsapor, Shapur's commander in the west, alongside the Sasanian governor of Mesopotamia, led the assault. Persian spies operated west of the rivers, relaying information about the disposition of Roman troops and their level of preparedness; one of these, a Roman Gaul born in Paris, who had deserted to the Sasanians, was captured by enemy soldiers near Amida.

The Romans knew the Sasanian hammer blow would fall hard upon them, though not where. The Persians initially achieved surprise. Ammianus Marcellinus described chaos in the Roman ranks at Amida. The historian was attached to the cavalry commander of the Roman armies in the east, Ursicinus, and thus witnessed many of the events of this campaign. The Armenian army, not wishing to wait for their Persian allies, whose crossing of the river had been delayed, elected to strike the Roman forces gathered around Nisibis. The Armenians alone attacked the Romans and inflicted serious losses and then withdrew carrying an immense quantity of plunder with them. The operations by the Armenians, omitted by Ammianus, explain why Ursicinus rushed to Nisibis; he viewed the Armenian onslaught as a prelude to a full-scale assault by the king of kings.

Believing that the Persian army would once more attempt a breakthrough at Nisibis, Ursicinus raced there accompanied only by his personal retinue. As the Romans prepared their defense of the city, they saw clouds of smoke and orange fires blossom on the plains to the north and east. Enemy raiders galloped as far as the gates of Nisibis itself; without a fast horse, Ammianus himself would have been captured or killed. On a fear-filled night lit by a full moon, probably July 26, 359, Ammianus ran away with the small troop of soldiers who had collected around him in the retreat from Nisibis, joined by the garrison of the fortlet of Amudis.[1] He fled on the heels of Ursicinus who had decamped across Mount Izala to the city of Amida.

From there, Ursicinus dispatched Ammianus to the neighboring province of Cordouene in Persian Mesopotamia, where the governor, the *satrap* Jovinianus, played to both sides. The satrap allowed Ammianus to scout the Persian army. The Romans looked down from a high bluff overlooking the plains of Nineveh. There they saw the whole of a vast imperial force, including a contingent of Chionite Huns and Albanians from the Caucasus Mountains. Ammianus thought he picked out Shapur from among them, "glittering in splendid attire."[2]

Ammianus sent fast riders to Roman Mesopotamia to warn the governor, Euphronius, and count Cassianus, who commanded the local troops. The Romans hurriedly evacuated the city of Harran (Carrhae), as its defenses were dilapidated and its garrison inadequate to withstand an assault. At the same time, legionnaires fired the crops. The standing corn was just ripening, and the plains, dry after the summer rains, roiled into flame, a belt of fire and ash cascading from the Tigris to the Euphrates.

In the face of the enemy stroke, Shapur halted. Persian troops traveled light. Like most ancient and medieval armies, the Sasanians relied on supplies of stores at defined points while traveling in friendly territory and then lived off enemy lands when in hostile country. By this time, likely in June, Shapur must have learned that the main Roman eastern field army was bivouacked at Edessa and thus in a good position to strike if he were to cross the Euphrates and move up the river as his ancestor Shapur I had done when he had captured Antioch a century before. Strategic realities therefore forced the great king to alter his plan for the offensive. Since the Romans were apparently preparing for an assault on Nisibis, which lay directly ahead of him, Shapur opted to turn his army north to strike at the Roman fort of Barzalo (today Killik in Turkey) where the crops still stood and afforded him ample provender for his mostly cavalry army.

Divining from Shapur's line of march that the Persian king intended to traverse the upper waters of the Euphrates, the Romans moved to destroy the river crossings at the city of Zeugma and the bridge of boats at Capersana. A squadron of Illyrian cavalry seven hundred strong and recent transfers to Syria were set to guard the road. These troopers later alleged they feared a night attack by Persian forces roaming nearby, which inspired them to abandon their posts. After darkness fell, Persian scouts informed Tamsapor that the route lay open; the Balkan cavalrymen were drunk and asleep. The Sasanian general marched his twenty thousand troops past the slumbering Romans, skirted the foothills to the east of Amida, and fell upon the unsuspecting Roman pickets there.

The general Ursicinus expected no action in his quarter; his scouts had brought him no news to change his mind about Shapur's intentions to cross the Upper Euphrates. Ursicinius gathered units to accompany him on a march to the city of Samosata, some 150 kilometers (94 miles) as the crow flies to the southwest of Amida. En route and just beyond the suburbs of Amida, the Roman general was shocked to see a horde of Persians. He stared in disbelief as he spotted among them the Roman traitor Antoninus. Ursicinus called out to the deserter and berated him and then watched in stunned silence as Antoninus bowed his face to the ground and retreated to the Persian lines, never ceasing to face the Romans as he did so. Cries went up from a body of Roman troops on a nearby hill, warning of an impending charge by a detachment of Tamsapor's cataphracts. In the melee of the ambush that ensued, the Romans retreated in chaos, some falling to their deaths off the steep banks into the Tigris, others drowning in the river, caught in the mud and trapped by the weight of their panoply. Ammianus and his comrades struggled to the city where, beneath the basalt walls, they cowered for the night, under constant Persian attack:

> Here, mingled with the Persians, who were rushing to the higher ground with the same effort as ourselves, we remained motionless until sunrise of the next day, so crowded together that the bodies of the slain, held upright by the throng, could nowhere find room to fall, and that in front of me a soldier with his head cut in two, and split into equal halves by a powerful sword stroke, was so pressed on all sides that he stood erect like a stump.[3]

From the walls the Roman defenders rained a steady fire of artillery into the mixed mass of Romans and Persians. Constantius had seen to the refortification of Amida, and the large, U-shaped towers were engineered to house the complicated torsion machines that were a hallmark of the late Roman arsenal. The two most common examples were the ballista, which fired a heavy bolt, and the onager, a stone-throwing machine.

Ammianus and those in his company managed to enter the city by means of a postern gate, despite its being thronged with civilians who had come to the annual city market fair, unsuspecting of Persian attack. Rarely do we glimpse the face of the Persian wars in such grisly detail.

Despite their failure to detect the advance of Tamsapor, Roman scouts and spies had not been completely idle. Based on the reports of his own spies and the intelligence provided by the deserter Antoninus, Shapur had expected to find the city defended only by a single legion, the V Parthica, which the emperor Constantius had based there as part of his general defensive overhaul of the eastern frontier. Instead, the soldiers of the great king gazed upward at black basalt crenelations manned by six additional Roman legions who had arrived at the city by forced marches, no doubt from army headquarters at Edessa, some 177 kilometers (110 miles) to the southwest, a distance which the legionnaires could have covered in as little as two or three days.[4]

Among the Romans units present at Amida were the X Frentensis, formerly based in Palestine and then moved south to Aila on the Red Sea by Diocletian, as well as units which had formerly fought for the usurpers Magnentius and Decentius whom Constans had defeated six years prior. Alongside them fought the XIII "Gemina" Legion, the XXX Ulpi Victrix, a storied unit first raised by Trajan and bearing the name of his family, the Ulpii. Auxiliary troops, called Superventores and Praeventores, probably represent vexallations of about a thousand men each of light-armed cavalry skirmishers and scouts. These troops were commanded by the count Aelianus, who in 348 had led some of these elements to deeds of heroism during the Battle of Sinjar. Additionally, Amida held a unit of imperial household cavalry, elite horse archers called *comites sagittarii*, who probably numbered around three hundred.

The Persians opened hostilities at Amida by seizing two nearby Roman fortresses where they captured many civilians who had taken refuge behind their walls, along with a quantity of wealth. On the third day the commander of the Persian army arrived:

> ... mounted on a charger, overtopping the others ... wearing in place of a diadem a golden image of a ram's head with precious stones, distinguished too by a great retinue of men of the highest rank and of various nations.[5]

The Persian king clearly expected the besieged to listen to his offer, but in this he was sorely disappointed. Rather than a parley, Shapur faced a hail of Roman arrow and ballista fire, a bolt from which rent one of his garments. Only the timely intervention of his guardsmen, who surrounded the royal person, saved the king from wounding or worse. The shahanshah retreated to the camp, humiliated and inflamed at the temerity of the Roman defenders.

The following dawn, the king of the Chionite Huns, Grumbates, "a man of moderate strength ... with shriveled limbs, but of a certain greatness of mind and distinguished by the glory of many victories," advanced with his countrymen to the walls to demand surrender.[6] With the Hun king rode a

The Roman walls at Diyarbakir (Amida) can still be seen today. (*David Stanley*)

body of attendants, among whom was his son. A Roman ballista crew targeted the tall prince and skewered him with a well-placed bolt. When the Hun royal fell, the king and his retinue scattered, but they soon returned to recover the body. A general melee broke out as the Huns and Persians determined to take the corpse and offer it a proper burial, while the Romans fought savagely to deny them the chance. This bloody contest raged all day until, "at nightfall the body, which had with difficulty been protected amid heaps of slain and streams of blood, was dragged off under cover of darkness."[7]

The following day both sides observed a truce, and the Romans turned into an audience of the spectacle of the mourning of the prince and his burial. Wails from women in the Chionite camp accompanied the display of the body on a high platform, surrounded by ten couches with effigies for all to honor. Finally, the body was burned on its lofty pyre and its ashes collected in a silver urn. Two days of rest followed, and then the Persians unleashed foragers to devastate the rich amber fields and orchards around the city. Then the Sasanians dug in to invest the city, throwing a cordon of troops around the entire five-kilometer circuit. The Persian forces were sufficiently numerous to surround Amida in considerable depth, as it would only take twenty-five thousand troops to form five ranks around the settlement. Shapur's army was certainly several times more numerous than this.

The plain below the city was filled with bands of horsemen, gleaming in the summer sun, who quietly took up their siege quarters assigned to them by lot: the Chionites camped on the east, the Gilani Hunnic allied hedged in the south, the Sakastanis from the east of the empire in what is today Afghanistan. Albanians from what is today western Azerbaijan on the western shores of the Caspian manned the northern quadrant of the siege. The Sasanians had brought with them elements of their elephant corps, the fearsome and strange beasts, topped with howdahs and packed with archers, inspired awe in the defenders and became a particular focus of their efforts. The Persian elephants suffered many casualties, though we hear relatively little of them. Most likely they were used in a support role, helping shift heavy timbers and artillery as well as the great wooden siege towers.

Following the seven days of truce, the Sasanians stood in an iron hedge around the city, like a steel garrot around the garrison's neck. They stood in their formations, quiet and maintaining order, not breaking ranks, until sunset. Near dawn, the sounds of Persian war horns split the darkness, and the encircling army began its assault. The armored cavalry advanced and cast a storm of arrows onto the battlements, while ballista and stone-throwing artillery swept the walls. The defenders, for their part, fought with their own war machines and bows, and the carnage was great on both sides. Though we are not told it specifically and thus cannot be certain, it seems that the Persians attempted to mount the walls with scaling ladders, as the deep slashes and wounds that Ammianus describes are more indicative of hand-to-hand fighting than missile weapons. For two days the Sasanians assaulted the walls in this manner, but they could not enter the city.

In the early days of the siege, a plague broke out inside the city. If the 120,000 souls trapped in the city is an accurate number given by Ammianus, then it is little wonder that pestilence struck, given the small size of the city and the obvious problems of sanitation. Dysentery due to contaminated water and food supplies is the most likely culprit, the worst of which passed at the same time that the defenders gained some respite from the heat, ten days after the end of the truce given for the burial of Grumbates's son.

The Persians worked tirelessly to gain egress to the city, surrounding the curtain walls with sheds and mantlets and raising siege mounds on which they would advance the wooden siege towers that they were constructing. The Persian siege towers were large, capacious enough to hold a ballista on the top deck from which to shoot down on the defenders, and armored with iron faces, with a drawbridge below from which the attackers could descend onto the ramparts.

In the middle of the siege, the Sasanians gained an advantage when a Roman deserter showed them an underground gallery leading from the city to the river so that water could be brought into the fortifications. Through an oversight, the Romans had failed to guard the gallery. In the dark of night, seventy archers from Shapur's bodyguard entered the tunnel and scaled to the third story of the towers on the south side of the city. At dawn, the Persian forces mounted a general attack, and the presence of the archers created confusion among the Roman ranks, while Sasanian troops with scaling ladders tried to mount the walls. Why Shapur was unable to use the secret passage to greater effect, to force entry for a larger troop into the city, is lost to history.

With the emperor still far from the theater of war, divisions among the Roman high command paralyzed plans of any relief to the besieged. Shapur's men were free to range throughout the countryside. The Sasanians captured the city of Ziatha (probably modern Harput, some 125 kilometers to the northwest of Amida). From the battlements of Amida, the Romans watched as Shapur had the prisoners paraded before them. The defenders were forced to watch helplessly as the Persians frog marched the prisoners, among them the old and feeble, off to captivity to the east. Enraged to the point of mutiny by the sight, the Gallic light troops who had been exiled to Syria by Constantius could not be checked by their centurions and fired out of the gates, intent on taking revenge. While the martial spirit of the Gauls was exemplary, their efforts were in vain. After they were driven from the field, their recklessness and constant agitation to attack forced the commanders of the Roman defense to lock them inside the city.

Shapur attempted another assault, this time employing his siege towers onto the earth works and ordering his men forward with wicker palisades and shields to cover the advancing dismounted cavalry troopers. On the upper decks of the siege towers, the Sasanian attackers overtopped the Roman walls and directed ballista fire onto the defenders that spread carnage among the Roman defenders. The assault burned like an inferno, drawing even Shapur himself and his bodyguard to the foot of the walls, where he:

> rushed into the thick of the fight like a common soldier . . . he was the mark of many a missile; and when many of his attendants had been slain, he withdrew, passing from one part of the troops under his command, and at the end of the day, though terrified by the grim spectacle neither of the dead nor of the wounded, he at last wounded, he at last allowed a brief time to be given to rest.[8]

At dawn, the shahanshah renewed the assault, determined to remove the thorn of Amida from his flesh. With his siege towers in ashes, the Persians completed their earthen siege mounds and overtopped the walls; there the battle raged desperate and bloody. Fortune favored the great king when the Roman siege mound, raised inside the walls opposite the Persian works, collapsed and overtopped the wall, creating a broad, level road for the Sasanians to enter the city. The shahanshah's men pressed forward with drawn swords in gory hand-to-hand combat until the city swarmed with Persian troops and "armed and unarmed alike without distinction of sex were slaughtered like so many cattle."[9] Ammianus, the doughty witness to these events, saved himself by escaping through an unwatched postern gate at nightfall and walked, exhausted, through the gloom to the tenth milestone from the city. There, as luck would have it, he was saved by the macabre appearance of a groom who had escaped on a horse without saddle or bridle. Having fallen from the horse, the man was torn limb from limb and dragged behind the animal until the mount had slowed. After another narrow escape from roving Persian cataphracts, the terrified Ammianus made his way to the west and the city of Melitene, where he found Ursicinus and joined him on his journey to Antioch.

It was now October 359. The Persian siege had consumed seventy-three precious days, and Shapur had paid a premium in Persian blood. Ammianus claims that Sasanian and allied dead tallied thirty thousand. Although well informed, there could have been no body count conducted by the Romans, the losers of the battle. Even if the mortality rate of one half of their forces, which implies many more wounded, the figure Ammianus provides would imply a force of at least sixty thousand, a not-impossible number but certainly the upper limits of a late antique field army. The Roman troops protecting Amida could have numbered no more than thirty-five thousand—again a very large force for the time—which means that the defenders would have killed roughly one Persian per soldier, an unlikely scenario. That the defenders were heavily outnumbered seems likely. Ammianus is clear in his sentiment, shared by all the defenders, that the Romans hemmed inside the basalt city perched over the Tigris held no hope to live; their only goal was to die courageously.

Whatever the true count, Sasanian losses had been sharp, even if many of the dead had been culled from the ranks of his allies to the north and east. The great king had further spent the campaigning season. When his men finally overtopped the black walls of the city, the season had turned to autumn and the sun paled with the approaching winter. In the mountain heights snow had begun to fall. Having pierced the veil of Roman defenses and liberally watered the ground with Persian blood, the shahanshah had to surrender the advantage he gained. Shackling his prisoners, he marched with his plunder back to the borders of his empire.

Whatever the final tally, and despite Ammianus's attempts to spin the battle as a Roman victory, Amida was a heavy Roman defeat. They had lost seven battle-tested legions, and with the emperor Constantius still campaigning in the Balkans against the Sarmatian menace, the hole in the eastern defenses would be hard to plug. Only in the spring of 360 did the emperor finally make his way east to shore up the empire's shaky position.

Shapur was not idle in 360. He seized and destroyed the Roman fortress in the salient at Sinjar. Advancing northward, the great king bypassed the bee's nest of Nisibis and instead invested a city to the north, Bezabde, a powerful fortress city lying on a high ground that sloped toward the Tigris. Where the settlement lay on lower ground, it was girded with a double wall. The Romans there were not unprepared. Three legions formed the garrison, the Second Flavian, Second Armenian, and Second Parthian. Alongside them fought numerous archers from the hinterland of the city. Shapur's direct assault, mounted by men with scaling ladders and covered by Persian stone-throwing engines and ballistae, failed. The Roman wall-mounted artillery and archers inflicted terrible losses. After the Christian bishop of the city visited Shapur, rumors of treachery circulated, as the Sasanians shifted the attention of their attacks to weaker areas of the wall on higher ground, accessible only via narrow paths. As the bitter struggle dragged on and winter approached, the Sasanians made a breakthrough. Persian sappers wheeled forward their largest battering ram, covered with wet bulls' hides and therefore protected from the boiling oil, flaming pitch, and fire arrows of the Romans. Under constant assault from above, the Sasanians swung the suspended metal beak into the foundations of a tower. The tower imploded, crushing or burying the defenders who crowded it, and the Persians poured into the city. After he watched his troops sack the city, Shapur announced his intention to hold the town. He rebuilt the fortifications, provisioned and garrisoned it, and then marched home, his plunder and captives in tow. Along the way, Shapur moved to reduce another powerful Roman fortress city, Birtha (today Tikrit in Iraq, birthplace of the infamous dictator Saddam Hussein). Birtha was superbly fortified, surrounded by ditches and moats, with double walls which converged at angles that offered the defenders superb fields of covering fire. The great king threw his forces at the ramparts but departed after a brief, futile siege.

Constantius, fresh off his victories over the Sarmatians, wintered in Constantinople. There the emperor took time to uproot what he believed was a major conspiracy against his rule. Late in the summer of 360, he marched into Roman Armenia and toured the shattered, burned-out husk of Amida. Only with the onset of autumn did the emperor pivot to the offensive against Bezabde. The Sasanian elite troops bivouacked there proved harder to dislodge than a barbed arrowhead. Despite being outnumbered, the Persians heroically staved off disaster through numerous sorties, the most devastating of which destroyed most of the Roman battering rams. With the Roman siege mounds already crested over the walls and the Persian defenders greatly diminished in number, the Sasanians mounted a desperate charge from a postern gate and fired the wood and cane substructure of one of the enemy siege mounds, collapsing it and inflicting considerable casualties. The Roman assault foundered and the shah's men lived to fight another day. Constantius had already invested many lives and wanted a return on the gold and blood he had spent. The number of dead and wounded, however, made him reconsider his tactics, and instead he settled down to starve the obstinate defenders into submission. When the autumn rains came, the fields around the city became a bog, making action nearly impossible. In failure, Caesar had to admit defeat, and he marched his men to winter quarters in Antioch.

The Roman enemy drifted from one crisis to the next. In response to the emperor's demand for legions from the west to make good some of his losses in the east, troops under the junior emperor in the west, the Caesar Julian, declared the latter emperor. Julian was a man of medium build with shrewd, piercing eyes. An overly large head for his frame, along with his scruffy beard, made him an awkward physical specimen. At the start of his insurrection in 360, the Caesar was just twenty-nine years of age, the ambitious, intelligent survivor of Constantius's bloody purge that he had orchestrated on the death of Constantine I. Julian had been raised by tutors in comfortable confinement, first in Nicomedia, then in the Cappadocian backwater of Asia Minor, far from friends and out of the minds of troublemakers.

As strange as the emperor's appointment of Julian as Caesar may appear, in keeping with the practice of his house, Constantius felt the job demanded one of his kin. Thanks to his killings among the family, there were precious few from among whom he could choose. The selection of Julian therefore smacks something of desperation, ignorance, or even hubris on the part of Constantius. No matter. Julian, whose arrogance and personal weaknesses have been expertly glossed over by admiring ancient historians and their modern followers, moved against his cousin in the summer of 361, after having been declared emperor by his troops in Gaul the prior year. Once more the Romans were on the precipice of civil war. Combined with the lion of Shapur who remained unchecked in the east, the Roman state faced a simmering, deadly crisis. Constantius at first made no moves against his younger cousin.

Shapur advanced once more to the Tigris frontier, but there he hesitated and never mounted the full-scale invasion that his enemy dreaded. Constantius could only send a skeleton force to oppose the shahanshah, while he prepared the bulk of his army to deal with his rival, Julian, who had crossed under arms into the Balkans and was preparing for the final confrontation. The Sasanians never crossed the river. Something was amiss in the Persian Empire.

There are several possibilities for the great king's halting maneuvers from 360–63. In light of the lack of internal sources, we are thrown back on speculation. One possibility is that the shahanshah, after more than fifty years on the throne, much of it spent in the saddle, facing enemies from Central Asia to Syria, was worn down with fatigue. He may have dealt with health issues, although the fact that Shapur would reign for another nineteen years after his capture of Bezabde in 360 argues against any life-threatening illness. Another more likely prospect is that the Persian victory and subsequent alliance with the Hunnic groups, led by the Chionites, had frayed after the Amida campaign. The great siege of the city had been a pyrrhic victory for the Sasanians, and during it their allies had suffered immensely. After the Amida campaign we hear nothing of his Hunnic allies in the subsequent campaigns, nor of the Albanians. The Armenian lords had again largely slipped into the Roman orbit, and they had been an important contributor of heavy cavalry to the Persian armies. Shapur was determined to bring Armenia and Iberia (modern Georgia) back into the Sasanian fold and made strenuous efforts to weaken the pro-Roman princes among them. The great king's loitering campaigns on the western fringes of his empire in 360 had much to do with his attempts to entice the Armenian king Arshak II back into the fight on his side; Constantius had sent large bribes and heaped honors on both his Armenian and Iberian allies in order to keep them from siding with the Persians. Shapur's growing concerns with access to Armenian and Iberian manpower, both of which provided excellent soldiers, is more comprehensible if his alliance with the Huns to the north and the east was crumbling, cutting off access to Hunnic recruits from among these superb fighters. Shapur's obsession with Armenia and Iberia would only grow in the later years of the 360s, likely due to heavy Persian defeats suffered at the hands of the Huns.

Constantius, active as always, marshaled his troops and moved to meet Julian. On November 3, while on the road near the foothills of the Taurus Mountains, Constantius II died at age forty-four. He had come down with fever when he had reached the nearby city of Tarsus, famous as the birthplace of the Christian apostle Paul. As the malady had deepened, the emperor, with his typical energy, had insisted on pressing forward to meet the threat against his person and his throne.

Strange indeed that Constantius, whom pagan historians paint as a dimwit and a hothead who foamed at the mouth when he heard of the rebellion, nonetheless patiently bided his time, making sure that there would be no Persian attack in the campaigning season of 361 before swinging his army westward to meet his rival with the outsized head and scraggly philosopher's beard that added to his ungainly appearance. Raised as a Christian, Julian harbored a deep passion for pagan philosophy. When he assumed the throne, he renounced his Christian religion and openly embraced the worship of the old gods. In a Roman world which had been held firmly in the hands of Christian emperors for thirty years, this sudden reversal came as a shock and led to conflict and opened fissures among Roman elites.

Julian, despite his arrogance and self-righteousness, possessed numerous strengths: intelligence, charisma, and courage among them. Whatever self-doubts he may have harbored, these he generally masked well enough, though his insecurities are on full display in certain petty actions and in his need to write long, defensive missives to the citizens of Antioch, who came to despise him during his stay there and to whom the emperor returned the favor. The great city on the Orontes, for all its pomp and wealth, was probably better off that the emperor never returned.

The young emperor inherited a strong Roman army, which, despite its recent battering, was competently led and logistically sound. Prior to his fateful march to meet Julian, Constantius had made a massive recruiting drive that enrolled thousands of infantry and cavalry back into the legions; many of these were likely to have been half-Romanized natives of Illyricum and Sarmatian and Gothic mercenaries. He stockpiled tremendous stores of equipment and supplies at Antioch and elsewhere throughout the east. While Constantius never managed a hallmark triumph over the Sasanians, neither had he suffered the kind of crushing defeat the empire had experienced in decades prior. In light of the forces ranged against him, both internal and external, Constantius demonstrated more than capable leadership. He was consistently able to hold the line against the Persians and, more importantly, replace Roman losses.

As inheritor of the capable, if not spectacular, Roman war machine, Julian immediately prepared for war. He ordered a fleet of ships built at Samosata on the Euphrates. The young emperor marched east from Constantinople with his western field army, many of the legions were battle hardened in multiple campaigns against the Germanic tribes on Rome's northern borders.

In 361 Shapur must have greeted the news of the ascent of Julian with mixed feelings. On the one hand, Julian's paganism was bound to cause internal dissent among the Romans; on the other, Julian's reputation for generalship and personal courage had, despite his brief experience, already been crowed from the rooftops by his pagan admirers and lionized beyond proportion. Like many of his predecessors, the emperor, raised on the Greco-Roman ideology of barbarian inferiority, likened the Persians to the Germanic tribes on the Rhine and Danube. This racist condescension, coupled with personal arrogance and an intractable personality, instilled an almost manic sense of destiny in the youthful Julian. Shapur, more than twenty years senior to his antagonist, was about to undergo another great test, perhaps the greatest of his reign.

Julian departed from Antioch at the end of winter in 363, having taken nearly two years to establish his reign and prepare for the expedition. Julian and his guard traveled overland to Hierapolis (modern Mambij in Syria) and then traveled on to Batnae on the Euphrates, which he reached on or around March 12. A forced march took Julian to Harran, which he reached on March 18. At Harran the emperor divided his forces. While at Harran, news apparently came of a Persian raid on Roman territory, and this is the reason given by some authors for Julian's dispatch of a strong force to Nisibis. In fact, it is likely that Julian wanted the Sasanians to believe, as Shapur would clearly come to think, that the Roman thrust would come across the Tigris; the great king naturally would have suspected a counterattack against Bezabde, which he still controlled and whose lands formed a Persian salient north of Nisibis. Julian dispatched thirty thousand troops to Nisibis to guard the city and to form a reserve force that could threaten the Persian territories across the Tigris. These reinforcements were led by the counts Sebastianus and Procopius, Julian's kinsman. This force was also to support Arshak and his Armenians. The strength of this northern division likely indicates that Julian's army was probably the largest seen in the region since the time of Trajan.

While at Circesium, the emperor ordered the king of Armenia, Arshak, to prepare for war and to be ready to join his invasion. Arshak's troops, descending from Armenia, combined with the Roman force at Nisibis presented a serious menace to Shapur and further reinforced in the great king's mind the Roman design to press him in the north. Hearing news of the Roman troop movements around Nisibis and that Roman cavalry operations, despite the earliness of the season, already ranged across the Tigris into Persian territory, the shah called up his forces and moved his army north, stripping many of the Euphrates garrisons to bolster his field units.

Julian now revealed his true design. By forced marches he moved swiftly down the Euphrates to Circesium, the last Roman bulwark on the river. Indeed, the emperor's strategy departed from the doctrine established by Constantine and Constantius, whose efforts had focused on the iron belly of Upper Mesopotamia, where vast quantities of Roman blood and treasure had been expended to keep out the Persians. His intention was to push through Assyria, through the fertile lands of Persian Mesopotamia, and surprise the Sasanians in the south. Julian aimed at nothing less than a knockout blow to the head of the Persian state; he intended to march down the Euphrates route used by Trajan and Gordian III and strike at the capital of Ctesiphon.

At Circesium arrived the Roman river fleet. More than 1,100 wooden and skin transport vessels had floated, and along with them came 55 warships. The Roman fleet included prefabricated pontoons to assist in bridging operations. Other ships followed carrying supplies, especially timber, siege engines, and food. Alongside this enormous fleet marched sixty-five thousand Roman troops. Leading the infantry ranks was the master of foot, the Sarmatian warrior Victor. The Germanic Dagalaifus led Julian's bodyguard and is seen in action alongside Victor with the infantry in the rear guard of the Roman host. Two commanders led the cavalry wings that would flank and shield the heavy infantry, among them the brother of Shapur, Hormisdas, who had decades before deserted to the Romans. Julian made no secret of his intentions to conquer the Sasanian Empire and place Hormisdas on the throne as his puppet, thus ending once and for all the Persian menace, or, as one historian recorded from the emperor's mouth, "We must wipe out a most mischievous nation, on whose sword-blades the blood of our kinsmen is not yet dry."[10]

Shapur was caught by surprise by the Roman advance. He had anticipated an attack in the north, and as the spring began the great king was in no position to counter the Roman stroke. The Sasanian king did not have the soldiers to match his enemies. Though modern historians follow some of their ancient observers in repeating the falsehood that King Arshak of Persia proved a traitor and did not intervene on behalf of the Romans, the Armenians did join the campaign on the Roman side. Arshak's Armenians drove off a Persian force in Cordovene and ravaged the territory of the great king there. If there was, as some ancient sources insist, a plan to link up the northern Roman and allied forces in Assyria, these could not be realized, and Julian, who by rapid marches entered the heartlands of Sasanian Mesopotamia, offered scant chance for any such unification of forces.

The Roman troops advanced with little resistance. Anatha, an island fortress in the middle of the Euphrates, offered no opposition to the imperial army and was simply bypassed, as was the next city downstream. Farther south, the Romans sent a portion of their troops across the river, and they skirted around some manned and hastily burned abandoned strong points; a clutch of these remain little more than names and have never been localized.

Command of the Sasanian defense fell to Suren, head of the prominent noble family of the same name and likely governor of Asoristan Province, in which lay the capital. The Persians, their soldiers scattered throughout various garrisons, could not match the strength of their invaders. Suren opted therefore for a campaign of attrition, contesting key fortifications and aiming to hold the royal city of Ctesiphon until Shapur arrived. Near the capital, Julian's troops laid siege to the key city of Peroz-Shapur (modern Anbar in Iraq), where the Sasanian garrison of 2,500 initially put up stout opposition, but then elected to surrender. After bridging lands flooded by the Persians' breach of weirs that managed the Euphrates and fed irrigation waters to the rich soils of Mesopotamia, the Romans stormed the city of Maiozamalcha on the Royal Canal. The city fell after the imperial troops undermined the walls. The invaders slaughtered the inhabitants with no regard for age or sex.

The Persians could not stop the enemy from clearing out a derelict canal which connected the Euphrates to the Tigris, and thus the Roman fleet was floated on the Tigris, and Ctesiphon lay only a few miles downstream. At night the Persians opposed a Roman crossing to the northern bank of the Tigris. There a strong Sasanian force was routed when attacked by the legionnaires from the front and by Roman light troops from behind. The way lay open for the advance on the capital. By late May 363 Julian's forces had arrived.

Julian stood on the threshold of the capital and the next day faced a Persian force drawn up in battle order. Suren elected to challenge the Romans, though his own force could scarcely have numbered more than fifteen thousand men. An eyewitness described the sight:

> The Persians opposed to us serried bands of mail-clad horsemen in such close order that the gleam of moving bodies covered with closely fitting plates of iron dazzled the eyes of those who looked upon them, while the whole throng of horses was protected by coverings of leather. The cavalry was backed up by companies of infantry, who, protected by oblong, curved shields covered with wickerwork and raw hides, advanced in very close order. Behind these were elephants, looking like walking

hills, and, by the movements of their enormous bodies, they threatened destruction to all who came near them, dreaded as they were from past experience.[11]

The ground and numbers favored the Romans, and the legionnaires closed the gap between the two forces on the double. Deprived of their ability to charge and with their advantage eliminated, the Persians panicked and gave ground. The retreat turned into a rout, a headlong flight to try to reach the safety of the walls of Ctesiphon, where the citizens looked on in horror as their defenders perished by the hundreds and the legionnaires threatened to crash through the gates with the throng of fugitives. The Persians were said to have lost 2,500 men while the Romans only took 70 casualties.

While encamped at the city, the emperor received an embassy from the great king. Shapur's legate offered territorial concessions in exchange for the end of the war and supposedly reminded the emperor that "To conquer is honorable, but to be more than conqueror gives occasion for envy," a clear message that the emperor's hubris, should he persist, would lead to his undoing. Julian rejected peace overtures and reiterated his desire to continue the war.

One of the more bizarre mysteries in history then unfolded. Julian, after his epic march, despite numerous skirmishes, sieges, and ambushes on the part of the Persians, apparently preserved most of his forces intact. The only sources we have—Roman ones—are tight-lipped about their own losses. Certainly the sieges had been costly, but the invaders had not been beaten in a pitched battle, and we hear nothing about disease or malnourishment troubling them. After his bloodying of the garrison outside of Ctesiphon, one would expect that Julian was on the verge of a great victory and the sacking of one of the wealthiest cities in the world. Yet, at a council of war on or around June 5, the Roman high command agreed to abandon the siege and march back home. What had changed?

Our sources are opaque to the point of complete blindness on the machinations which took place. The high command argued, we are told, that Shapur lurked nearby with powerful forces. He was unbroken and ready to strike. The Romans found the country into which they were now mired far more powerfully fortified than they expected, and the prospect of being trapped between the hammer of the army of the great king and the anvil of the troops inside his capital was real. Julian made the fateful decision to abandon his objective and retreat. He chose to march home by a different route. Burning their transport fleet, the emperor swung his still formidable host into the lands by the Diyala River, which flowed down from the Zagros Mountains. There, a Sasanian attack failed and the Romans won another victory, but the season was hot and the Romans began to suffer from incessant Sasanian cavalry attacks, which harassed them without respite. Ahead of the Roman line of march, the shahanshah's troops fired the fields and cleared out the civilian population. The invaders soon found themselves running out of supplies, oppressed by the heat, and facing the enemy in a long-running battle as they marched up the Tigris. Arabs allied to the Sasanians made lightning raids along the sprawling Roman columns, picking off stragglers. The Persians relentlessly turned the screws, with ambuscades, hit-and-run raids, and night attacks that wounded, killed, and exhausted the already fraying enemy.

The Sasanians offered battle about fifty miles north of Ctesiphon. Led by the *asped* Mirena of the famous Mihr family of nobles, commander of the Sasanian cavalry, and accompanied by two of Shapur's sons, a strong Persian army faced the Roman lines. Julian countered the Sasanian army by forming his forces into a crescent. In so doing, he ended any hope the Persians harbored for a cavalry attack. If Mirena had chosen to charge, his heavy horsemen faced the risk of envelopment by the Roman mounted men, placed on the right and left wings and extended to the front. Julian thus negated the superior Sasanian cavalry and was, with his infantry, able to close to hand-to-hand fighting. Over the course of a hard-fought day, the Romans won a victory. About twenty miles upstream, near the future site of the Islamic city of Samarra, the Persians again attacked the Romans while they were on the march. Hearing the rearguard was under attack, the emperor rushed to the fray without equipping himself with his mail shirt and protected only by a shield. As he rushed to the back of the army, he learned that the Persians had struck at the front of the formation and that his troops there were hard pressed. No sooner had the emperor ridden to the rear when a troop of Persian mailed cavalry and elephants fell on the center of the Roman army. Roman skirmishing troops drove them off, but Julian, whose bodyguard had scattered in the melee, was caught amidst the retreating Persians, and one of them ran him through the side with his lance. His soldiers rushed the stricken emperor to his tent.

The Sasanians locked with their foe in savage battle, their archers said to pour so many arrows into the Romans that they could not see the enemy bowmen. Under a hail of missile fire, the Roman infantry nonetheless inflicted serious damage on the Persian army. Mirena was among the dead, as was a Persian governor, likely the same who accompanied Tamsapor in the siege of Amida four years prior. The Roman sources do not admit defeat, but they lost the battle. Their army was split in two, their losses considerable, and their emperor dead. It was not merely the starvation, heat, and the loss of their delusional emperor which brought the Roman army to its knees but the sanguinary clash on the Tigris on June 25 that convinced the invaders to parlay for their lives.

At midnight, Julian's wound burst open and he bled to death. His army, now trapped, starving, and thirsting, had to find a way out of the iron maw of the Sasanian beast. Shapur, who made no appearance in the campaign, remained in the north, facing the Armenian raiders of Arshak and the Roman garrison at Nisibis. The season was still young enough that the strong forces under Julian's relative Procopius could have crossed the Tigris and likely would have done so had they been aware of the dire straits of their comrades. Whatever the reason, the strong Roman forces at Nisibis stayed in their quarters, oblivious that the triumphant dispatches they had received were long out of date.

While the accounts, most of which are friendly to Julian, portray the legions as unbowed and unbroken, Christian sources, usually disregarded because of their hostility toward the polytheist emperor, tell a different story. The bishop of Antioch, John Chrysostom (347–407), said that Julian bungled the entire expedition:

> as if he was accompanied by an army of women and young children rather than men. For one thing, he brought them to such a pitch of desperation through shortage of provisions that they were reduced to consuming some of their cavalry horses and slaughtering others as they wasted away of hunger and thirst. You would have thought Julian was in league with the Persians, anxious not to defeat them but to surrender his own forces, for he had led them into such a barren and inhospitable region that he in fact surrendered without ever being defeated.[12]

The battle on the middle reaches of the Tigris left the invaders in bloody shock. Bereft of their courageous leader and staggering through the heat of the wilderness, the legions were in danger of collapse. After electing a new emperor, the Christian imperial guardsman Jovian, the Romans decided to resume their march. On June 28, the Sasanians waited at the ready for the Romans, who broke camp in the early morning hours. The advancing legions ran headlong into the Sasanian elephant corps mixed with heavy cavalry. The Romans managed to kill two of the pachyderms and the Sasanians gave way. Under harassment, the Romans moved about ten miles up the river and were able to find a suitable level area beneath some higher ground; there they dug a ditch and created a palisade of sharpened stakes to impede attack. As night came, Sasanian troops broke through one quadrant of the camp and nearly fought their way to the emperor's tent before they were finally driven back.

Under constant strain, Jovian knew the likelihood of the legions reaching the safety of the frontier was nil. Caught between the Scylla of Shapur's host and the Charybdis of starvation, it was the Romans' turn to sue for peace. Unlike the haughty Julian, they found the shahanshah receptive. His terms were heavy. In exchange for their lives, the Romans would cede their suzerainty over Armenia and Georgia and hand over the territorial gains made east of the Tigris in the Peace of Nisibis won under Diocletian. There would be a truce for thirty years. To ensure adherence to the treaty, both sides agreed to an exchange of high-level hostages. Despite the humiliating terms, which choked the emperor like the dust of the desert plains through which he marched, Jovian had few choices. Pressing onward meant almost certain annihilation of his army, and perishing on the dusty plains of Mesopotamia was the only real alternative to swallowing the wormwood of the proposed treaty. Once Jovian accepted the terms, the Romans were fed and treated honorably. A Persian force escorted them the 550 kilometers (340 miles) upriver to Nisibis. There the shamed emperor refused to enter the city. The stunned inhabitants were told to pack their things and leave the city and a Persian garrison moved to install itself.

Streams of ink have flowed telling the tale of the courageous, youthful emperor, tragically struck down by a Persian spear thrust in the sands far from home. Many praise the prince's valor, his quick, active mind, his steadfastness, and his fortitude. Few, however, understand what Julian hoped to accomplish, and the historians who preserved the memory of the disastrous campaign, several of whom had participated in it and survived, offer no insight on the question. The emperor is said to have declared that he would place Hormisdas on the Persian throne, but it is difficult to comprehend that he intended to do so: Hormisdas must have been, by 363, at least well into middle age, having arrived in Roman territory when Constantine was still alive—and that emperor had died in 337. If true, the installment of such a monarch was but a short-term expedient which, in the longer term, would have done little or nothing to advance Roman interests.

If Julian's aim was the capture of Ctesiphon—which appears likely—inspired, after all was the emperor by Trajan's great feat of arms, then the harsh light glowers even more brightly on the emperor's mismanagement. Ctesiphon was clearly not the city it had been. The Sasanians had seen to its safeguarding since their rise to power. It could have been no surprise that the capital would be obstinately contested and studded with multiple rows of defenses, yet having arrived at its gates, which his men nearly entered after the fight with Suren, the emperor and his war council suddenly decided to turn tail. Nor could Julian have been surprised that Shapur's army remained intact and menacing to him—he himself had planned for his attack to catch the enemy unawares—from the early departure date, to the sending of a powerful decoy force to Nisibis—the deception had been well planned and executed. Perhaps the suddenness of his arrival was nothing more than a grand cast of the die? If so, once the throw went against him and the surprise capture of the capital failed, Julian simply intended to declare victory and march home. There are indications that he envisioned a large-scale, punitive raid rather than a conquest, namely his orders that winter quarters be prepared for his army on the Cilician Plain. This speaks of an emperor who planned on being back in Roman country well before the first rains of autumn soaked the muddy ground between the rivers.

Finally, what of the lack of coordination and the waste of twenty to thirty thousand Roman troops, not to mention his Armenian allies, in the north? Nisibis lay more than 670 kilometers (416 miles) from Ctesiphon. Optimistically, the Roman troops in the north would have taken nearly forty days to reach the Persian capital. But what about when the expedition foundered? One would have thought thirty thousand legionnaires might prove useful, but when Julian elected to steal the march on the enemy and rely on secrecy and surprise, he rendered this entire army useless. In Procopius, the emperor saw fit to install as joint commander of this troop a man whom he promised the imperial throne, yet not one whom he entrusted an offensive against Shapur. Timely action by the army in the north could have saved Julian and his wretched band from destruction.

Through sound strategy and patience, Shapur had won the greatest victory of his reign. He and his lieutenants lost battles but won the war, outgeneraling the soldier's emperor. Distance, heat, and hunger proved his most powerful allies in an unequal contest. Using the strategic depth his empire afforded, the Persians waged a relentless war of attrition. Except on a few occasions, when they felt they had no other choice or that the situation favored them, the Sasanians avoided direct confrontation. Instead, they neutralized the numerical advantage through their persistent use of ambush tactics, coordinated, small-scale attacks, night battles, and skirmishing. The great king's victory had restored the reputation of his kingdom to its lofty place in the minds of his enemies, pushed the frontiers of the empire far to the west, and placed the Romans on the defensive. He had been restored a free hand in Armenia and Iberia, where he could turn his attention to grinding to dust the Christian and pro-Roman families, resistors to Zoroastrianism and his rule. In one bloody stroke he had captured the Roman eagle in a snare of their own devising, sacrificing cities and fortresses to enemy depredation while he played the long game.

Following conclusion of the war with Rome, Shapur fixed his gaze on Armenia, vital to Sasanian interests for its strategic position and its manpower. Armenia offered a bulwark not only against the Roman Empire; along with Georgia, it formed the line of first defense against the nomadic tribesmen of the north who traveled through the Caucasus passes as if through a funnel, emerging into the shah's lands where they threatened the heartlands of the empire. Armenia was divided between the pro-Roman nobility, many of them Christians, and the pro-Persian polytheist or Zoroastrian nobility.

In 364, Shapur launched the first of many Sasanian incursions into Armenia. One Armenian historian chronicles twenty-seven such raids over just a handful of years, most conducted by Armenian loyalists to the great king and Sasanian forces led by the family of Suren. Under their banners, much of the country was burned to ash, and the descent into murderous civil strife forced Arshak, after bitter years of resistance, to finally submit to Shapur's boot on his neck. In 368, Shapur's men dragged the hard-luck Armenian king to the infamous prison, the Tower of Oblivion in Khuzestan in southwest Iran. There the unfortunate prince committed suicide.

The turmoil in the Caucasus had great potential to spread like a brush fire over dry ground. There independent princes, whose principal hobby was violent competition, could barely be kept in check by any central authority, much less a weak one. Shapur hastened to fill the vacuum left by the fall of Arshak, but he was not long over the carcass of Armenia. Having, he thought, settled the Armenian question, he had to contend with a trifecta of events that threatened his hard-won hegemony there. First, Pap, son of the deceased King Arshak, appealed to the Romans. As Christians—and as a power whom Sasanian influence in the Caucasus directly threatened—how could the Roman eagle sit on its perch while Armenia bled? Concerns mounted in the west with the successful Sasanian siege of the Armenian fortress of Artogerassa. Persian troops hauled queen Pharantzem off to captivity in Persia, where, in 370, the former consort of Ashak was raped and killed by Persian troops.

Having crushed what he thought was the last of the Armenian *nakharar* nobility, Shapur had also recently installed his client king, Mihrdat III (365–380), in Iberia. Likely the old king, in his seventh decade on the throne, believed that Persia's ferocious labors in the Caucasus had tipped the balance of power there to his lasting advantage. Then again, long experience also taught him that the Armenians were as fractious in equal measure to the lofty heights of the mountains in which they dwelled. Moreover, they had an old ally, bloodied but unbroken, to which to turn. Considering the time ripe for imperial intervention, in 371 the emperor Valens gave ear to the appeals of Pap and his supporters and dispatched an expeditionary force. In the summer of 371, the Sasanian troops under Shapur clashed with the Romans and their Armenian allies who supported King Pap. No reliable figures for the opposing forces are given, and the details of the battle are scant. The Romans and Armenian cavalry, fighting as dismounted infantry during part of the battle, battled with distinction, forming a shield wall which stymied Sasanian attempts to rout their force. Shapur suffered defeat and had to withdraw:

> . . . just as a storm blows the leaves from the trees of the forest, so they quickly dismounted from their horses with their lances and cut them as cold corpses to the ground before they could reach their own line. When the Persians began to surround ours, they withdraw the protective shields of the Romans, as into a fortified city, and suffered no harm.[13]

The battle at Bagavand did not, however, end the conflict. Undeterred, the great king launched more raids to pressure the Armenians and attempted to lure King Pap to his cause. Alarm spread among his Roman sponsors. After they had regained some of their influence in Armenia, the Romans feared that Shapur's honeyed promises would entice their ally to switch sides. In 374 King Pap visited a Roman military camp and feasted with their generals, where, well into the merrymaking, imperial axe men cut him down.

The war in Armenia dragged on, a taste of gall and wormwood in the mouths of the would-be Sasanian conquerors. Under the capable Armenian lord Manuel Mamikonian, who led the Armenians after the exile of King Varazdat, the mountaineers inflicted several defeats on Persian forces. In one engagement in 379, Manuel surprised and captured the Sasanian *marzban*, the lord of the Armenian march Suren, perhaps the same nobleman who had fought against Julian. The Sasanians were in no position to take revenge. Shapur, who had chosen war nearly every year of his reign, faced in the east a grave challenge to his power.

The sources allow for little precision, but it appears that, by the end of his life, Shapur had been fighting on two fronts for the better part of a decade. In the west, the Armenian situation see-sawed, first to the Sasanian and then to the Roman advantage. In the east, in the region of Tokharistan, in the great embrace of the Pamir Mountains and the southern fold of the Hindu Kush, where the ringlet of oasis cities had been under Sasanian suzerainty since the days of the great Ardashir, the local population sniffed the air and whiffed freedom. The arrival of the Chionites, and likely subsequent waves of nomadic invaders in the long escalator shifting peoples across the steppelands of central Eurasia, had brought fresh warlords into the region. They sensed Persian vulnerability and saw the rivers of wealth that poured in via India and China on to Persia and the west.

The Kidarite Huns had invaded from the north and steadily gobbled up the Kushan lands and challenged the Kushano-Sasanian rulers in the far east. Just after his capture of the Armenian king Arshak, a Sasanian force had been annihilated in the eastern regions, probably north of Balk in the borderlands of the old region of Bactria. In 375/76, Shapur seems to have suffered another serious blow with the loss of Balkh, the anchor of Sasanian administration in the eastern regions and the bulwark against the Hunnic peoples who menaced the heartland of his empire.

Shapur died in 379, after seven decades on the throne. His long reign, far longer than the lifetime of most people in those days, was one of constant, almost superhuman struggle. The unquenchable energy and spirit of the king shows through in his incredible tenacity. Here was a monarch who knew little more than war. Though we lack the sources to count the campaigns he personally waged, it is likely the great king fought in something close to fifty engagements. The physical demands of travel alone, on horseback, over thousands of kilometers with few amenities save what his servants could carry, smacks of one possessed of an almost superhuman will. By turns clement and cruel, the great king had to balance the political realities of the day, knowing when to forgive and when to strike the enemy at the head and the heart.

The long, bitter war of attrition in Armenia was likely a factor both of temporary Sasanian weakness, during which they were forced to fight on two fronts, and Armenian intransigence, for which the doughty warriors were famous. Had the great king simply tolerated Christianity there, rather than launch a wave of persecutions, the path to Persian overlordship would likely have been much smoother. But Shapur was no absolute monarch. He had to play to the interests of the Zoroastrian priestly classes in order to prop up a key pillar of his rule. In the eastern provinces, while his forces were able to avoid total collapse, the cracks in the foundations of Persian rule were already well advanced and threatening to topple the whole structure of Iranian political power. A young Shapur no doubt would have risen brilliantly to the challenge. But in his last years, the best that he could hope to do was hold the line and trust that his successors would restore the greatness of the king of kings across the broad arc of lands from Merv to the Pamirs.

His greatest success, to be certain, came in the autumn of his rule during the invasion of the Roman emperor Julian. A worldly man, by then well-versed in the arts of war as well as intrigue and diplomacy, it could have scarcely come as a surprise to the Shahanshah when the Romans once more went on the offensive against his empire. While the gains of the Treaty of 363 were whittled back in the Caucasus, the lands across the Tigris nearly all held firm under Sasanian rule, anchored by the great prize of the fortress city of Nisibis. That great frontier barb would remain an ache in the flank of Rome for the next two centuries, and in all that vast span of time, thanks largely to the Herculean labors of Shapur, no Roman army would set foot into the heartlands of the empire of the great king.

CHAPTER FIVE

The Frontiers Erupt

O n the death of Shapur in 379, his brother Ardashir II seized the throne. Ardashir supposedly had agreed to his elderly brother's wishes that he would rule only until Shapur's minor son, who bore his father's name, reached his majority and could ascend to power. Ardashir II had spent his career in the western regions of the empire where he served as governor of Adiabene, a province lying north of the Tigris, astride southern Media, which stretched as far as the historic city of Arbela on the Great Zab River. As lord of Adiabene, Ardashir had battled the Roman forces of Julian in the great war of 363.

In present-day western Iran, in the heart of the Zagros Mountains, lies Taq-e Bostan, the "Arch of the Garden," an ancient caravan halt and campsite on the former Silk Road. A great spur of rock juts out of the earth amidst an archipelago of sacred springs that water the spot and fill it with lush greenery. A spring still flows at the foot of the great stone slab. There, framed by a deep, elegant arch cut from living rock, Ardashir is depicted looming over the fallen emperor Julian, eternal testament to the feats of arms accomplished by the Sasanian lord during the defeat of the Romans. It may well have been Ardashir who was the shadowy figure who tore at the heels of the westerners as they staggered up the valley of the Tigris and whose elephants and steel-cased horsemen delivered the victory of the century amidst dark days for the kingdom.

Stone relief of Shapur II and Shapur III at Taq-e-Bostan. (*Philippe Chavin*)

Almost nothing is known of Ardashir II and his policies. Recent Persian trouncing at the hands of the Kidarites, who had destroyed the Persian client kingdom of the Kushano-Sasanians no later than 370, undermined royal authority and sapped morale. Defeat at the hands of nomad powers, the agents of the evil spirit Ahriman, the master of disorder, undermined Sasanian legitimacy and bred doubts about their fitness to rule. More widely, the conquest of former Iranian territory by non-Iranians sent tremors throughout elite society: many would have questioned not only the fitness of the Sasanian line but the worthiness of the Iranian mandate from heaven to rule the world. Ardashir II could not conjure the galvanizing spirit of his ancestral namesake, nor recreate his successes. Under his rule, there would be no eastern victory. The usurper reigned just four years, dying in 383, four years in which the Sasanians were happy to hold the line against the Kidarites. In the north, the oasis bastion of Merv in Khurasan, the Sasanian bridgework into the lands of the Oxus and beyond, remained as one of their last bulwarks against the rising tide of Kidarite power.

With the old warrior's passing, Shapur II's son took the throne as Shapur III (383–388). At Taq-e-Bostan, like his uncle, Shapur III's image is memorialized in stone. He would be the last king to have himself represented thusly for two centuries. Shapur stands in frontal pose on the right hand of his father. Son, like father, has long plaited hair, a full beard, and a powerful

The Klimova plate showing Shapur III killing a leopard. (*Joanbanjo*)

build. He holds a straight Persian longsword before him, the sword of authority but also the symbol of his martial prowess. Shapur no doubt trusted in his skills to emulate some of the success of his father. Shapur III also appears on the famous silver Klimova plate where he is a dynamic force, legs set, his tasseled trousers flowing, as are the long, elaborately decorated neck guards of his headdress. With his left hand, the king grasps the head of a rampant leopard. With his right, he deals a mortal blow to the beast with a saber plunged into its heart. Shapur embodies the archetype of the hunter, like the mythical Nimrod of ancient days. He is the killer of wicked things, of servants of Ahriman, those who follow the Lie. The leopard is more than mere quarry. The great cat, tense and powerful, seeming to threaten to leap out of the frame, represents chaos, the darkness that threatens to swallow the great king's orderly realm and the enemy of civilized peoples. Only in these pictures did Shapur enjoy such total victory over the forces ranged against him.

Like his father, Shapur III faced the dragon fire of war on two fronts and the serpentine coils of a fractious aristocratic *wuzurg*, the independent noble families whose disobedience threatened to choke his rule. While Rome had recently been struck a heavy blow, it was staggered but not felled. In 378, an army of Goths had crossed the Danube and annihilated the forces of the Eastern Roman Empire. The Battle of Adrianople claimed nearly the whole of the eastern field army and alongside it the life of the emperor Valens, whose body was never found. Gothic warbands fanned out over the Balkans, spreading carnage as they roved. At the same time, the internal discord of the Iranians is revealed by their inactivity in the west from the final year of Shapur II's government through the short years of Ardashir II's reign. Division stayed the Persian hand against a tottering Rome. Under the soldier emperor Theodosius I (379–395) the Roman eagle again took flight, a phoenix from the flame. Theodosius's army, renewed by a throng of Gothic mercenaries, soon menaced the Sasanian borderlands and revived Roman claims in Armenia.

There, three rival kings wrestled for supremacy: the brothers Arshak III (378–387) and Vagrash III (378–386) supported by the Romans (in this era often referred to as "Byzantines") and the Sasanian-backed candidate, Khusrov IV (387–389).[1] After a cascade of diplomatic exchanges and with the threatening war clouds growing darker on the horizon, Shapur III adapted a policy first proposed by his father. Not long before his death, Shapur II had forwarded to the Romans the idea of abolishing the Arsacid kingship of Armenia and dividing the land, leaving the noble houses and their imperial loyalties intact but under the domination of Persia and Rome. Shapur III and Theodosius thrashed out an agreement whereby the kings remained in power and their territory divided. The Roman-sponsored king would rule lands anchored on the region of Akilisene in the west of the country, while the Armenian vassal of the Sasanians would hold the south and east from their base in Ayrarat. Shapur's man, Khusrov IV, lorded over the more populous and larger territory. Through their agreement with Rome, the Sasanian crown attempted to cut the apple of discord that had led to so many bloody conflicts. In doing so, the Persians maintained their bridgehead against Rome and access to the rich recruiting grounds of the redoubtable, skillful heavy cavalry and horse archers of the Armenian mountains. The Sasanians also maintained a gateway to the north Caucasus, a strategic corridor for trade and the projection of power and influence that naturally demanded heavy defense: the passes at Darial and at Darband were major travel and invasion routes for north-south travel, including by nomadic groups which threatened the settled southlands.

In the east, the Kidarites and the local peoples of the Kushan lands assailed the Persian Empire with fire and sword. Having prized from the Sasanians power over their eastern capital of Balkh during the waning years of Shapur II, the Kidarites established their dominance in the northeastern marchlands and severed the Silk Road routes to China. The remnants of the Chionite tribal confederation, known as the Red Huns, or Alchon Huns, smashed through the defenses of the far eastern regions, capturing Kabul from Shapur III's men, and then pushed south.

Shapur III died in a palace coup, smothered, it is said, while hunting. It might be said that the leopard of chaos, whom he destroys with such ease on the Klimova plate, had turned to strike him and his royal order to the ground. During the night assassins collapsed the king's great tent, crushing the royal personage. A troubling sign for the Sasanian monarchy and a fate Shapur III shared with his ancestor, Hormozd, was the inability to quench the unbridled ambition and meddling of the noble factions in the affairs of the kingdom. Shapur's son acceded to the throne as Bahram IV (388–99). Bahram had been the governor of Kirman in the southeast and thus had some administrative experience when he assumed power, though little is known of his life and reign.

As the fifth century dawned, on all fronts tremendous clouds of war thundered over the Persian Empire. The shahanshahs faced a deepening gloom. Against an array of greedy aggressors, the kings of kings knew that they must choose their battles carefully or be swept away. Despite numerous setbacks, especially at the end of his reign, Shapur II had managed to keep his kingdom on a permanent war footing. To do so, the hoary old king had checked the powerful noble families and maintained them in the field of battle, a feat his successors could not equal. Bahram needed victory and the plunder that came with it, but to do so he would need the landed aristocrats to buy into his program, and in this, like his predecessor, he failed.

In 395, a large Hun army struck into the Near East. Twenty years prior the "European Huns" (so called to distinguish them from the Hun groups in the east) had migrated across Central Asia to pastures between the Don and Manych Rivers and near the Sea of Azov to the west. About their origins there are many theories and few facts. Most likely, the Huns of the fourth and fifth centuries can be historically linked with the tribal confederacy known from Chinese sources as the Xiongnu. These tribal groupings, sophisticated in their organization and military capabilities, lived on the western borderlands of China, whence they migrated deeper into Central Asia, the eastern marches of the Sasanian Empire and into northern India. Other groups ranged much farther west to the Volga and Don Rivers in Europe. From their encampments, Hun raiders struck south, first appearing in Armenia circa 363.

From the grass sea of the south Russian steppe, these ultimate agents of chaos crossed the Caucasus and pierced the Sasanian defenses at the Darial Pass at the base of Mount Kazbek, a strategic ingress the Persians called Dar-I Alan, the Gate of the Alans, after the Iranian tribes in the Caucasus region. During their migration some twenty years prior, the Huns had broken the power of the Alan tribes of the Caucasus and absorbed many of their impressive cavalry into their own ranks. Incorporating subject peoples expanded the Hunnic reach and grew their military capabilities, though it is doubtful the core Hunnic ethnic confederates were very numerous. Despite the stereotype of popular imagination, which conjures nomad hordes swarming over the steppe like locusts, the grasslands never supported large populations. However, since all able-bodied males of suitable age fought, nomads competed militarily with much more numerous settled populations.

Analogous to the Huns was a later steppe power, the sixth-century Avars who would play a major role in the drama of Roman-Persian warfare that unfolded in the early seventh century. Only about twenty thousand Avar warriors migrated westward into the lands north of the Danube River. Nonetheless they conquered the Hungarian Plain and terrorized the much more populous Byzantine (East Roman) Empire for decades.

Hun raiders, mounted on indefatigable, hardy ponies, relied on their mobility and swift tactics to evade and shock their enemies, making lightning attacks against civilians, scooping up goods, cattle, and captives, and then escaping before the more ponderous settled powers could react. Peerless horsemen and, like the Persian nobility, their cavalry raised from men trained to ride and fight from boyhood, Hunnic tribal armies would prove the bane of Europe for the next century. In combat Huns swarmed the enemy, using arrow storms fired from short, powerful composite bows to cripple and kill men and horses. To the settled Roman and Persian societies of the south, the Huns were so strange as to be otherworldly, and their ferocity in battle and their customs made these exotic newcomers objects of derision and fear. The Roman historian Ammianus effectively demonized them for posterity in a vitriolic, exaggerated, and evocative image of the Huns. In a more measured fashion, Ammianus also described their fighting habits:

> They also sometimes fight when provoked, and then they enter the battle drawn up in wedge-shaped masses, while their medley of voices makes a savage noise. And as they are lightly equipped for swift motion, and unexpected in action, they purposely divide suddenly into scattered bands and attack, rushing about in disorder here and there, dealing terrific slaughter; and because of their extraordinary rapidity of movement they are never seen to attack a rampart or pillage an enemy's camp. And on this account you would not hesitate to call them the most terrible of all warriors, because they fight from a distance with missiles having sharp bone, instead of their usual points, joined to the shafts with won-

derful skill; then they gallop over the intervening spaces and fight hand to hand with swords, regardless of their own lives; and while the enemy are guarding against wounds from the sabre-thrusts, they throw strips of cloth plaited into nooses over their opponents and so entangle them that they fetter their limbs and take from them the power of riding or walking.[2]

The range of skills and fighting style of the Huns, striking from a distance with powerful, short, composite bows or close with swords and lassos, made them versatile and deadly. Horse archers were new neither to the Persians nor their Roman enemies, but the Huns represented a new, potent, and unique antagonist. Late Roman writers memorialized the superb fighting skills of the Huns: during the Gothic invasion of Italy in 409, the Romans dispatched 300 Huns who cut down 1,100 of the enemy, suffering 17 dead themselves. In the sixth-century Byzantine invasion of North Africa under the famous general Belisarius, his 300 Hun mercenaries annihilated 2,000 Vandal lancers.

In 395, a drought had led to famine on the steppe and drove the unified war bands together with a common purpose to enter the settled lands to the south and plunder as much as they could carry home. A large Hun army, led by two chieftains named Basich and Kurisch, descended through the Darial Pass, crossed through Armenia, and fell upon the Roman lands of Cappadocia and Mesopotamia. Pinned down in the west by the Gothic menace which had broken out anew, the Romans stood by helplessly as the Huns ran riot, raping and killing as they went and sweeping up thousands of captives and cattle. The famous Christian writer and translator of the Bible into Latin, St. Jerome, wrote from distant Palestine, "Behold the wolves, not of Arabia, but of the North, were let loose upon us last year from the far-off rocks of the Caucasus . . ."[3]

By the upper waters of the Euphrates, the Huns divided. A throng of riders galloped south and crossed the frontier into Persia. There they pressed deep into the heart of the empire, harrowing the towns and villages along the river and burning their way into the fertile Mesopotamian breadbasket of the empire. Along the way they seized immense spoils and finally arrived at the gates of Ctesiphon itself. There the Huns could not tarry, as their scouts reported a Sasanian army had mustered and marched against them. The nomads fled, but the pursuing Persians caught and destroyed one of their columns. The remaining raiders were forced to abandon their prisoners and return home via the pass at Darband on the Caspian, likely because a Sasanian and Armenian force blocked the Darial Pass through which they had originally plunged.

Their defeat at the hands of the Persians was remembered by the Huns nearly fifty years later when, at the court of the infamous Attila, they recounted the story of the expedition against Persia to a Roman ambassador. The long shadow cast by the battle and the desperate straits that had launched the expedition imply an extraordinary Hunnish army, numbering perhaps ten thousand warriors. The Huns were no doubt caught by their heels because of the huge haul of prisoners they dragged with them; Bahram's men were said to have freed more than eighteen thousand of these, a great many of them Romans. Of Bahram's other campaigns, only vague mentions survive, and he is said to have combatted vigorously the enemies of the realm.

Hunting was the sport most enjoyed by the Sasanian nobility. The king took solace in withdrawing from the cares that weighed heavily on his shoulders, and with a throng of attendants, servants, beaters, and animal handlers, the royal hunt resembled a small army unleashed to wage war among the animals of the carefully managed game parks and wilds of the kingdom. Hunting offered the space to retreat from the court with its tentacles of intrigue shrouded in the fog of conspiracy and the unhealthy city with its stench and clamor. Among his trusted companions, the king wielded bow, spear, and sword in a show of skill and strength. The hunt was warfare of a different kind. Unfortunately for Bahram, his love of the hunt and trust in intimates exposed him to the same murderous palace plots that had extinguished his father's life. During a hunt in 399, Bahram fell, shot through the throat with an arrow—a terrible accident one author would later claim, but the truth, recorded by another, was that a "group of murderous evildoers" brought Bahram's life and rule to an untimely end. It was just punishment, claimed a later historian, for Bahram's execution of more than twenty thousand people. Casting aside the number as fantasy, there is nonetheless the glow of fire here beneath the smoke, and the likelihood is that Bahram, successful in stemming the tide of the enemy advance, attempted to cut down his internal foes, root and branch.

Bahram's successor, probably a son of Shapur III, was Yazdegerd I. Yazdegerd, whose name means "God-made," has left a complex and contradictory legacy. On one hand, he is called "the Sinner" due to his errors and weakness in tolerating minority faiths in the empire, especially Judaism and Christianity, which flourished early in his reign. Yazdegerd's dramatic ideological pivot is best seen in his coins. Until his day, the coin of the realm, the silver drachm, bore alongside the bust of the king the inscription, "Mazdaworshipping divine king of kings of the Iranians and non-Iranians whose lineage is from the gods."[4] Yazdegerd altered this long tradition with another inscription, "Yazdegerd, who maintains peace in his dominion."[5] The great king, a messenger of peace and stability, began his rule with clemency and compassion, but the court swarmed with intrigants, and corrivals swarmed in the provinces. The young monarch's patience was soon to be exhausted.

First, though, the great king had to forge a new course amidst the storm from the east that threatened to swamp the ship of state. Since the days of the mighty Ardashir, Sasanian kings had claimed lordship over Iran and non-Iran, as power brokers for the entire world; Yazdegerd sought a different ideology from which to galvanize his rule. The immediate catalyst for sweeping changes that the great king effected were the Huns. Following multiple defeats under Shapur II and steady Hunnic pressure that can be surmised throughout the reigns of Yazdegerd's immediate (murdered) predecessors, the fire of the Sasanian star had faded.

It is true that the nobility still partnered with the House of Sasan, consistently electing one of the family to rule when candidates from the other great houses certainly offered viable alternatives. Thus, despite the troubled times of the fourth century, the partnership of lords and kingly dynasty remained intact. But it was not an equal marriage. Increasingly, the great families reserved for themselves the privilege of kingmaker. Such a relationship between crown and court was as tenuous as it was treacherous. It was not lost on Yazdegerd that many of his line had met untimely deaths through an uncanny, even farcical series of "mishaps." Under such cheerless conditions, Yazdegerd could hardly expect to grow old.

Not least of the strands of the Gordian knot with which the great king was confronted was the poisoned thread of defeat at the hands of the Hun. The king keenly sensed the threat to Iranian prestige represented by these eastern and northern military opponents and even the existential threat they posed to Iran. He also realized the peril posed by the Magian priesthood and the landed aristocracy. Finally, he had to deal with a seemingly pathological urge among his own leading men to smother him in his sleep, or otherwise do away with his kind.

Yazdegerd addressed the Hunnic problem with the pen. Warfare was not the only, nor the best, option available to him. If Shapur II had set a grinding pace for his aristocratic cavalrymen and their retainers engaged in the fight over years and even decades, his successors had no such ability. Defeat bred demoralization, defeatism, and defection. Yazdegerd established an ideological foundation, brick by brick, to which his successors added, which would scaffold the Sasanians to the peak of their power, embedding as it did the king and the nobility in bonds of reciprocity articulated in ancient stories. Yazdegerd established a regime in which life paralleled ancient stories and in turn reinforced their overarching centrality. The great king, supreme guardian of order on earth, mirrored the heavenly Ahuramazda, and like him and the great kings of myth, the shahanshah required noble helpers to maintain the cosmic order, to play out the drama fought between good and order, between Iran and Turan, where dwelled the Huns and the other forces of chaos. In return the nobility would receive titles, lands, gifts, prestige, and plunder.

As the fifth century dawned, the Sasanians prioritized their own survival in the face of the threat from nomadic groups and dynasties to the north and east. Yazdegerd recognized that he could not act militarily on two fronts— something of which earlier Sasanian kings had also recognized and seen, for example, in Shapur III's peaceful partition of Armenia with his Roman adversary. During Yazdegerd's reign, the Persians launched an internal propaganda program, recasting the ancient Roman enemy as a lesser state but a brother nonetheless, one they claimed was mentioned in the Avesta, ancient Zoroastrian scriptures. The great king launched a charm offensive against the Eastern Roman Empire based in Constantinople, repatriating thousands of captives taken by the Hun raiders of 395. The Romans, shaken by internal revolt, the collapse of the western half of the empire, and war without end against the Goths and Franks, welcomed the prospect of peace on their eastern borders. Stories even circulated that Yazdegerd stood as guardian of the boy king Theodosius II (402–450), whose father, the emperor Arcadius (383–408), fretted about the child's fate after his own death would come to pass. The great king is said to have sent a tutor for the boy emperor and a letter in which he addressed the East Roman senate in Constantinople in which he issued a grave warning: if anyone harmed a hair on the emperor's young head, they would have to deal with Yazdegerd and the might of the Sasanian army.

To take on the nobility and priestly opponents, Yazdegerd appointed a capable, devoted, and steely nobleman, Mihr-Narseh, to the office of *framadar*. The title means "lord of many," and its holder's function was that of grand vizier or prime minister. At royal banquets the framadar took his seat after only the king and the princes of blood, before even the great priests and generals of the realm—a clear indication of his power and standing. Mihr-Narseh belonged to the powerful Suren clan and hailed from the village of Dast-e Barin in southwestern Fars, the heartland of the Sasanian dynasty. He traced his lineage to ancient ancestors of legend and was well connected to the powerful families of the south. Of his time in office, which spanned not only the reign of Yazdegerd, the urbane, educated Mihr-Narseh stood in contrast to the great king's bloody hostility to the great houses. Nonetheless, Mihr-Narseh aided the king in his religious reforms and in his attempts to curb the power of the Persian aristocrats.

Yazdegerd's war was firstly an internal one, a fight in which he demonstrated acute awareness of the complexities of rule. Yazdegerd's conflict with the Zoroastrian priesthood is manifested in his initial tolerance of Christianity. For the first time, Christians could freely and openly rebuild ruined churches, and their bishops could travel freely on their business. On more than one occasion, Yazdegerd employed the supreme Christian bishop of Ctesiphon, including a delicate negotiation between the king and his estranged brother in Pars. He was so popular among them that they offered daily prayers for the "victorious and glorious king."[6] In the Babylonian Talmud, compiled by the Jewish sages of Sasanian Mesopotamia, he was called the new Cyrus, recalling the ancient Achaemenid Persian king who restored the Jewish exiles to their homeland after their deportation to Babylonia by the infamous King Nebuchadnezzar II. In this highwire balancing act, playing off one faction against another, the king performed without a net. His grooming of Christian and Jewish favor, as mentioned, helped earn Yazdegerd the infamous epithet of "the Sinner."

Although the extent of Yazdegerd's failed revolution cannot be fully appreciated due to the sorry state of the few sources that detail his reign, the king appears to have attacked his internal problems with vigor. Nor did he escape the treatment historically reserved for most revolutionaries. In 417/18 the catholicos Yahballaha I, chief bishop of all the Christians of Persia, arrived in Constantinople seeking peace and reconciliation. His task was to maintain the status quo between the two great powers which recent events had threatened to destabilize: the likelihood is that the Magians took umbrage at the conversion of Sasanian elites to the alien religion.

By 420, a wave of conversions among prominent Iranians had frayed the cord to breaking. Christian zealots had audaciously destroyed a fire temple. In the face of such a heinous act, the king could not look the other way, and so Yazdegerd (or one of his immediate successors) imprisoned and tortured some Christians in the kingdom.[7] To spare themselves from Persian wrath, Christian refugees fled from Sasanian lands to the East Roman Empire, and the news of their ordeals further scraped at the sinews of the relationship between the Christian Roman Empire and the Persians.

In the autumn of 420, Yazdegerd traveled to Hyrcania, the remote mountainous north of Iran by the Caspian. His journey there was likely dictated by the desire of the great king to strengthen the empire against the Kidarite foe. During his journey, a cabal of nobles murdered the shahanshah. Just as his three predecessors had fallen victim to conspiracy, Yazdegerd could not escape the murderous intentions of the aristocracy. Later generations comforted themselves with the story of the Sinner's demise. In this tale, in answer to the prayers of his oppressed subjects, namely the Zoroastrian clergy and the nobility, a magical horse emerged from a spring, heaven sent. No one among the king's retinue could tame the steed, so the king himself tried. As he saddled it, the horse kicked him on the chest, a blow that stopped the monarch's heart. After its divinely inspired act of regicide, the horse galloped away, never to be seen again.

Three of Yazdegerd's sons vied for power. Shapur, lord of Armenia since 416, rushed to Ctesiphon and had himself crowned Shapur IV, but he found his support built on quicksand. The new shahanshah fell prey to a claque inside the court who assassinated him in a matter of months. The second brother, Narseh, also failed in his bid for power. Instead, the nobles preferred an obscure Sasanian, perhaps a son of Bahram IV, named Kusrow, who attempted to consolidate his rule.

But the sons of Yazdegerd were not finished. A black sheep of the family, long before ostracized by his father and banished to live among the Arab tribes on the fringes of the kingdom, named Bahram saw his moment had arrived. Bahram was the son of Yazdegerd and his wife Shushandukht, daughter of the Jewish exilarch Huna bar Nathan, leader of the Jews of Babylonia. Upon the news of the chaos that enveloped the royal court and the elevation of Kusrow, Bahram resolved to make a bid for power.

Bahram's chief backer was the Arab lord and Sasanian vassal Mundhir ibn al-Nu'man I (418–461). Mundhir belonged to the family of Lakhm, an Arab clan who had come into Sasanian service at the end of the third century. In the wake of the demise of the Palmyrene Kingdom, the Lakhmids filled the power vacuum along the desert fringes of Syria. There they forged their rule over the tribes of northern Arabia and established themselves at the town of Hira on the western banks of the lower course of the Euphrates River. Like the Palmyrenes of Syria before them, the Lakhmids were town dwellers; agriculture and trade were their sources of wealth. They policed the frontier and guarded the caravans that plodded across the desert to Arabia and Rome beyond.

The Lakhmids drew their military power from among allied Arab nomads and hired foreign mercenaries. Shapur II had found the Lakhmids capable and trustworthy, and he elevated their chiefs to kingship. The Sasanians integrated Lakhmid forces into the southern shield of the empire. As loyal servants, Lakhmid troops served alongside a permanent garrison of Sasanian heavy cavalry, and together these maintained the peace along the vast imperial frontier with Arabia.

Bahram marched on Ctesiphon at the head of ten thousand Arab and Persian horsemen. Upon his arrival the nobles, who had deposed his brother Shapur and installed Kusrow in his place, agreed to accept Bahram only if he submitted himself to trial by ordeal. The crown and regalia, so the colorful story goes, was placed between a pair of hungry lions and their cubs and the two claimants, Kusrow and Bahram, invited to seize the symbols of power; whoever succeeded would be king. Bahram, whose physical size and beauty made the onlookers marvel, set upon the lions with a mace and slaughtered them. After such an awe-inspiring display, Kusrow was the first among the Persians to acclaim Bahram king. Whatever the truth of the matter, at age twenty, Bahram ascended to power as Bahram V, nicknamed Gor, the "wild ass," an epithet he earned for his hunting prowess. The unfortunate Kusrow is never heard of again.

After the relative peace that had prevailed under his father, Bahram immediately faced war in the west. The young Roman emperor Theodosius II had, despite the protection extended by Yazdegerd and his tutoring at the hands of Persian sages, embarked on war. Stories of Persian persecution of Christians circulated at the imperial court, and the victims called for intervention. When the Sasanians demanded the emperor return the Christian refugees to their lands, Theodosius refused. The Persians had responded with additional insults, refusing to return Roman miners they had hired to work newly discovered gold veins in Persian Armenia. They also robbed Roman caravans and detained the merchants. The emperor's decision to break the peace was likely deeply influenced by news that reached him of the anarchy that reigned within Iran—two kings had been crowned within a matter of months and Bahram would make a third.

Theodosius ordered his eastern field marshal, the Alan general Ardaburius, to the frontier. In the spring and summer of 421, at the head of the Roman eastern army, Ardaburius marched into Armenia and pillaged throughout the district of Arzanene in Persian Armenia. There, in mid-August 421, the Persians, led by Narseh, confronted him. Much later sources consider this Narseh to be Mihr-Narseh, the former vizier of Yazdegerd. It is equally likely though that Bahram's full brother Narseh was meant and whom the king of kings almost certainly established as lord of Armenia, the customary holding for the foremost Sasanian male after the shahanshah himself. Ardaburius and the Romans defeated Narseh, who retreated into Persian

Mesopotamia and there planned a counterattack across the border.[8] The defeat the Sasanians suffered, announced in a victory bulletin in the East Roman capital in Constantinople on September 6, was minor. After the engagement Narseh maintained sufficient forces to contemplate a counterstroke into Roman Mesopotamia, which the Romans feared. The Roman general Ardaburius had clearly achieved strategic surprise, and his invasion was made with enough power to throw the Persians onto the defensive.

Ardaburius pressed the Roman offensive, marching about 120 kilometers south to invest Nisibis, a trip that took the Romans perhaps ten days, and thus the last week of August or first week of September saw the foe encamped on the hot, dry plain outside the city. Nisibis comprised the keystone to Sasanian defenses in Upper Mesopotamia and a bridgework that the emperors fervently wanted to seize and thereby reverse the strategic situation. Narseh sent overtures to Ardaburius, asking his enemy to set a time and place for a trial by battle, but the Romans refused. On the Persian side, we hear no more of Narseh, who may have been posted elsewhere or returned to Ctesiphon to manage affairs of state. Bahram was away to the northeast, dealing with an invasion by the Kidarites, who, like the Romans, sought to take advantage of the anarchy surrounding the youthful shahanshah's rise to power. Facing a two-front war, the Sasanians were hobbled. Bahram could not commit his full power to the west to fight the Roman invasion, and he had to quickly make terms with the Kidarites. An army of twenty-five thousand eastern foes smashed through Sasanian defenses at Merv and raided all the way to Rayy (near what is today Tehran). The great king had to swallow the humiliation of paying tribute to his enemies—a move that exemplifies Sasanian weakness and desperation. If the king could not settle affairs in the west swiftly, he would not be able to free himself of the Kidarite yoke, a failure that would spell certain doom to his kingship and possibly the end of the dynasty.

As usual, for much of what we know of Roman-Persian warfare, we have only the Roman side presented to us. The Roman church historian Socrates, our major source for the war, reports that the Romans learned of the Persians mustering their whole army, and thus Theodosius ordered reinforcements to the east. These additional troops could not have been raised and transferred across Anatolia during 421—the campaign season was too far advanced by the time the Romans began to invest Nisibis.

The next phase of the war began in the spring of 422. Socrates wrote that Bahram V, out of fear of the Romans, hesitated to take the field himself but instead sent the "Saracens" to raid through Mesopotamia. Saracens, a term for Arabs in the Roman sources, likely means the follower of the Lakhmid prince of Hira, Mundhir, who had aided Bahram in his rise to power. The idea of a hesitant monarch, caught up in the pleasures of the harem and the hunt, is a cliché in later tradition attached to Bahram; there certainly is little evidence of it during this war. Bahram planned two strikes, the first led by his faithful lieutenant, the Arab prince Mundhir, who struck across the Euphrates, aiming for the great Syrian city of Antioch. Though the cause is unclear, Socrates mentions that, on hearing rumors of an impending Roman attack, the Arabs panicked and drowned in large numbers in the Euphrates—the Lakhmid thrust into Syria was a dismal failure. Bahram, meanwhile, moved to relieve Nisibis at the head of a large Sasanian force. On hearing of the shahanshah's approach at the head of a host that included a brigade of elephant troops, the Romans were terror struck and abandoned the siege.

The two sides began negotiations shortly after this, though the fighting was not finished. While a Roman peace embassy was greeted favorably by the young king of kings, there was clearly a strong pro-war coterie amidst his courtiers and officers. The two sides decided on a trial by duel and each selected their champion. The Persians chose Ardazanes, an otherwise unknown figure but a member of an elite guard cavalry unit. Ardazanes fell, defeated and killed by a Goth in Roman service named Areobindus. Undeterred, Bahram turned to fresh cavalry reinforcements and attempted to surprise the Romans with a two-pronged attack. While his main force of infantry, elephants, and cavalry attacked Ardaburius's front, a second wave rode to outflank and ambush the Romans in the rear. Miraculously, a second Roman force led by the magister Procopius surrounded and destroyed the Sasanian ambushing force, and the main attack also failed, apparently falling into a Roman trap set by Ardaburius. The encounter left many dead and seven thousand Persian prisoners in Roman hands. Faced with the heavy reversal, Bahram agreed to a peace treaty that merely restored the situation ante bellum. A major concern from the Roman side, which they achieved, was freedom for their Christian brethren inside the Persian lands to practice their faith unmolested. Despite its unpopularity, the trial by arms forced the king of kings to accept the terms in the interest of expediency.

After the large-scale confrontation, fought over two years in 421–22, the Romans had earned the victory. In the years that followed, the great powers once more resumed something akin to their traditional hostile stance, but neither found itself in a position to seek vengeance. Afterward Bahram settled affairs to his liking in Armenia, deposing the last Armenian king, Ardashir V, and installing a *marzban* in his place. Persian Armenia thus formed a regular province inside the Sasanian realm, a move that the great king hoped would quell internal dissent and end Roman meddling in affairs there. Bahram then turned his gaze north and east; the Romans would be dealt with in due time.

Whether or not the great king was the layabout of lore, he had to pivot from matters in the west to face down the Hunnic menace. While the scant sources portray the king, roused from his love nest and hunting grounds to a higher purpose, gliding over the field of battle to a swift, decisive engagement, the reality is likely far messier. All we know for certain is that the centerpiece of the war against the Kidarites occurred around 427, when Bahram marched with his forces through Armenia, skirted across the mountains south of the Caspian, and marched on the large oasis of Merv, the former Persian dike against the waters of the barbarian tide. At the village of Kushmayhan at the edge of the desert oasis, he launched a surprise night attack and routed the enemy, killing the king of the Kidarites and driving them from the Merv oasis and reestablishing at least some Sasanian control of the lands up to the Oxus. The great spoils seized from the Kidarites were the objects of marvel. Bahram gifted the dazzling rubies and other gems from his vanquished opponent's crown, along with the fallen king's wife and servants, to one of the great fire temples of the empire, Adur Gushnasp, built on the stunning site of Takt-e-Solayman in western Iran.

Bahram's victory over the Kidarites, while impressive, was not total. While we know of this one signal victory, the city-based Kidarite Huns continued to rule over the rich and important cities of the eastern lands of Bactria and Gandhara, and they pressed the fight throughout Bahram's reign. In response the great king shored up Persian defenses around the Merv oasis and appointed his brother Narseh *marzban*, warden of the marches. It was likely Narseh, too, who followed up Bahram's victory with at least one invasion across the Oxus, a punishing raid in force that aimed at further shaking the Kidarite grip to the north and east. It was likely Narseh's foray into Transoxiana, the alien land of Turan, cast in Persian ideology as the realm of barbarian darkness, that led to a treaty that established the borders between the two kingdoms. But these maneuvers did not end the conflict, and the Sasanians had to prioritize their eastern affairs over all others up to the very end of their rule.

To the west, the Roman threat waxed and waned. In the early 430s, the general Anatolius yomped east with a train of architects, engineers, and masons. High in the mountains, 1,900 meters above sea level, atop a crest astride an ancient Armenian city, Anatolius and his legionnaires split stone, worked cranes, and slaked lime for mortar. Block by block the Romans erected a new fortified city, in honor of the reigning emperor, named Theodosiopolis (today Erzerum in eastern Turkey). These massive remodeling, extension, and addition works, accompanied by the repopulating of the city, would turn Theodosiopolis into one of their most important and powerful bases on the eastern frontier. Lying as it did about 460 kilometers (285 miles) north of Nisibis, the fortress could not make good the loss of the latter city, but by virtue of its strategic situation, the city guarded one of the northern invasion routes. Its refurbishment, while certainly directed first and foremost against the Sasanians, also provided a bulwark against future threats which might arise beyond the Caucasus. The Roman-fortified base broke the spirit, if not the letter, of the peace treaty of 422, the text of which does not survive. Though Bahram certainly took notice of the violation, the Sasanians did not interfere with the building work. In 438, before the king of kings could strike against the new Roman barb in the flesh of his kingdom, aged just thirty-eight, Bahram Gur, the "wild ass" of Persia, died. His passing, like that of his father Yazdegerd, is covered in a shroud of stories and tales woven after the fact. Given his youth and the history of ill will of elements within the Persian noble houses, we can safely doubt one version that has the shahan-shah dying peacefully in his sleep.

The mantle of kingship fell to Bahram Gur's son, Yazdegerd II (438–457) who was aided by the faithful, venerable vizier Mihr-Narseh. With the coronation of Yazdegerd, Mihr-Narseh began service to his third generation of the House of Sasan. Unlike the policies of his father and grandfather, Yazdegerd II moved to impose Zoroastrianism on the people of the empire and, in doing so, took principal aim at the Christians and Jews in the western lands.

Freed for the moment from his troubles in the east, Yazdegerd struck against Rome. Religious affairs likely played a major part in his decision to attack; the growing power of Christianity in Persia, the meddling of the Romans on its behalf, and the insoluble tensions between powerful Zoroastrian elements and their religious rivals could be eased somewhat by humbling the Christian emperor. Equally importantly, Yazdegerd aimed to batter down the newly built city of Theodosiopolis, destruction of which would humiliate the long-reigning Theodosius II and suture a weeping sore on the frontier.

Yazdegerd's advance on Theodosiopolis occurred in 440 and is mistakenly attributed to Bahram during the war of 421–22.[9] The strategic situation favored the great king's plans. Throughout the 430s, barbarians battered and bloodied the body of both eastern and western empires. For the Romans, vexed by wars against the Goths and other Germanic tribal confederations, the fifth century unfolded in a cascade of bloody crises. The Huns established themselves in the middle Danube River valley from which they were free to strike a blow at either the Western or Eastern Roman Empire. After 434 the Romans staggered under blows delivered by the Huns under the two brothers who ruled them, Bleda (434–ca. 445) and the infamous Attila (434–453). In 439, the Romans suffered yet another catastrophe, this time in the rich provinces of North Africa, which fell to the Germanic Vandal confederation under their adventurer king, Geiseric (428–477). With Roman forces spread like butter over bread, the east was largely denuded of troops.

Learning of the fires that blazed throughout Roman lands and that the Romans dispatched their armies to fight elsewhere—and possibly too because the Romans did not forward payment they had agreed upon to subsidize Persian defenses of the Caucasus—in the spring or early summer of 440, Yazdegerd broke the treaty and marched to attack Theodosiopolis in Roman Armenia. A poor start, fouled by heavy weather that saw the Sasanian advance slow to a crawl, foretold of the campaign to come. Despite the Roman frontier being manned by skeleton forces, Eunomius, the Christian bishop of the city rallied the garrison and townspeople in a fervent defense of the town, which he cast as a war between Christ and the devil. Faced with a "barbarian chief" who shouted from below the city battlements that he would bring destruction to the house of God inside the city, the fiery Christian bishop had his artillerists man their ballista, the heavy stone-throwing machines the Romans had mounted on the walls of the city. Taking careful aim the holy man unleased a shot that smashed the skull of the Persian who threatened desecration of the holy places and "sprinkled his brains on the ground."

Amidst the siege, the Roman general Anatolius, who for twenty years had been in high command in the east, arrived under a banner of peace, with full authority to negotiate terms. The Romans bought off the Persians, offering (or renewing) subsidies in gold—five hundred Roman pounds annually (160 kg) to the Persians, which allowed Yazdegerd to claim victory and cast the Romans as servants of his empire. The great king, eager to claim a propaganda victory, put the gold to good practical use.

The Hunnic threat, amplified by their successes in the east and west, waxed under Yazdegerd and extended now to the Caspian whence they threatened the lands of the Iranian heartland. Attila, the terror of Europe, threatened invasion of Persia. In response, Yazdegerd fortified the Darband pass against them. On the western coast of the Caspian, 20 kilometers (12 miles) south of the pass, the great king built Shahrestan Yazdegerd, a massive fortress in mud brick, covering an area of 100 hectares (247 acres) with walls 10.2 meters (33.5 feet) thick, studded with 144 projecting towers.

Drachma of Yazdegerd II, minted at Gurgan or Qom between 439-447. (*Classical Numismatic Group*)

Having accomplished little in the west, but fulfilling his objective of triumph through tribute, the great king marched home to face the demon to the east, the Kidarites. Unlike his predecessors, who had at various times paid humiliating and deeply unpopular tribute to the Kidarites to buy peace and bring an end to Hunnic predations, Yazdegerd would brook no such slight to his honor. He refused to make the payments to the Kidarite kings and braced for war. In 441, Yazdegerd established himself at Nishapur (the "New City of Shapur") in the northeast region of Iran known as Khurasan. From 441–448/49 Yazdegerd's armies made annual attacks to the east and made considerable inroads.

> [When Yazdegerd learned that] . . . in every region his empire lived in peace, and that he had put the king of the Huns [the Kidarites] into even greater straits since he had ruined most of his provinces and had prevailed over his rule, then he sent messengers throughout all the fire-temples of his land . . . .[10]

Triumphalism and the victory bulletins sent to the Zoroastrian houses of worship aside, the empire remained under the specter of war. In 449, Yazdegerd once more marched from Nishapur to strike against the Kidarites. On the approach of the Sasanians, the Huns fled into the desert lands and refused battle. The great king changed tactics; he unleashed troops of raiders who fanned out across Hun territory, plundering freely and pillaging several

Kidarite towns and fortresses, leading a train of prisoners in their wake whom he deported to Persia.

Despite the ongoing stalemate in the east, and—after years of campaigning—his successes limited, Yazdegerd nonetheless exerted strenuous pressure on the Jews and Christians of his empire, particularly his Armenian subjects, whose nobles (nakharars) he forced to convert *en masse* to Zoroastrianism. Given that Christianity now moved to convert among its adherents not only the Armenian and other Caucasian vassal lords but also increasing numbers of Persians along the northern frontiers of the empire, in places like Gurgan and in the Merv oasis, the tone-deaf policies dictated by the Zoroastrian elites, religious authorities and nobles alike, were certainly short-sighted, as it was from these frontier populations and the Caucasus that the Sasanians drew a considerable portion of the manpower for the wars. Despite his persecutions, the king of kings managed to avoid the permanent alienation of the Caucasian nobility. On those cavalry forces Yazdegerd fundamentally relied for his wars in the east, which he was forced to wage nearly every year of his reign.

On their return home, some of the Armenian nakharars forsook their new religion and returned to Christianity, and thus openly revolted against the shahanshah. It was no small undertaking. Troops were led by prominent Armenian Christian lords, Vardan Mamikonean and Arshavir Arsharuni and others. In the summer of 450, at Khalkhal, north of Lake Sevan in Armenia, the rebel forces met Yazdegerd's *marzban*, the Sasanian commander over the Darband Pass. The Armenians smashed the Persian right wing and drove it back on the troops on the army's left flank, which soon collapsed. In the flight and confusion that followed, the Armenians pursued the broken enemy into thick forests and cut them down. Many more Persians drowned as they tried to cross the Lop'nos River. Vardan then marched north, stormed the Sasanian fort at Darband, and slaughtered its garrison. From Darband, the rebels sent negotiators to the European Huns or Alans to the north of the pass and coaxed them into an alliance against the Persians. Hun military support was especially crucial as the Romans, to whom the disaffected Armenians had also made overtures, refused to aid them.

Yazdegerd sent his old war dog, the vizier Mihr-Narseh, with numerous troops and an elephant corps, to the borders of Armenia. From his Armenian base the king's man sowed further dissension in the rebel ranks and drew to his side numerous nobles from the Caucasus, undermining those lukewarm to the cause through threats or bribes as the need arose. In 451, at the Battle of Avarayr, southeast of Mount Ararat, the Persians routed the Armenian Christian coalition and killed or captured many of them. The Sasanians seized numerous hostages, especially the sons of the noble rebels. These and others were deported to the east where the great king intended to press forward the bitter struggle against the Kidarites.

Yazdegerd again took the field in about 454, the sixteenth year of his reign, and invaded Bactria from Khurasan. Once more, the Huns refused open battle, relying on their tactics of harassment and ambush in which the Sasanians were bested. At the end of the campaign, however, the Huns counterattacked. Relying on surprise attacks, hit-and-run strikes, and sudden raids to grind the imperial army down, they raided deeply into royal territory:

> For the enemy did not battle with the Iranians face to face. Instead, they unexpectedly fell upon one wing after another, putting many men to the sword, while they themselves returned unharmed, and vanished. Doing this for many days, they defeated the Iranian troops with severe blows.[11]

In 456 the great king again sojourned in the east, prosecuting the war in which no end was in sight. The shahanshah had discontinued tribute payments to the Huns, apparently part of a treaty arrangement agreed upon in the wake of the Persian embarrassment in 454.[12] The following year, while sojourning in Pars, in the homeland of his dynasty, the shahanshah died. Two of his sons, Hormizd III (457–459) and Peroz I (459–484), fought for control of the empire. Peroz sought allies in the east and found succor among the Hepthalite Huns. With their aid, Peroz established himself on the throne. Doubtless the young king, fresh off his victory over his rivals, could have foreseen that his reign would collapse in ruin after he tried to break free of his former allies.

The Hephthalites, called the "White Huns" by a later Byzantine writer, who also claimed that they, unlike other Huns, had Caucasian features, formed a ruling dynasty who had entered the Sasanian orbit. Around 425 the Hepthalites had entered the Transoxanian lands bordering the Kidarite kingdom. In 456 a Hepthalite embassy arrived in China, and it is from around this time that the dynasty seems to have established itself in Bactria and have driven out at least some of the Kidarites.

Thus, one group of Central Asian migrants had finally accomplished the task which the great king and the Iranian lords, despite their herculean efforts, had ultimately failed—to break the Kidarites. Kidarite power was now caught between the hammer of the Hephthalites in the east and the Sasanians, and by 466 Kidarite rule was broken and Sasanian authority was once more restored over a wide area. If, as the sources assert, Peroz ceded the city of Talo-qan in northeast Afghanistan to the Hepthalites in return for their support in his dynastic dispute with his brother, the Sasanians had benefitted from their alliance with the White Huns and regained extensive lands in the east. These gains would be short lived.

Once he grasped the reins of the state, Peroz had to contend with centripetal forces at the western edge of his lands. In the northwest the king of Albania revolted in his enclave in the Caucasus, a region astride the southern extension of the mountains, the Ceraunian range. Albania was bounded by the valley Kura (Kor) River and the borders of Iberia (modern Georgia) in the west and the Caspian in the east. In the chaos that descended on the Sasanian Empire following the death of Yazdegerd, the Albanian king, Vache II (440–462) broke free from Persian rule. At the heart of his disaffection lay the ongoing conflict between the Zoroastrian and Christian religions. Under pressure from Yazdegerd II, Vache, who was the son of one of Peroz's sisters, had converted to the Iranian national religion, but he soon apostatized and raised the flag of revolt.

The Persian general Raham, member of the Mihran family, who had close ties to the king of kings and whose clan had supported Peroz's rise to power, led a Persian host into Albania. There Raham defeated the forces of Vache and made his son prisoner. Despite the reversal, Vache persisted in his rebellion, enlisting mysterious "eleven mountain kings" and further inviting a group of Huns to seize the fortress of Darband. Exasperated by his erstwhile vassal's stubbornness, Peroz again turned to the Hepthalites, whom he sent a vast treasure to buy their service against Vache. The Hepthalites marched through the Darial Pass and fell upon the Albanian forces, burning and destroying much of the land, but Vache nonetheless resisted. He finally ended his rebellion by handing over his mother and daughter to the shahanshah. In 462, Vache gave up the struggle and retired to a monastery, and Albania would do without a king for the next thirty years.

After he settled the crisis in Albania, Peroz marshaled against the Huns at Darband, apparently those whom Vache had called to his aid. He sent embassies to the Byzantine emperor and as far west as Pope Leo I (457–474) making familiar pleas for money: the spilling of Persian blood in campaigns against the Huns spared the Romans from bleeding in turn. In response, the emperor dispatched a high-ranking official to deal with Peroz, and he finally caught up with the great king in Gurgan. The sources conflict, though it seems that the Romans, in keeping with their long-standing practice, did in fact deliver money which the shahanshah employed in the campaign. Probably in 467 or 468, Peroz proved victorious in his Caucasian foray and regained control of Darband.

Meanwhile, in the east, Hepthalite power grew. As the Kidarites before them, the White Huns pressed westward into Khurasan and the territory the shahs considered core Iranian lands. Peroz ceased tribute payments and braced for war. The Hepthalites had expanded their power far to the west—likely embracing even the Merv oasis and other Sasanian lands in Khurasan, since Peroz's campaign, launched in 473 or 474, was waged from Gurgan by the Caspian. Details are sparse, but it seems Peroz won initial successes before being trapped by the Hephthalites and captured. The great king had marched his army deep into enemy territory in pursuit of his most bitter foes. Along with him was all the might of the Sasanian Persian army, a mass of iron-cased cavalrymen, skilled with bow and lance, and infantry from all over the empire. As his enemies retreated before him, Peroz marched on, leading his mighty host farther and farther into a remote mountain valley flanked by thick woods. Thinking the broad valley open and his foes in flight, the monarch rushed headlong, determined to seize the victory. Gradually, his men sensed something was wrong; perhaps they glimpsed movement in the trees or had the feeling of being watched or simply the foreboding that comes before battle in a strange land.

One source relates that, after being approached by nervous Persian noblemen about their push into hostile territory, an ambassador from the Roman Empire, who happened to have accompanied the expedition, rode to the side of Peroz and told the king a story: Once, said the Roman, a lion chanced upon a goat, tied down and bleating on a mound of earth. The lion rushed to seize his prey and fell into a deep circular trench that the owners of the goat had dug for the purpose of catching the lion. When he heard the story, the king halted the host in fear that he had led his men into peril. Too late; the enemy revealed themselves. His host was surrounded. Messengers arrived from the Akhshunwar, the Hephthalite king, and chided Peroz for his carelessness. They announced, however, that all could be forgiven if the Persian king agreed to bow before the enemy leader. Peroz took counsel with the magi. The great king decided that he would comply but arranged to prostrate himself before his nemesis as the sun appeared in the sky, since each morning Zoroastrians customarily bowed before the rising sun. The Persian monarch thus comforted himself with his deception, having bowed only to the great star and not to the foe. This version of the story, no doubt concocted to save some face for the Sasanian monarch, could do little to mask the truth. The Hepthalites demanded ransom in gold, and Peroz paid dearly, even aided, it is said, by payments from the new Roman emperor Zeno (474–491). Humiliated and held hostage, Bahram could not suffer such indignities if he expected his reign to continue and his family to continue to hold the throne of Persia.

The tale of the king, thoroughly embroidered by ancient and medieval hands, is embroidered with myth and spun into a moralizing fairy tale. After his first capture, so the story goes, Peroz returned a second time to attack the Hephthalites, was again captured, and was forced to pay an even larger ransom than previously, as well as leave his son with the enemy as a hostage. Nonetheless, as we have inherited the tragic story of Peroz, historians agree that the great king mounted a second campaign against the Hepthalites. According to a later Islamic-era account of the fateful expedition, the king of kings had responded to a nomad incursion into Khurasan, the frontier region around the city of Nishapur in northeastern Iran. Peroz had hastened with his army to meet the threat. This time, to gain surprise, the king advanced through the desert on little-used trackways, hoping to shock the enemy by appearing to their rear, but in the difficult and unfamiliar terrain, his guides lost their way. The Sasanians found themselves in a shambles, stricken with thirst and unfit to fight. Taken prisoner once more, to gain his freedom Peroz was forced to make a humiliating peace, paying a massive indemnity and regular tribute and ceding a vast expanse of former Persian territory. The Hepthalite king demanded thirty mule loads of money, likely gold, since we know that the Sasanian gold dinar underwent substantial debasement during his rule, and even in these diluted coins, the great king could muster only twenty of the thirty mule loads promised, forcing him to leave his son hostage with the Hepthalites.

Word of the vanquishing of one of the world's great monarchs soon spread far and wide. One Armenian historian recalled:

> Even in time of peace the mere sight or mention of a Hephthalite terrified everybody, and there was no question of going to war openly against one, for everybody remembered all too clearly the calamities and defeats inflicted by the Hephthalites on the king of the Aryans and on the Persians.[13]

In 484, the great king again marshaled his forces, intent on exacting revenge and recovering his honor. The power of the army was clearly impressive, numbering as many as fifty thousand men. However, experience with the Hephthalites, and the hard lessons of the previous decade, had struck deep. Despite the presence of the full panoply of Sasanian arms, including large numbers of war elephants, morale was poor and fear reigned. The Persian host marched "more like men condemned to death than warriors marching to war."[14] As he approached the frontier, Peroz reached the tower built

by his predecessor, Bahram Gur, in Khurasan, the Land of the Sun, the eastern province of the Persian Empire comprising the contested lands behind
the Oxus River. Bahram's tower marked the border, and under a previous
treaty both sides had agreed not to cross beyond it in anger. So that he would
not be in violation of the treaty, according to a fanciful later tradition, the
king had a border tower mounted on a mobile platform and dragged ahead
of his army by three hundred men and fifty elephants.

The king of the Hephthalites, the scourge of the Persians, sent an embassy
to Peroz and reminded him of his obligations: the two sides had agreed on
firm borders and on peace, and Peroz had promised never to wage war on
him again. The Persian king received the embassy and, in the memory burned
brightly enough to be memorialized in the Persian national epic poem, the
Shah-nama, the great king replied:

> Behold! I lead a vast, a noble host
> And warriors bent on fight, and I will leave not
> For long on earth the shade of Khushnawaz[15]

When he received the great king's reply, Kung-ki (called mistakenly here
Khushnawaz) is said to have mustered his forces and ordered the treaty his
foe had brazenly trampled "set on a spearhead like a shining sun." Upon the
approach of the Sasanian host, the Hephthalites dug a trench "lasso-deep
and twenty-cubits wide." The battle was joined, and Warner's beautiful old
translation of the *Shah-nama*'s account is worth quoting at length:

> The drums and trumpets sounded in both hosts,
> The air was ebon with the armies' dust
> And from them both such showers of arrows rained
> That blood ran down like water in a stream
> Then, like a dust-cloud, Shah Peroz advanced
> With mace and Ruman helm, and as he drew
> Anear to Khushmanawaz, the Turkman's chief
> Retreated, turned his rein, and showed his back.
> The foeman followed fiercely. Shah Peroz
> Spurred forward with few followers and fell
> With others—chiefs and Lions of the day
> Of battle—in the fosse . . .
> Now Shah Peroz, that chief of chiefs endowed
> With Grace and state, had broken head and back,
> While of the princes, save Kawad, none lived:
> Thus host and empire went adown the wind.

Thus ended the reign of Peroz, choked on his own blood in the bottom of a pit in Central Asia. His life and end served as a fitting metaphor for the Sasanian monarchy in the fifth century: constant struggle and ultimate failure. As the fifth century entered its last decades, now a tributary of the mighty Hepthalite state, could the empire survive?

CHAPTER SIX

The Struggle with Rome

The brutal and untimely death of Peroz left the empire in turmoil. The king of kings had perished in a ditch in the far east, near Balkh, and his body was never found. Along with him perished four of his sons and brothers. Like a whirlwind, the Hepthalites swept over the realm, seizing the great cities of Herat, Nishapur, and Merv. Under the weight of this catastrophe, the kingdom staggered, and the miracle was not only of Persian survival but that the House of Sasan would continue to hold the throne.

The magnates of the empire placed Balash (484–488) on the throne of his brother Peroz. Making peace with the Armenian rebel Vahan Mamikonean, Balash employed a host of Armenian cavalry in his fight for the throne against his brother Zarer, whom he defeated and killed. The king of kings, his treasury empty, could not count on the loyalty of his troops. Balash found himself increasingly at odds with members of the seven great *wuzurgan* noble families, namely the powerful magnates Zarmihr Sokra, from the House of Karin, and Shapur Mihran, from the House of Mihran, who had supported his ascent to the throne. Zargmihr had levied fresh forces and halted the advance of the Hephthalites following the disastrous final expedition of Peroz. Balash also ran afoul of the magi, who opposed the shahanshah's desires for good relations with the Christians, as well as his efforts to install Roman-style bath houses in Persian cities, which offended Zoroastrian ritual sensibilities. Balash lasted just four years before he was deposed and blinded by the nobility and magi in favor of his nephew, Kavad.

Kavad, son of Peroz, was sixteen years old and thus had attained manhood just one year earlier. During the reign of his father, perhaps after the second time the great king had been captured, Kavad had lived as a hostage among the Hepthalites. It is possible, as Arabic authors later report, that Kavad was adopted by the senior wife of the Hepthalite king, who persuaded her husband to provide an army for the Persian youth with which to contest the throne. On his march to seize power from his uncle, Kavad is said to have remarked of Balash, "I knew well that his death would be my life."[1]

In the first decade of his reign, Kavad relied on the tutelage and material support of the leader of the House of Karin, the kingmaker Sokra. Likely in a vain attempt to undermine the power of the Zoroastrian magi, Kavad supported the heresy of Mazdakism, which embraced some notion of redistribution of property and the ability for women to marry outside of their class. During his period of Mazdakism, Kavad is said to have become vegetarian, an astonishing practice for anyone at the time, much less the shahanshah.

The great king's dalliance with this destabilizing ideology led to his overthrow. The great king's younger brother, Jamasp (496–499), was placed on the throne. Kavad was imprisoned in Susiana, in the southwest of the kingdom, in a place which Byzantine sources colorfully called the "Tower of Oblivion," so called because the names of those interred there could never be spoken again. In an episode as if out of a fantasy novel, Kavad was freed by his beautiful wife with whom the jailer became infatuated. Taking advantage, she had Kavad rolled in a carpet and smuggled out by a servant. When the jailer asked about the bundle, Kavad's female accomplice replied that her servant carried the bedding on which she had slept during her night visit to the king's cell. She was, moreover, menstruating. This unwelcome revelation persuaded the warden to want no part of inspecting the rug, given that it was ritually unclean according to Zoroastrian belief.

After his picaresque prison break, Kavad made his way to the Hepthalite court where King Kun-khi warmly received the fugitive, so warmly that he married Kavad to one of his daughters. The Hepthalite king provided his new son-in-law with twenty thousand Hepthalite cavalry.

By the time Kavad reached the frontier, the magnate families had made their choice. Facing a bloodbath at the hands of their former king and his Hepthalite horsemen, their decision was an easy one. Jamasp was persuaded to step aside and return to private life, and a civil war was thus averted. While his brother avoided his wrath, the Zoroastrian priesthood did not: Kavad turned on them with savagery, executing or imprisoning a number of them and thus freeing himself, for the time being, from their interference in his affairs. Internal affairs settled to his liking, and war in the east out of the question, Kavad looked westward where he would cast the die and end the long détente with the Romans. In 502, the great king, his power secure at home, marched against Rome.

At the head of a combined Sasanian-Hepthalite force numbering at least thirty thousand and as great as fifty thousand, Kavad crossed the border from Persian Armenia and struck the city of Theodosiopolis in Roman Armenia, which, after a few days, the governor Constantine betrayed to the Persians. Kavad's men plundered and burned Theodosiopolis and, leaving a garrison there, the great king marched on. He struck south into the Roman region of Oriens, a super province comprised of much of the eastern Roman lands in the Levant. Though he could not have known it, of course, Kavad's pivot to the west marked a turning point in history. The start of the campaign would initiate over a century of intermittent war, in turns both bitter and brutal, that would eventually bring the superpowers of the late antique world to their knees.

The mood in the Roman east was apocalyptic. A local prophecy allegedly foretold of the misery to be visited upon the Christians of the frontier on account of their sins, "And the Persians will rise up in [Anastasius's] time and trample on the cities of Oriens by the sword along with the greater number of the soldiers of the Roman empire."[2] John, the bishop of the Roman city of Amida, had a vision on the eve of Kavad's attack in which he saw an angel standing beside the altar of the city cathedral. The angel informed the holy man that Amida would be cast down to ruin as divine retribution against the wealthy of the city who had refused to give grain to the poor during the famine that had stricken the land over the past two years.[3]

Despite the lateness of the campaign season, Kavad pressed his offensive. The Huns and Persians sacked the city of Martyropolis (today Silvan in Turkey) and arrived outside the gates of Amida on October 5, 502. The Roman emperor Anastasius (491–518), one of the great monarchs to sit on the imperial throne, was a septuagenarian, but his rule had been firm and he was no dotard. While the emperor was many things, a man of war he was not, despite his having been forced to fight a long, difficult civil war against the tribal mountain people of Isauria in southeastern Asia Minor. By 502 that conflict was five years in the past, and the Roman army was a peacetime army, not prepared for a major war.

Peace with Persia had lasted for decades and made the East Romans feel too at ease. After all, the last time a Persian army had appeared on the frontier was in 440, during the reign of Yazdegerd II—so long ago, in fact, that it was beyond the living memory of nearly all who dwelled along the borderlands. The Persian bogeyman must have seemed to the generation of 502 like a long-slumbering dragon from some children's tale. The appearance of the Sasanians with their Hepthalite allies from the distant east terrified the Romans. Roman defenses were run down, and the army in the east hardly prepared for war. Despite this, Anastasius decided to press his luck, since he had received more than one embassy from Kavad, requesting money to refill his empty treasury.

These proposed payments, the Byzantines knew, were to pay debts Kavad owed to the Hepthalites. Rather than send Roman gold to cement the relationship between the Sasanians and the Hepthalites, Anastasius determined to drive a wedge into what he considered an unholy alliance. Thus, the emperor viewed Kavad's attack as the turning of the screw, a shakedown intended to force Caesar to open his purse strings. Anastasius hastily dispatched the patrician Rufinus bearing a quantity of gold with instructions to persuade the king of kings to stop outside Roman territory and return home. By the time Rufinus arrived in the great city of Caesarea of Cappadocia on the eastern Anatolian plateau, events had overtaken him. There Rufinus learned of the shahanshah's capture of Martyropolis and march south. He left the gold in Caesarea and hurried to Kavad in a vain attempt to persuade the great king to accept the payment and abandon his invasion.

The Romans remembered a strange tale of Kavad's march on Amida. A day's journey from the city a band of Hepthalites came upon the simple enclosure of a holy recluse, the monk Jacob, who had spent years in seclusion and quiet prayer in devotion to God. The Hepthalites rode up to the flimsy enclosure surrounding the monk's shack and drew their bows to kill the old holy man. They were immediately stricken with paralysis and could not release their weapons, no matter what their brains willed. The story of their miraculous discomfiture came to the ears of Kavad himself, whose curiosity was piqued by the strange tale. The great king himself came and conversed with Jacob and, having seen the holy life the old man lived, asked the monk what he desired. Anything, Kavad said, that the monk asked for would be granted to him. He expected the recluse to ask for a large sum of money or some earthly treasure but instead was surprised to be asked only that any fugitives who escaped from the Persian advance be spared and be permitted to remain under Jacob's care. No doubt in part because the old man's words offered an omen of impending victory, Kavad happily assented. The mercy he showed to the aged monk would not be extended to the citizens of Amida.

By October, winter has already come to the Armenian highlands, though along the banks of the Tigris, the autumn weather was pleasant, sunny, and with temperatures in the sixties or seventies Fahrenheit (16–26 Celsius). In the mountains to the west, snow was falling in the heights, and the passes would soon be closed. Rufinus and the Romans knew there could be no relief army marching from the west; aid could only come from Syria in the south. At Amida, the weather would soon turn, and the Persians were not equipped for the cold, having only flimsy clothing, and Kavad fretted about the coming of cold season. He wished for a quick victory and ample spoils so that he could return to Ctesiphon and sojourn the winter there.

Kavad soon learned of the meager enemy strength at Amida, likely consisting of the small garrison and the handful of guards in the service of the Roman governor Cyrus, who was present in the city. Roman forces likely numbered fewer than two thousand trained men. Certainly, no high-ranking officers were present, but Roman claims that there were no soldiers present are likely exaggerations. The stubborn defense the enemy mounted against the Sasanians had to have been directed by experienced soldiers, despite their being heavily outnumbered. Added to the sprinkling of soldiers were throngs of men and women who manned the tower and battlements of the city. After Shapur II's 359 sack of Amida, Roman engineers had built a newly strengthened curtain wall in the hard, local basalt, and the walls remained in good repair, strengthened by towers and artillery.

Kavad pressed the siege with repeated attacks using battering rams against the fortification. His men began to build an earthen siege mound by which the Sasanians aimed to overtop the walls. The attacking force brought several battering rams to bear against the walls, but their efforts were thwarted by the civilian defenders, who used bundles of reeds suspended on chains to cushion the walls against the battering engines while pouring down stones and missiles on the heads of the besiegers. The Sasanian siege mound progressed toward the city wall, where the citizens, who had joined the fight with alacrity, watched in alarm as the mound grew higher. The hard-pressed Amidenes rushed to strengthen the threatened bulwark, hastily throwing up a new rampart to match the height of the siege ramp. They also dug beneath their walls and began to mine below the enemy works, hollowing out a cavernous space and shoring up the void with timbers.

In the midst of the siege, Rufinus arrived from the Roman side with an offer of gold in exchange for the Persian withdrawal. Kavad, in no mood to parley, held the ambassador hostage and continued his attack. By early November, Persian engineers completed the earthen incline, and Kavad's troops pushed forward battering rams to smash down the ramparts. Kavad oversaw the assault with five hundred picked men, heavily armored and covered by thick, continuous fire from Persian archers lining the plankway atop the ramp. In the desperate melee that unfolded, the defenders dumped oil mixed with resinous plant material and cast raw oxhide onto the gangway, making the approach slick and treacherous for the ponderous siege towers the Persians brought to bear; on the soaked planks the Persian sappers inched forward under heavy attack from the civilians crowded on the walls.

The Sasanians courageously pressed the attack for more than six hours, struggling in the face of a barrage of arrows and stones fired from Roman artillery and blocks of stone hurled from the battlements. During the Persian assault, their rams knocked down a portion of the new, hastily built upper walls whose mortar had not yet dried. The Amidenes fired the timbers beneath the Persian siege mound. The props burned up and the mound collapsed, crushing a large band of Sasanian attackers in a day in which the shah's army had suffered heavy losses.

Thwarted in the latest assault, the great king turned to Nu'man, the Lakhmid king of the Arabs, ordering his Arab vassals to raid south into the territory of the ancient city of Harran, the scene of so many confrontations between the Persians and their Roman foes in the third and fourth centuries. Kavad needed supplies for the winter, and he sent foraging units ever further afield. One strong force of Sasanian raiders reached as far as Constantina (today Viranshehir), some hundred kilometers (sixty miles) south. On November 19, at Bismedion (Tell Beshmai), fifty kilometers (thirty-one miles) to the northeast of Constantia, a squadron of Persian cavalry encountered the forces of the Roman duke (*dux*) of Mesopotamia, Olympius of Constantina and his fellow commander, Eugenius, the *dux* of the Roman province of Euphratesia based at Melitene (Malatya, Turkey). The Persian foraging parties were beaten and driven back. Roman scouts brought word of five hundred Persian cavalry encamped in a nearby valley, but discipline among the Roman troops disintegrated, and they fanned out to strip the corpses. As darkness fell, the Roman duke ordered trumpets to sound and the kindling of a signal fire in order to call for the scattered Romans to reform.

The Sasanian *marzban* immediately understood the signs of Roman disorder and formed his Sasanian cataphracts, Hepthalites, and Arab light cavalry for the attack. A sixth-century Sasanian military handbook survives which details military protocol for night attacks of the kind undertaken at Bismedion:

> And part of the army must move against the middle of the enemy and the rest around them, and let those in the middle be the first to attack in order, that shouts and noise should be heard from that place and not from the flanks. And, before attacking, let them drive forward one after

the other the most swift of the mounts, cutting off their reins and pricking them from behind with spurs, so that they should get frightened and rush forward and make a noise; and one of the warriors should rush forward and make noise; and that one of the warriors should shout "O warriors, hasten, hasten! He is already killed, your chief so-and-so! And many are slaughtered! And many are fleeing!" And another should shout: "Oh man! For God' sake have mercy on me." And another should say "Mercy, mercy!" . . . And it must be known, that night attacks are necessary in order to frighten and to terrify the enemy; and let them abstain from gathering the possessions of the enemy, from catching their mounts and from taking spoils.[4]

Sasanian doctrine therefore relied on shock and disinformation to sow confusion and break down enemy order. Under the cover of darkness, the cavalry troopers struck hard against the enemy center, where they expected the presence of the enemy commander. The initial cavalry charge conducted by Sasanian heavily armed and armored *savaran* was accompanied by shouts from troops pretending that the enemy officers were being killed or had fallen in battle, with others playing the role of the "afflicted" enemy. This valuable snapshot shows a number of interesting and important insights into Persian night battles—namely the reliance on the cover of darkness to create confusion and disorder and the expected presence among the Sasanian ranks of men who could speak the language of the foe—these men must have either been bilingual native Persians or, in the case of the Battle of Bismedion, Roman deserters.

As the Persians advanced, the Roman cavalry saw they were outnumbered and turned tail. The Roman infantry, belonging to the *I Legio Parthica Nisibena*, had no such luxury—to break formation was to be ridden down and slaughtered. About a thousand fighting men closed ranks into the testudo "tortoise," a shield wall in which the front ranks used their shields to protect the face of the line, while the men behind held their shields overhead. From behind this shield wall, the Roman front presented a thicket of spears. The Persians peppered the infantry shield wall with a storm of arrows and javelins, but the foe stood firm. Finally, under repeated charges by the Sasanian heavy cavalry, the lines broke and the Romans were scattered. In swooped the Arab light cavalry who rode down the broken legionnaires as they fled. Most of the foot soldiers were killed and the rest taken captive.

A week later, Nu'man's cavalry raided deep into the territory of the city of Harran and ranged even further afield, approaching the lands of the famous

Christian city of Edessa, renowned for its early conversion to Christianity under King Abgar and the glory of its shrines and churches. One of the most important cities of the Roman East, the city's hinterland offered tempting pickings for Nu'man's rangers, who seized captives and rustled cattle. The Lakhmids carried away 18,500 captives, along with numerous goods and cattle.

Against the Persian threat to the city, the *dux* Eugenius mobilized the people of Edessa, forcibly collecting iron to bar the watercourses in the city where streams passed beneath the walls and digging trenches outside the city to further strengthen its defenses. The city gates were rotted away and unserviceable, so they were blocked with stones and rubble. Eugenius then marched against the Persian garrison at Theodosiopolis (Erzurum) and restored the city to Roman rule. This move, a march far to the north, placed the duke much closer to his headquarters in Melitene but removed him from any action at Amida. The Romans clearly hesitated to confront Kavad directly—they were too demoralized and outnumbered to offer effective opposition.

Kavad had now besieged Amida for more than a month, and as November passed, he grew increasingly impatient. His men were exposed to cold, and the inactivity associated with sieges threatened discipline. Despite the success of Persian foraging expeditions, supply shortages posed a real threat to his large army, and with winter bearing down and his assaults thwarted, the great king considered abandoning his investment. Part of the shahanshah's frustration was the skill demonstrated by the besieged, who thwarted the king's men as they attempted to repair the destroyed siege ramp by filling it with sacks of dirt and debris in order to quickly effect its rebuilding. For their part, the enemy employed artillery to destroy the Persian works, crushing and killing the crews of the covered battering rams and assault towers.

A contemporary writer on the Roman side, an unknown author from Edessa traditionally called "pseudo-Joshua" but otherwise unknown, describes this artillery:

> The Amidenes then devised a contraption which the Persians called "the striker," because it impeded their work and devastated them. With this contraption the Amidenes could hurl enormous stones each weighing more than three hundred pounds, and as a result the cotton covering under which the Persians sheltered was burst and those who were standing under it were crushed. The battering ram was also wrecked by the continuous, incessant barrage of stones. Indeed, the Amidenes could not injure the Persians in any other way as much as by the enormous stones,

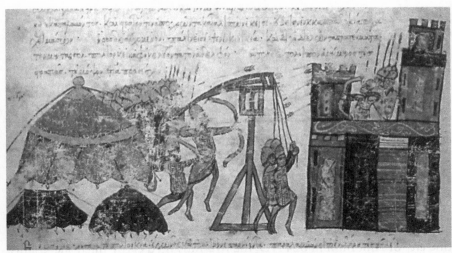

Traction trebuchet from an illuminated manuscript depicting a Byzantine siege of a citadel. (*Skylitzes chronicle, Madrid, National Library of Spain*)

because the Persians had been pouring water on the cotton covering which had been patched together many times above the mound, and it could be damaged neither by arrows, on account of the thickness, nor by fire, because it was wet. However, these enormous stones launched from the striker shattered both the men and armaments underneath it.[5]

The striker could not have been, as is usually supposed, the conventional Roman torsion engine called the *onager*, "wild-ass," so called because the hair rope coils that, under immense torque, when released propelled a swinging arm that launched a projectile from a sling. On its discharge, the force of the flying arm caused the rear of the engine to buck off the ground—because of this heavy recoil the torsion engine received its moniker. Ammianus describes in some detail the operation of onagers during the fourth-century Persian attack on Amida. The engine he observed was placed under such stress during its handling that the frame shattered, killing its crew.

The stone missiles of the size described by pseudo-Joshua in the 502 siege were far too large to have been launched by onagers, whose normal projectile weight was around forty *minae* (17.44 kg or 38.45 lbs).[6] The novelty of the machine, evident in the description, whose tone implies wonder at the device, as well as the mass of the projectile involved, indicates the device was relatively new to the Romans. The best candidate for the striker is the traction trebuchet, used in China from at least the fourth century BCE. Despite their not being known as great masters of the siege, it seems likely that, in the fifth century, the Huns brought knowledge of the machine west where the Romans adopted it. The traction trebuchet comprised a heavy wooden pivot, ending in a sling fitted on a metal pin. A large wooden cross beam provided the fulcrum and was in turn anchored to a larger wooden frame. Once the arm of the engine was lowered to the rear, the crew, standing in front of the trebuchet, used ropes to heave the arm forward. At the top of its arc, the pocket containing the projectile slipped free of the pivot end and, like a giant sling, fired the rock along the desired path. The range and trajectory of the missile could be altered by adjusting the sling attachment.

The weight of projectiles recorded in the 502 siege—some three hundred Roman minae (pounds), about 131 kg, is within the capabilities of the weapon known from other historical instances. During the Arab siege of the Byzantine city of Amorium in 824 AD, the Muslims fired earth-filled sheepskins, each weighing 100–150 kg.[7] The siege of Amida would mark the first historically known use of the machine in the Middle East and would imply a traction trebuchet likely crewed by around a hundred men. Whether the Persians deployed the machine at this time is unknown, but if they did, it seems that Kavad had nothing of the size of the trebuchet the Roman enemy wielded against him.

As morale flagged and the season drew on, the great king considered abandoning the siege. At that moment, so one story goes, the shahanshah, who was certainly no Christian, saw a vision of Jesus Christ telling him that the city would soon be delivered into his hands. More colorful is the story that, when the Persian siege works were destroyed, the citizens on the walls heckled the besiegers. Among them were prostitutes who lifted their dresses to reveal their private parts as they mocked their attackers. The magi accompanying the king told him that the omen was a good one and that the secrets of the city would soon be open to him. Not much later, due to lax discipline, the Persians found a weakness. Whatever the truth, Kavad sent a delegation to the city on January 7, 503, and promised he would depart the city in exchange for a small gift of silver. The officials and elders, including the governor Cyrus among them, rejected the king of king's demands.

Soon after, a high-ranking Persian officer, called in the sources Kanarak the Lame,[8] indicating his title as the *kanarang* or margrave of the eastern borderlands along the Hepthalite frontier, became aware of an unguarded sewer on the western side of the city. On the cold, rainy night of January 10, while the monks who guarded this section of the wall were drinking, probably in continued celebration of the feast of Epiphany, the Sasanians gained the sluice, entered the tower, and slaughtered the drunk and sleeping monks to a man. Aware of the fighting, defenders from the adjoining tower rushed to the attack, and they battled the Iranians who nearly lost their narrow hold on the wall.

Intense fighting continued through the morning hours, as the Persians threw ladders against the wall and forced the attack, Kavad himself, sword drawn, threatening and cajoling his troopers forward. At dawn the battle hung in doubt, as both sides fought ferociously. Heavy fire from the neighboring towers inflicted losses on the Sasanians who had recently scaled the walls. As in the first Persian siege of the city in the fourth century, the Romans turned artillery from the flanking towers on the Sasanians, who measured their gains in dead men for each foot of wall they seized. In the melee Persian archers from the captured segment of the wall seriously wounded Cyrus, the Roman governor who had come to support the defenders. The Amidenes fought like cornered animals. Civilians entered the ground floor of the captured towers and began to pry stones from the vaults in an effort to collapse the floor from underneath the Iranian attackers who clung to their hard-won gains.

In murderous hand-to-hand combat, Kavad's men gradually extended their hold on the walls. As darkness closed on the first full day's fighting, the Iranians held five or six towers. After two more days of savage combat, the great king's men commanded the walls to the west gate, and only then, once they opened the gate, did they finally storm the city. On January 12, Kavad's forces mastered Amida. After such a bitter siege, the bloodletting was severe. In the midst of the carnage, Kavad heard the pleas of a Christian bishop who had taken refuge in the city and who begged the great king to spare the Church of the Forty Martyrs and those who had sought refuge inside it. The shah agreed and those fortunates were spared, but most were not. Over the traditional three days allotted to pillage, the Persians, Hepthalites, Armenians, and Arabs looted, murdered, raped, and burned—these were the horrors of war throughout the ages. The old and infirm were slaughtered, and those left alive were clapped in irons and herded out of the city to face the long march to Persia. The numbers given in the Roman sources—some eighty thousand dead—are open to question, but certainly thousands of civilians perished. The eighty thousand, a very high number for the physical size of Amida is certainly plausible if it included the number of those taken captive.

After mostly emptying the city, Kavad left a three-thousand-man garrison. The shah released the Roman dignitary Rufinus with instructions to return to Anastasius and report to him what he had seen. Kavad then departed with his troops toward Mount Singara in the Syrian Desert. In about six-months' time, the great king had achieved a great deal: he had refilled his empty treasury and thus fed the dragon of his Hepthalite allies with loot that mollified this cagey and unpredictable ally. He had taken tens of thousands of captives—farmers, taxpayers, tradespeople, and potential soldiers—ripped them from the belly of the Romans, and installed them in Persia where they could help to grow the royal economy. Crucially, the shahanshah had dealt a vicious body blow to the Romans who had slumbered under the false assumption that the Sasanians wanted peaceful coexistence as badly as they did.

In April 503, Kavad again sent an embassy to the Romans, demanding tribute. The Romans refused, Anastasius having spent the winter months recruiting forces and marching his armies east. In May, a huge Roman army descended on the east. Not since the days of Shapur II's great contest with Julian had such an imperial host been seen in the eastern lands, some fifty thousand men.

Roman forces, likely numbering around twenty thousand men, were led by the generals Hypatius and Patricius. The latter is described as the great *strategos* (general) of the Romans, "an old man, upright and trustworthy, but with slight intelligence."[9]

> They gathered and made war on the city (Amida) with wooden towers and trenches and all kinds of engines. They set fire also to the gate of the city, which was called that of the house of Mar Za'uro, in order to come upon the Persians, but they were hindered because the Romans were resting, and they did not go in, for the Persians shut the gate.[10]

While Hypatius and Patricius slothfully pursued the siege of Amida, Areobindus Dagalaifus Areobindus, the *magister militum per orientem*, supreme commander of the eastern armies, marched on Nisibis. Areobindus bore the name of his grandfather, the Gothic warrior and Roman hero who had defeated the Persian champion decades prior in 422 during the invasion of Bahram V. Alongside the Gothic Roman general marched the Arab leader Aswad, leader of a tribal confederation from central Arabia whom the Romans had drawn into their orbit, no doubt in part to offset some of the strategic and tactical advantages Lakhmid Arab auxiliaries had rendered the Sasanians.

When Persian spies reported to Kavad that Areobindus's army only numbered twelve thousand, the great king dispatched twenty thousand troops. Along the Roman route of march between the village of Dara in the uplands of the Tur 'Abdin, the Sasanian force intercepted Areobindus's Romans but were driven from the field. At least one Persian *marzban* fell in battle, killed by a Goth in Roman service who collected the fallen Sasanian lord's sword and bracelet; these were sent to the emperor as a token of the victory. By May, Areobindus's army had dug in beneath the walls of Nisibis and tightened their noose around the city.

At Amida, Hypatius and Patricius had constructed three large wooden siege towers and sheathed these in iron to protect them from flaming missiles. These expensive and impressive towers had just been completed when the generals received desperate messages from Areobindus to the south at Nisibis. The generals are said to have burned the siege towers and left a small force behind under the command of a Roman federate, a Laz named Farzman, who continued to pressure the Sasanians trapped inside, luring some into ambushes and cordoning off the city so no supplies could enter.

In July, Kavad received the musters from his Lakhmid vassals in Hira, and alongside these, the return of a strong force of Hepthalites. The shah rallied his Persians and marched against Areobindus who now found himself outnumbered on the order of three to one. The Roman marshal dispatched pleas for reinforcements from Amida. Hypatius and Patricius apparently refused. Kavad's men fell upon Areobindus, and the Romans broke and fled, scattering to take refuge in the cities of Constantia and Edessa. The Persians took rich plunder from the abandoned Roman camp. When news reached the generals Hypatius and Patricius at Amida, they burned their precious siege towers, left a small force behind, and marched south to block a possible Sasanian thrust into the region of Constantina (Tella).

Kavad now unleashed his Lakhmid cavalry who, under their king Nu'man, ranged to the south and advanced along the Khabur River, which drains into the Euphrates. The Persian Arabs intended to slip into Roman territory between the city of Theodosiopolis (Resh'aina) and thus enter the gap between the hills of the Tektek Dagh and Jebel 'Abd al-'Aziz. There Nu'man encountered the Romans under the *dux* Timotheus, whose forces included numerous cavalry units. In this portion of the theatre of war, along the great southern bend of the Euphrates, the Romans employed another wing of their Arab allies, the federate tribal group called the Ghassanids, who were to play a major role in the clashes along the western borderland of the Sasanian Empire for well over the next century. Under their leader al-Harith, the Roman Ghassanid Arabs raided down the Euphrates and attacked the Lakhmid capital of Hira, which was abandoned after the inhabitants, forewarned, had fled into the desert. The Ghassanids therefore returned from their raid empty-handed, except for a caravan they had seized, and without attacking the town itself.

Kavad continued to draw his forces to his side, determined to pummel the enemy until they acquiesced to his demands. Troops of Armenians, Kurds, and Hepthalites strengthened the ranks of the shahanshah, and his Sasanian cavalry fanned out in pursuit of Areobindus's battered army whose combat effectiveness the Persians had shattered. The Roman general could do naught but watch as Sasanian raiders pillaged the landscape around Constantina and wrought havoc along the frontier. Patricius with the bulk of his forces descended into Mesopotamia and thus was not far away. The Roman army had taken over the village of Opadna (modern Tell Harzem), the former marching encampment of Areobindus on his route to Nisibis, about forty kilometers west of the Dara bivouac.

There, in the early morning, a Hepthalite vanguard, eight hundred strong, stumbled upon Roman forward units and was slaughtered. As the hours passed and no more enemy appeared, the Romans decided there were no more enemy in the vicinity and settled down for lunch. Under the brutal sun, many men took the opportunity to cool down in the waters of a nearby stream, probably the modest Cordes River. On the march farther south Kavad soon learned of the butchering of his Hepthalite mercenaries, and as his forces trudged by the river, the muddying of the waters soon alerted him to the Roman presence upstream. He hurried north and surprised the enemy who were caught completely by surprise and immediately fled. Many Romans threw themselves off the nearby heights in their panic, and the broken remnants took flight to the west where they hid themselves behind the walls of Samosata at a vital crossing on the Euphrates. Persian losses were light, but a serious one was the wounding of the Nu'man, king of Hira; he would die of his injuries at the first siege of Edessa.

After his second major victory, Kavad turned west and approached Constantina where the Jewish inhabitants of the city offered to give up the city into the great king's hands. A Roman prisoner among the Persians managed to have a message secreted into the settlement, which revealed the planned betrayal. Kavad lingered for a short time at the city. There, the Jewish treachery aside, he found Roman morale was high, as the populace had been roused by their fiery bishop Bar-Hadad. Supplies from the pillaged countryside were scarce, and so Kavad hurried westward and arrived at the walls of the great city of Edessa in September.

The great king arrived at Edessa, the "God-guarded" city, so named due to its reputation for holiness among the Christians, whose tradition held that their ancient king Abgar had corresponded with Jesus himself and had been the first to lead his city to the new religion. Due to the divine protection afforded it by God, Edessa was considered impregnable. In more practical terms, Edessa held, alongside its local garrison, thousands of Roman troops who had gathered there from the plain of Nisibis with Areobindus along with its local garrison, and the men had not been idle. Along with the Edessene population, the Romans destroyed buildings built against the fortification walls and razed the suburbs, denying the Sasanians any possible place of refuge. The defenses, too, were well prepared, the battlements bristling with artillery. Those manning the walls screened the crenelations with curtains of fire-resistant goat hair, which offered additional protection from the renowned Persian archers.

Faced with the unpalatable prospect of another lengthy siege, Kavad dispatched heralds to the city to call for negotiations. If his delegation were allowed inside the walls, the great king is said to have secretly ordered them to suddenly attack and hold the gates until he could arrive with the mass of the army. If their admission was refused and Areobindus came outside to meet them, Kavad directed his men to seize the *magister* as a hostage, one for whom he could strike a greater bargain.

Areobindus refused to host the Persian delegation within the city, and instead he left the town to the rendezvous at a church not far from the fortifications. There, the Persian *spahbed* Bawi, a top-ranking commander, met for the parley, during which the two sides haggled for hours. The Persians demanded ten thousand pounds of gold to withdraw; the final Roman offer was seven thousand pounds. Areobindus had arrived with a strong bodyguard, and the spahbed Bawi hesitated to carry through with the planned kidnapping. In the face of such staunch resistance, and perhaps because his supplies were short or he was troubled by the death of his staunch servant, the Lakhmid Nu'man, whose death the Christians among the Persians attributed to the God-protected status of the city, Kavad broke camp and marched on Harran.

The great king ordered his Lakhmids to the city of Serug (Batnae), and he advanced on Harran, where his Hepthalite vanguard was surprised by Rufinus, the local Roman commander there (probably the same notable Kavad had held hostage the previous year, as the great king knew him). The Roman cavalry killed sixty Hepthalites and captured their leader. When Kavad arrived, he announced to the citizens that, if they returned the Hepthalite chief to him, he would not attack their city. The citizens returned their hostage and sent fifteen hundred sheep and other presents to the great king. Meanwhile, the Lakhmid cavalry had encountered Roman reinforcements from the west, led by the patrician Patriciolus and his son, Vitalian. In a fearless attack the Romans crossed the Euphrates and caused heavy losses among the Lakhmids, who were driven from the field.

His tour of the Roman east continued largely unimpeded, as Kavad was well informed by spies and deserters of dissension in the enemy ranks, and while the westerners in the theatre of war outnumbered the Persians, Roman bickering and blundering forced them on the defensive. Kavad pivoted his host from the banks of the Euphrates and once again made for Edessa. It is doubtful he ever intended to assault the city; else he would have surely done so during his first siege.

On September 17, Kavad once more reached Edessa. The Persians found the gates of the city open—a sure invitation to attack and a sign of the confident spirits of the denizens of the "God-guarded" city. Kavad hesitated, apparently uncertain of the best way to strike the fortifications. The Daisan River flowed around a considerable portion of the city walls. These gates could only be reached by crossing bridges. On their approach the Sasanians would be funnelled into narrow columns and forced to endure withering Roman artillery fire, of which the Persians maintained a collective memory of more than a century of bitter experience. Crowded on the crossings, Kavad's men would have suffered terribly before even hoisting their ladders at the base of the walls.

Again, Kavad initiated negotiations with Areobindus and reached terms: the Roman handover of hostages and Persian prisoners captured in the skirmish with the villagers and the handover of two thousand pounds of gold. But the king was in a rush, and when he sent his officer Hormizd to collect as much gold as he could prize from the Edessenes, the city elders flatly refused. If the shah were foolish enough to attack, they reasoned, Christ would protect them. Furious, the great king marched his army from their nearby encampment and surrounded the city on September 24. Among the army was now the royal elephant corps, whose presence, as usual, awed and terrified the Roman onlookers, most of whom had never seen the strange-looking beasts.

While the Persians remained quiet, Areobindus ordered his troops not to engage the superior force he faced. A group of especially cocksure villagers who had taken refuge in the city, though, sallied through the gates: "A few of the villagers . . . went out against him with slings and felled many of his [Kavad's] mailed men, while suffering no losses themselves."[11]

The modest sling, a weapon of great simplicity and extreme antiquity—its use stretching back in time to at least ten thousand years ago—is a little-considered tool of war, despite its appearance on battlefields throughout Eurasia from the Bronze Age into the medieval era. The sling—a length of leather or plant fiber with finger holes to secure the weapon to the hand and a pouch to hold the projectile, was a weapon of rustics, typically. Its extreme simplicity and cheapness of manufacture made it a favorite arm of peasants and especially shepherds. Among rural folk, endless hours of boredom spent tending their flocks allowed them to master the weapon for use on the occasion when predators—usually humans but sometimes wolves, lions, leopards, or bears in the Middle East—interrupted their idylls and forced the herdsmen to defend themselves and their animals. In the hands of a skilled user, a sling projectile, usually smooth river rock, left the weapon at speeds over 90 m/s, superior to arrows fired from bows. Arrows had the advantage of a much smaller projectile point and thus superior penetrating fire, while sling stones or cast lead shot were more aerodynamically efficient. Slingshots, although they hit their target over a wider surface area than an arrow and thus dissipated more energy, still hit home with 125 percent more kinetic energy than arrows. Expert slingers—which included most slingers in antiquity due to the hundreds of hours of practice the typical user invested—were often lethal.

In the early antiquity, among the favorite recruiting grounds of slingers were the Balearic Islands off the coast of the Iberian Peninsula, where the locals honed their skills on game, especially on difficult-to-strike hares destined for the cooking pot. In the famous encounter between the Greeks of Sicily and the Carthaginians at the Battle of Himera (480 BC), the Carthaginian general Hamilcar found his troops under continued threat from the Greek skirmishers and hoplites:[12]

> But when Hamilcar saw that his men were being overpowered and that the Greeks in constantly increasing numbers were making their way into the camp, he brought up his slingers, who came from the Balearic Islands and numbered at least a thousand. By hurling a shower of great stones, they wounded many and even killed not a few of those who were attacking, and they shattered the defensive armour of most of them. For these men, who are accustomed to sling stones weighing a *mina* [about 425 grams or 15 oz] contribute a great deal toward victory in battle, since from childhood they practise constantly with the sling. In this way they drove the Greeks from the camp and defeated them.[13]

Much later, in the first encounters in the New World between the Spanish Conquistadors and the Aztecs, the Spaniards experienced the unpleasant force of the Aztec slingers, whose projectiles shattered swords and slaughtered horses with a single strike.

Closer in time to the encounter in Mesopotamia, the Roman writer Vegetius (fourth century AD) wrote:

Soldiers, despite their defensive armor, are often more aggravated by the round stones from the sling than by all the arrows of the enemy. Stones kill without mangling the body, and the contusion is mortal without the loss of blood.[14]

The Persians, as all societies in Eurasia, were familiar with the weapon, but it did not feature among their troops on this occasion, at least. Faced with the insolence of such a rabble, the Persians would not suffer the insult. The Sasanians reacted with a mad rush to seize the gates. Persian infantry dashed to the attack, protecting themselves in a shield wall formation like the Roman *testudo*, and Sasanian cavalry soon joined the scrum. In the chaotic brawl the charging horsemen entangled themselves among the Roman slingers. Hepthalite cavalry used maces or clubs in their assault of the Roman peasants, while the swift Arab horse unleashed a torrent of javelins and spears into the ranks of the enemy rustics. The Edessene villagers expertly handled their slings and struck down horse and riders alike. Unable to inflict much damage to these doughty peasants, the Persians could only extract a measure of revenge by burning suburban churches and monasteries that had remained standing.

After his slapdash rush on the fortifications of the God-guarded city, Kavad packed up his tents and his elephants and marched back to the Euphrates, sending warnings to Anastasius that he expected to experience Roman hospitality in the near future. As a parting gift, the great king once more dispatched his Lakhmid raiders to harrow what was left of the stricken Mesopotamian countryside. Sasanian and Arab cavalry galloped to Serug where the mortified inhabitants, amidst the crumbling conditions of their neglected fortifications, understood they could offer no resistance and so handed over their town to the Persians.

Kavad's hasty departure was due to the news he received of a Hunnic invasion. While this expedition is thought by some to have been due to an incursion by the Sabir Huns, who lived north of the Caucasus, more than likely it was the Hephthalites, perhaps alarmed by initial Sasanian successes in the far west, who invaded. In 503, the Hepthalites held sway over a vast territory stretching from the Pamirs to the Caspian, including the vital former Sasanian marchlands centered on the Merv oasis, and it must be they who are referred to as the "Huns" in the sources.

As 504 began, the Persians therefore found themselves in quicksand. Roman troops still surrounded Amida, where the Sasanian garrison was cut off and starving. Anastasius, whose famed financial skills had provided the empire with ample resources, sent still more forces east, among them troops commanded by Celer, his master of offices, who shared joint supreme command with Areobindus and whose presence ensured resupply and the smooth movement of men and materiel into the war zone. In the spring of 504, Celer led a strong Roman raid-in-force behind Nisibis into the region of Beth Arabaye while Areobindus launched an attack into Persian Arzanene, the region east of the Tigris beyond Amida. Even the bumbler, Patricius, managed to inflict damage on the Sasanians—attacking across the Batman Su River into Persian Arzanene beyond. There, cavalry led by the Persian *marzban* of Persian Armenia or Azerbaijan surprised the Roman column, which retreated to the river. Patricius's men could not cross the water, raging as the waters were with rain and snow melt. Forced to fight or drown, the Romans fought with savage desperation and severely defeated the Persian provincial troops. With these expeditions, Persian losses mounted, as numerous villages and towns fell to the sword, with the accompanying loss of life and enslavement of their people. Matters were made worse by the defection from the Persians of several important figures and their retinues.

Faced with renewed war on his northern frontiers with the nomads, and unable to fight a two-front conflict, as the battle seeped into his own domains, Kavad sought peace. The great king dispatched a *marzban* to negotiate the surrender of Amida, and to arrange a truce. The negotiations dragged on, interrupted by various turns. Only in 506 did hostilities officially end.

That Kavad was involved in a war in the east during this period finds additional support in his weak response against the Roman building of the city of Dara at the site of a former village at the base of the scarp called the Tur 'Abdin, the traditional haunt of many Aramaic-speaking Christians. It was also the site of the Roman encampments where, in the previous war, Kavad ran off Areobindus. Acting with his typical energy, the wily old Anastasius paid outlandish sums to laborers who were willing to build his new fortress city. Dara, staring opposite the plain from Nisibis, would become, like Tolkein's Two Towers, the scene of bloody contention between the two great powers. The great amber ashlar walls and impressive towers—testaments to Roman engineering—still stand today. In 505, however, besides having his garrison at Nisibis harass the workmen, from which they were shooed away by the Romans like so many pesky flies, the great king could do little but watch and fume.

So strong was Kavad's desire for peace that the building of Dara did not stand in the way. Under its terms, the Romans would pay 550 pounds of gold annually, the equivalent of 39,600 gold *solidi* (the Roman coin of the realm). It also appears that Kavad agreed to restore those prisoners from Antioch remaining in his possession. If the outcome of the war was all that Kavad had hoped, it nonetheless provided some material relief as he sought to replenish his empty coffers and provided a powerful propaganda tool, allowing the great king to justly claim that he had humbled his powerful western foe who was now a tributary state.

While the Romans, for their part, also claimed victory, their crowing rang hollow. Despite their massive efforts and overwhelming superiority in numbers, the armies of Anastasius had accomplished next to nothing. In crucial moments, the best that could be said of the enemy performance was that they demonstrated gross incompetence. On occasion, for example at Harran and Serug, the local population simply disregarded the imperial officers on the scene and brokered their own deals with the great king's men. The lessons the Persians learned were, like their forebear Shapur II, through capable, assertive action, the Sasanians could certainly go toe-to-toe with their Roman adversary.

What knowledge Kavad had gained, moreover, he soon put to good use. It was not that the Persians needed schooling from the Romans in military affairs, far from it. After all, for more than two centuries, the Sasanians had been locked in hostilities with sophisticated opponents from the Caucasus to the Indus. Kavad, however, seems to have internalized a number of lessons he learned during his years fighting, especially against the Romans. In case the great king needed prompting, he was reminded of the value of strong static lines of defense like those he encountered first at Amida and then Edessa, where a determined population, whether backed by large numbers of professional troops or not, could offer stubborn resistance and blunt any offensive capability the Persians (or the Romans, for that matter) brought to bear. In these circumstances, the Sasanians, though skilled in siege warfare, were often at a disadvantage, favoring as they did excellent mounted troops whose advantages were lost the moment they were forced to fight on foot.

As their critical eastern frontiers extended to the steppe lands of Central Asia and confronted by the vast distances to be covered even within their own borders, the Persian war machine was predominantly a cavalry army. Infantry played an important but secondary role in the great king's wars. While the lands of the Kidarites and the Hepthalites contained cities—and some wealthy and strong ones at that—one needed to get there. The distance from Balkh to the Caspian was nearly 1,200 kilometers of harsh but relatively open country. Crossing this expanse was a task best accomplished on horseback, and the rapid strikes of Hunnic horsemen constantly reminded the Persians of their need to cultivate and maintain their own equestrian culture and skills. The Sasanians thus required two entirely different forces—one mounted, built for speed but stout enough to match the hybrid forms of warfare of their eastern enemies to fight both at range with the bow and then in shock combat with the lance. Such a host must be able to match the sudden movements and unexpected thrusts of large formations of steppe cavalry and support itself from the land. The second army the Sasanians increasingly required was an army of siege, conquest, and occupation, and for this, infantry was best suited. How the Sasanians were to manage these disparate demands can be seen as the sixth century unfolded.

The next, long obvious, lesson Kavad absorbed was that his western opponent had deeper pockets than he, the result not only of a more populous, more urbanized empire but of a better-managed one with a state bureaucracy with relatively efficient access to tax revenue in part because the emperor was not aided nor thwarted by a cabal of extremely powerful noble families. This disparity in wealth would have been especially apparent when fighting Anastasius, who was rare among emperors in his ability to cull large fiscal surpluses from his citizens and not foment massive tax revolts, even as his administration met every emergency, be it the unexpected war with Persia or acts of god which afflicted the empire. Whether or not he borrowed his ideas directly from the Romans, it is true that the reforms Kavad initiated during his second stint on the throne left his empire resembling the westerners in more ways than one.

Among the vital improvements which Kavad likely instigated was the creation of a bi-partite tax system based, on one hand, on taxation on the land and, on the other, on the taxes on persons (the head or poll tax). The head tax had already existed in Sasanian Iran and was not a novel invention of Kavad. But it seems likely that Kavad initiated the ground shift of state management in this direction; such is known from his instigation of a gargantuan cadastral survey of his empire, in which all lands were measured and assessed according to their productive potential. These assessments were not completed upon Kavad's death and would await the enthronement of his son, Kosrow I, to see fruition. Roman taxation was organized along similar lines: a land tax assessed on the productive environment on one hand and a tax on heads on the other. It is difficult to fathom that Kavad, through his personal experience, the reports of spies and merchants, and his discussions with well-informed prisoners like Rufinus, had remained ignorant of the Roman system and its benefits.

About the years immediately following Kavad's destruction of détente with the Romans, next to nothing is known, especially from the vital eastern regions where the Persians still endured the open sore of the Hepthalites, to whom they were tributary and of whom the humiliation and death of Peroz in 484 was scorched in living memory. Archaeological evidence indicates that Kavad did not remain idle and, in fact, enjoyed some important successes. After the death of his father Peroz, no Sasanian coins from Merv are known until the second decade of Kavad's reign, the year 512, to be precise. The recovery of Merv, indicated by the reestablishment of a royal mint there, indicates that, after his war with Rome, Kavad somehow wrested a large portion of the former northern and eastern frontier lands from his former Hephthalite allies. Persian royal mints began to issue coins farther east as well, in Herat and Abarshahr, administered from Nishapur.

The results of the conflict could not have been decisive, however. While the minting of the coins of Kavad in these eastern cities is a clear gauge of a restoration of royal authority, it is virtually certain that the Persians continued to pay tribute to the Hepthalites throughout Kavad's reign, Sasanian propaganda to the contrary. While the Persians established royal mints in areas previously lost, the continued payment of tribute under Kavad indicates that the outcome of the war was a treaty, one for which he gained territorial concessions but continued to pay drachms as a vassal of the Hephthalites. Another scrap of evidence indicates ongoing hostilities between the Hepthalites and Kavad's Sasanians—while the first embassy of Hephthalites arrived in the Chinese court of the Northern Wei in 456, the next known diplomatic mission arrived only in 507, perhaps indicating that the Huns viewed their troubles with the Sasanians as finally settled.[15]

The peace settlement held far longer than the seven-year term to which the Persians and Romans agreed. From 504 to 527, Kavad remained occupied with internal affairs and in shoring up his position in the east. Already, in 520, his health may have been poor; the great king sent a delegation to the emperor Justin to adopt Kavad's youngest son, Khusrow, but Justin was advised against it and refused. By 525 relations between the two states, which had been quiet, took a sudden turn. Iberia, the region south of the Caucasus between the coastal kingdom of Colchis and the inland kingdom of Caucasian Albania, had long been a Sasanian vassal state. Like his predecessors, however, Kavad made the mistake of attempting to impose Zoroastrianism on the population of Iberia, who were mainly Christians. Kavad's troops crushed the Iberian rebellion but did not stop there—they pressed into the kingdom of Lazica (today western Georgia) where the king, Tzath I, appealed for aid to the emperor Justin I (518–527) whose nephew, the ambitious and autocratic Justinian, was so prominent that many considered him the actual ruler. Justin sent aid to Lazica in the form of Roman officers and Hun mercenaries, but in the border war that followed the Romans and their Laz allies lost two key frontier fortresses while the Romans did nothing to pry Iberia from the Sasanian orbit.

Kavad, again wanting Roman gold, sent delegations to Constantinople to press his demands. His ambassadors found Justinian unreceptive. Unsatisfied with the negative response, in 527, Kavad commanded al-Mundhir III (503–554), king of the Lakhmids, to raid Roman territory. The Romans immediately launched their own counterraids across the Tigris and behind the territory of Nisibis. Generals picked from the personal bodyguard of Justinian, Sittas, and Belisarius rampaged through Persian Armenia and took great plunder and numerous captives. In 527, the Romans, led by the general Libelarius, led a strong invasion force into Nisibene country but failed to do any damage, and a Sasanian attack inflicted heavy causalities on the Romans. By now, the old emperor Justin had died, and Justinian (527–565) ascended to power.

Early in 528, the Sasanians learned of new Roman fortification works at Thannuris (Tell Tuneinir, Syria) on the Khabur River in the Syrian Desert, about seventy-five kilometers south of Nisibis. The Persian garrison at Nisibis attacked and disrupted the building efforts, and as a result of these skirmishes, Justinian ordered reinforcements to Thannuris to screen the fortification project, a force comprised of elements from the Roman field army under the command of several frontier *duces*. Outside of Thannuris the Sasanians dug a line of trenches, filled with sharpened stakes, and lured the Romans forward. The first wave of Roman horsemen, unaware of the ditches which had been concealed, fell headlong into the pits and perished. The rest of the cavalry, including the *dux* of Mesopotamia, Belisarius, fled from the scene and the Roman infantry who remained were trapped and butchered. Later in the year, the Persians defeated a second Roman force at another fort near Nisibis called Minduos. The only effective attack by the Romans this year was a strong winter raid into Lakhmid territory by the Ghassanid federates, who made a long chevauchee into Lakhmid and Persian territory where they plundered and seized captives.

After these victories at Thannuris and Minduos, Kavad again sought a compromise. The great king sent a delegation to Constantinople to negotiate. Justinian, facing famine in many places due to a severe winter, along with a series of devastating earthquakes that had leveled cities in Syria that required rebuilding and tax relief, was in a poor position to begin a war. Nevertheless, the payment of money to the Persians had long rankled conservatives in Roman circles, and the emperor had to tread delicately. After initial exchanges,

Kavad's diplomats delivered an ultimatum: Justinian could behave like a good Christian and avoid war by parting with some of his gold; otherwise, in one years' time he could expect a visit from the Persian army. Justinian sent officials east for further discussions but the time had expired. True to his word, Kavad had marshaled his army and marched to strike a blow against the Romans.

In 529, the Lakhmid lord al-Mundhir slipped past the Roman frontier with a combined force of Persian and Arab cavalry. The king and his forces penetrated deep into Roman territory. Moving at speed, the enemy was unable to react to this sudden Sasanian thrust, which advanced far to the west beyond the border fortresses and Roman troops stationed there. Mundhir raided the territory of the great city of Antioch, setting fire to the crops, plundering the villages, and taking booty and prisoners.

The sixth-century Roman historian Procopius wrote of al-Mundhir as:

> A man who for a space of fifty years forced the Roman state to bend the knee. For beginning from the boundaries of Egypt and as far as Mesopotamia he plundered the whole country, pillaging one place after another, burning the buildings in his track and making captives of the population by the tens of thousands on each raid, most of whom he killed without consideration, while he gave up the others for great sums of money. Al-Mundhir . . . ruled over all the Saracens [Arabs] in Persia, and he was always able to make his inroads with the whole army whenever he wished in the Roman domain; and neither any commander of the Roman troops, whom they call duces, nor any leader of the Saracens allied with the Romans, who are called phylarchs, was strong enough . . . to array against al-Mundhir . . . .[16]

The Sasanians took aim at the new fortress city of Dara. There the former *dux* of Mesopotamia, Belisarius, had been recently posted to supreme command as the emperor's eastern marshal, having long served alongside Justinian when his benefactor held high command. Belisarius had, two years prior, fled the field at Thannuris along with the rest of the Roman cavalry. In June 530, the Roman forces braced to receive the Sasanian assault. The Romans numbered twenty-five thousand infantry and cavalry; among the latter were considerable numbers of foreign mercenaries, especially Huns and Heruls (a Germanic warrior nation).

The Persians were led by a general whose name the Roman sources misunderstood, taking the Mihran aristocratic family as a royal title, calling the Persian commander *mirranes* (Mihr-Mirhroe), "Peroz by name," according to the sixth-century writer and eyewitness to the battle, the historian Procopius of Caesarea, who served at the time as the Roman general Belisarius's personal secretary.[17] Peroz was accompanied by the one-eyed veteran commander Baresmanas as well as a leader who Procopius calls "Pityaxes," which is likely not a name but rather a title, *bidaxsh*, denoting a margrave or even a royal viceroy. The army they led was a powerful one, at the outset of their engagement said to number forty thousand.

At first the Sasanians hesitated, perhaps because the enemy were assembled in a novel fashion, uncharacteristic of the Roman armies they had recently encountered. In the Roman center stood the infantry legionnaires, armed with spears and packed in close order so that their phalanx presented a hedge of iron through which the Persians would have to cut. On the Roman left, Belisarius had stationed two squadrons of cavalry, one comprised of Romans along with the Germanic Heruls, and on the Roman right stood a force of Hun horsemen from which they could flank an attack. The Roman right was identically disposed, with Belisarius and his elite household troops, the so-called *bucellarii* ("biscuit eaters," named after the soldier's hardtack bread) behind.

Throughout most of the day the armies stood at the ready, but neither side opened the fight. Finally, in the late afternoon, the Sasanian commanders ordered an advance. They did so according to established military doctrine in which the right of the army was normally the strongest and offensive wing of the force. The Persians were thus arrayed in conventional manner, cavalry in front, infantry behind, with their best troopers on their right, facing the Roman left. As the Persian right advanced, the Roman cavalry on the right fell back to the cover of their infantry phalanx. When the Sasanian cataphracts halted and did not press their attack, the Romans surged against them. In this initial skirmish seven Persians died against an unknown number of Roman dead. The Persians, however, were merely probing the enemy; they had been ordered not to force a general engagement, and so they fell back to the cover of their own infantry.

The Persians waited, and at length, sent forward a champion, a young man who rode up and down the Roman lines, taunting them and calling one of them out to battle. In what might serve well in a Hollywood sword-and-sandal flick, only one Roman had the courage to face the Sasanian rider; this was Andreas, a professional wrestler and trainer, the servant of one of the Roman commanders. Though supposedly not a soldier, Andreas hurled a spear and wounded the Persian hero, pulled him from his horse, and, in the grisly description of Procopius, "with a small knife slew him like a sacrificial animal as he lay on his back."[18] Shamed by their showing, the Persians sent forward another champion, a large and experienced soldier, but he, too, Andreas dispatched. In the face of this humiliation and under such a bad sign, the Persians refused to fight and instead withdrew to their encampment. Did the Sasanian commanders sense something amiss and thus hesitate? Were they surprised, as Procopius claimed, at the uncharacteristic steely discipline of the enemy, whom many of these same troops, no doubt, had pummelled only two years prior? A simpler answer seems at hand, since the following day, ten thousand reinforcements arrived from Nisibis, swelling the Sasanian ranks to fifty thousand, and they now held a numerical advantage of two to one.

Seeing the odds now even worse, Belisarius and Mihrhan Peroz exchanged a series of letters throughout the day. The Roman general reminded the Sasanians that the Romans desired peace and that the Persians should withdraw and wait for the Roman diplomat Rufinus, who was nearby. Peroz's response, preserved in Procopius, is likely legitimate, reflecting as it does Persian notions of truth and their belief that his western enemy often dealt in bad faith: "I should have been persuaded by what you write, and should have done what you demand, were the letter not, as it happens, from Romans . . ."[19] Peroz finished the exchange by instructing Belisarius to make ready a bath and lunch inside Dara, where he intended to take them the next day.

The Romans drew up as they had two days prior. The Persians advanced only after midday, as they counted on the Romans, who had taken no food, being weakened from heat and hunger. The Persians employed lines of archers in rotation to launch a steady hail of arrow fire into the enemy ranks, but due to a wind that blew against the Sasanian lines, the efficacy of their missiles was minimal. On the Persian right, the Sasanian *bidaxsh*, with his Kadisene (possibly Kurdish or Iranian mountaineers) inflicted heavy losses on the Roman left wing, which broke and attempted to flee. While the Persian right were engaged in what looked like the start of a general rout, the Roman mounted troops stationed along the center left of the Roman lines charged them. At the same time, a troop of Herul cavalry, who had concealed themselves behind a neighboring hill, rode down on the rear of the Persian left wing, spreading slaughter and panic among the Kadisene. As the Persian left buckled under the pressure, the Sasanian right wing also failed in the face of Roman resistance and, after a particularly bloody confrontation, retreated to the safety of their infantry lines, leaving three thousand of their dead on the field.

Faced with this reversal, Mihran Peroz committed his reserve cavalry, in this case a large body of elite *savaran* cavalry, the troopers who wielded bow, lance, mace, or sword with equal skill. Armored from head to toe, and riding barded horses, these professional horsemen were drawn from the minor aristocracy and trained for war from an early age. These troops thundered to reinforce the Sasanian left wing, for despite the initial struggle going to the Romans, the Persians refused to concede the field. The Romans, however, realized this and moved their forward cavalry squadrons on the edge of the Roman right wing and further reinforced their cavalry with a portion of Belisarius's household men.

The Sasanian charge was not a single compact mass but in two waves, the first, led by the commander Barsamanes and finding itself opposed by the reinforced Romans whose flight was probably feigned, turned to face the front of the first Persian wave. At the same time, the enemy cavalry on the Persian right flank closed and cut the Sasanian attack in two. One of the Roman leaders, the Hun Sunicas, cut down Barsamenes's standard bearer and then killed the Sasanian commander himself. At the loss of their standard and the death of their general, the Sasanians tried to flee the encirclement but perished in large numbers; as many as five thousand died.

Belisarius now threw the whole of his army against the broken enemy but soon called off the pursuit. His ill-disciplined troops, he feared, would scatter and invite the Persians to regroup and snatch victory from the ashes of defeat. The Sasanians, badly beaten but not destroyed, withdrew to Nisibis.

In June or July, the Iranians made another thrust to the north into the mountainous northern borderlands, where his troops had enjoyed prior success against the Romans and their allies. Under the leadership of Shapur of Rayy, the *artestaran salar* or the supreme commander, the Sasanian army numbered thirty thousand, comprised of Persians, Suanians from the mountains of western Georgia, and three thousand Sabir Huns from north of the Caucasus. Shapur led this host west into the region of Theodosiopolis in Roman Armenia. There he made no effort to siege the city, instead bypassing it with the plan of inflicting severe damage to the lands behind the frontier. Deeper inside Roman territory, far to the west, at the city of Satala, Shapur established his camp, where a weaker enemy army was penned inside the walls. The following morning the Sasanians started trenches and emplacements around the curtain walls in preparation for a siege.

Unknown to Shapur, whose precautions were lax or whose scouts had failed him, a Roman army of ten thousand under the command of Sittas, chief general of the mobile Roman field forces, and thus the *artestaran salar*'s opposite number, had screened the Roman approach behind the mountainous terrain. Sittas and the westerners suddenly appeared to the Persian rear; as they marched down from the heights, the soldiers and their train raised a great cloud of dust in the summer sky.

The Persians, ignorant of the strength of the enemy, and judging from the great billows of dust, feared a large enemy force was upon them. Shapur hastily drew up his fighters in the narrow plain of Satala, where his cavalry was cramped and unable to make their sweeps and flanking attacks on which Sasanian offensive relied. As the Persians retired from the walls and hurried to establish their battle lines, and as Sittas descended from the high ground his army commanded, the Roman garrison from inside the town threw open the gates and rushed forward, fully armed and at the ready.

The two forces clashed in gory hand-to-hand fighting, each side making repeated charges across the small area of flat ground. A Roman officer led his forces against the Persian center, where Shapur fought with his best men. The Romans managed to kill Shapur's standard bearer and seized the Iranian marshal's banner. Shapur's guard pursued the retreating Roman and cut him down, but with the banner now fallen and trodden in the dust, the Persian army fell into confusion, fearing that their general lay dead. Despite the chaos, the Sasanians were able to withdraw to their camp, and at night the two sides separated. With the dawning, Shapur broke off the campaign and led his defeated troops eastward.

As the campaign season closed in autumn 530, the two sides again came to the peace table. Kavad naturally insisted that the Romans tear down the fortress city of Dara, which had become a new bugbear with which he had to contend, as the army stationed there menaced Nisibis and provided cover for Roman operations across a great swath of northern Mesopotamia. The Romans, moreover, should resume their tribute payments so that the Persians could continue to man the Caucasus defenses, which, they repeatedly reminded the Romans, benefitted both peoples. As nothing came of these talks, the war entered its fourth year.

While the Persians had confined themselves to operating in Mesopotamia and the north, in the spring of 531, Kavad sent a Persian force of fifteen thousand men into Syria. Inspired, it is said, by the advice of his faithful servant, the Lakhmid king Mundhir, the route they traveled, up the Euphrates, was less heavily defended and Sasanian prospects for success better. Kavad likely needed little persuading. Whether for reasons of health, age, ideology, or some combination of these, the great king entrusted the command of the mission to his *hazarpet*, Azarethes and Mundhir, whose five thousand Arab horsemen formed a third of the host. The presence of "Huns" in the Persian army, noted by Procopius, could denote either Sabirs from the north or Hepthalite mercenaries. The expeditionary army crossed the Euphrates at the Roman fortress of Circesium. The Sasanian strike force long met no organized Roman resistance and plundered far and wide.

At Dara, Belisarius, marshal of the eastern armies, heard of the Sasanian stroke and swiftly moved south to intercept them, calling to his side the armies of the provincial *duces* from around the region. He ordered the local commanders around the Euphrates not to engage but to await the mustering of the field army, which he led along with Hermogenes. Disobeying orders, the Roman *dux* Sunicas, who had fought with distinction at the Battle of Dara the previous year, harried the invaders as they marched through northern Syria. Despite this harassment, behind Roman lines panic gripped the population as far west as Antioch, whose citizens had only recently suffered under the blades of the Lakhmids. Refugees thronged in droves through the north of Syria toward the Mediterranean coast.

Many of the people made captive by Azarethes and Mundhir had only recently been ransomed at great cost, and when Belisarius arrived, the local commanders urged him to free these unfortunates again. He must, they argued, pursue and bring the retreating Persians to battle. Reluctantly, Belisarius agreed to shadow the Persians as they withdrew and finally caught up with their columns at Callinicum (modern Raqqa) on the south side of the Euphrates. Belisarius, since the Iranian-Arab army was returning home, likely felt that his mission was accomplished, and vacillated. The general was all too aware that it was Holy Week, just before Easter, and the Roman soldiers, as Christians, were fasting. Added to his worries were the presence in the ranks of green infantry from Asia Minor. Despite his well-founded reluctance, his subordinates cajoled the hesitant marshal to action, and after consulting with his troops, who shouted their eagerness to fight, Belisarius agreed to attack.

The Romans formed up with their infantry on the left, pressed against the Euphrates. Belisarius and the Roman cavalry apparently drew up in the center next to the infantry, while on the Roman right were the Ghassanid Arab auxiliary light cavalry. Late in the day, when the Romans were further weakened from hunger, Azarethes led the Sasanian heavy cavalry on the Persian left, opposite the Ghassanid Arabs, and Almundhir and his seasoned Arab horsemen rode on the right. The Sasanians opened their attack with their customary arrow storm, which this time was notable for its effects, especially on the shaky Roman infantry. Under the early charges of the Sasanian heavy cavalry, the Ghassanids gave ground and opened a gap in the enemy line, through which they rode and attacked the rear of the Roman cavalry, nearly all of whom had fought valiantly at Dara less than a year before. On that cold day in April, panic seized them, and the Roman cavalry fled the field, leaving their infantry to be swarmed and ridden down. Only penny packets of the westerners offered resistance, including the new Isaurian recruits from the hill country of Asia Minor, "and almost all the Isaurians fell with their leaders, without even daring to lift their weapons against the enemy. For they were thoroughly inexperienced in this business, since they had recently left off farming and entered into the perils of warfare . . ."[20]

So much for Caesar's legions. After the battle, Belisarius was recalled to Constantinople to account for his ignominious performance and, after an inquest, relieved of his command. Though the general blamed indiscipline, which is likely, the charges of treachery laid at the feet of al-Harith, the Ghassanid Arab leader, were unfounded.

His victory at Callinicum was of little consequence, however, except in the removal of the talented Belisarius from the front. The Persians had not managed to collect much wealth from the Romans, and the defeat was not so heavy as to change Kavad's bargaining position. Despite this, after Callinicum, Justinian received a letter from Mundhir by the hand of a Christian deacon, Sergius, sent by the Lakhmid king. This extraordinary step indicates not only Mundhir's standing in the circle of trust of the great king but perhaps, too, that Kavad was ill or mistrustful of certain men at court. The Roman emperor and empress sent lavish gifts to the Sasanian court along with the diplomat Rufinus to broker a peace, and the emperor also gave Sergius rich presents to convey to Mundhir. Rufinus's party arrived at Edessa but were refused entry by the Sasanian border guards.

The delay was caused by Kavad's wishing to further strengthen his bargaining position, to which end he had ordered troops against the Roman city of Martyropolis (Silvan). While the Sasanians struggled in their advance, due to the onset of the autumn rains and snows that turned the route into a marsh, the new eastern general, Constantine, ordered the general Sittas with reinforcements northward. En route the Sasanian troops learned of the death of the king of kings. The Persians turned and went home.

CHAPTER SEVEN

Defending the Empire

After the passing of Kavad in 531, his son, Khusrow I, aged seventeen or nineteen, would reign for nearly fifty years (531–579). Khusrow I was not the eldest son of the great king Kavad, and his appointment to power was therefore somewhat irregular; tradition had dictated that the throne fell to the oldest son. Thus, around 520, Kavad had supposedly negotiated with the Roman emperor Justin to take the boy under his wing and back Khusrow's right to rule. The Romans declined to intervene, and this fact created a source of great tension and frustration within the Sasanian court. Khusrow himself would not forget the slight. Nevertheless, the youth's elevation was accomplished, and Khusrow would go on to be arguably the greatest Sasanian monarch, renowned for his energy, the splendor of his court, and the vitality of his empire. Little wonder, then, that Khusrow is remembered by his epithet, *Anushirwan*—"he of the Immortal Soul." Due to the energy and reputation of the great king, carefully managed over his long reign, we are better informed about this shahanshah and his military actions than those of many of his predecessors.

Khusrow undertook numerous restructurings in the kingdom, which his father had likely begun. In his military reforms he was helped by a certain Babak who was entrusted with the overhaul of the institutions within the army. Babak and Khusrow created new military commands which streamlined imperial organization and the ability of the state to respond to the numerous threats that the Iranians confronted. The *Eranspahbed*, the office of the commander in chief of the Sasanian military, was replaced by four *spahbeds*, generals commanding forces, each leading troops in one quarter of the empire. The spahbed of the west held military power in the core lands of Iran and Iraq. The spahbed of Azerbaijan held sway over the regions of Armenia and the adjacent lands, such as Iberia and Albania, including the passes through the south Caucasus. The spahbed of Khurasan managed forces along the great northern front against the Central Asian steppes, though the Sasanians preferred not to refer to this marshall of the north as such, as the term "north" was loaded with negative connotations, being the domain of demons and utter chaos.[1] Finally, the spahbed of Nemroz guarded the southern shield of the kingdom, along the great belt of the Arabian Desert bordering the fertile farmlands of Mesopotamia, the breadbasket of the empire. The responsibility of the spahbed of Nemroz included the southern shores of the Arabian Gulf, through Bahrain to Oman and Yemen. The special commands of the *marzbans*, the margraves, of the frontiers, fell under the direct command of the king of kings.

The troops were regularly drilled and the cities equipped with horse courses where cavalry trained. Both foot and horse soldiers were regularly inspected to make certain they were properly equipped and in fighting condition. Babak personally inspected the cavalry regiments who paraded before him. Pay, standardized and delivered from the fisc, for the cavalry was high, up to four thousand drachms (for some perspective, a basket of dates could be had for one drachm).

Khusrow further oversaw a general expansion of the military and wider recruitment, especially among the Daylami mountaineers from around the Caspian. These folk, who had long served in the shah's armies, would provide the finest infantry forces in Persian service and play a pivotal role in Khusrow I's wars and in the wars to come. A sixth-century Roman historian offers a description of these troops during their conduct in the Lazic War (541-562):

> The Daylamites are among the largest of the nations on the far side of the Tigris whose territory borders on Persia. They are warlike in the extreme and, unlike most of the Persians, do not fight principally with the bow and the sling. They carry spears and pikes and wear a sword slung over one shoulder. To the left arm they tie a very small dirk and they hold out shields and buckler to protect themselves with. One could hardly describe them simply as light-armed troops nor for that matter as the type of heavy-armed infantry that fight exclusively at close quarters. For they both discharge missiles from a distance when the occasion

arises and engage in hand-to-hand fighting, and they are expert at charging an enemy phalanx and breaking its close-knit ranks with the weight of their charge. They can re-form their own ranks with ease and adapt themselves to any contingency. Even steep hills they run up without difficulty thus seizing in advance all points of vantage, and when put to flight they escape with lightning rapidity whereas when they are the attackers they press the pursuit with perfect timing and co-ordination. Well-versed as they are in practically every type of warfare they inflict considerable harm on their enemies.[2]

Around the king's person, Khusrow established a permanent corps of professional cavalry called *aswar* (*savaran* in later Persian; *aswaran* in Arabic). These men were drawn from the ranks of the great noble families and their households. Soldiers were enrolled from the provinces and recorded in muster rolls. They were paid regular salaries and provided arms and horses, the supply of which was levied from the local populations who had to furnish the materiel of war as part of their tax or rent obligations. *Aswar* troopers were equipped with a full panoply that included a helmet with chin straps, mail armor worn beneath a breastplate (probably of lamellar or scale), greaves over the legs, arm bracers, lance, sword, mace, battle-axe, two bows in their cases with spare bowstrings, and a quiver with thirty arrows. A lasso was sometimes also carried.[3] In the guard cavalry units, horses were also armored. To carry such warriors, armored and armed to the teeth, Persian mounts must have been large, heavy boned animals and extremely rugged.

During his reign, Khusrow built or expanded the linear defenses of the state, which, under his rule, took their final shape. Massive state investment and gargantuan building works with few parallels in Eurasian history were designed to provide security to the Sasanian Empire along its frontiers. As has been noted, earlier kings had built and repaired vital military installations, especially in the south Caucasus, a primary invasion route for seminomadic and nomadic groups from the steppe lands to the north. Among these huge projects was the wall at Darband, which ran from the western edge of the Caspian Sea to the pass. The wall extended some 46 kilometers (28.5 miles) and rose to a height of 15 meters (50 feet).

The great king likely ordered the construction of another huge fortification on the northern frontier, known today as the Great Wall of Gorgan or Gorgan Wall.[4] This fortification, with elements comprising a linear brick wall, supporting forts and waystations, ditches, and complex water supplies fed by dams and canals over considerable stretches of the barrier, was an engineering marvel of the day, extending from the eastern shore of the Caspian Sea to the foothills of the Elburz Mountains, a distance of more than 195 kilometers (121 miles), making it longer than the more famous Roman fortified line of Hadrian's Wall in northern Britain (117 kilometers or 73 miles) and the Raetian *limes* of Rome along the German frontier (166 kilometers or 103 miles). The scope of building undertaken by the late Sasanian kings, almost unknown and unappreciated in the west, is truly astonishing, implying as it does not only the marshaling of vast economic resources but logistical support for builders, engineers, and military personnel on an enormous scale.

Immediately after his accession to power, though, Khusrow I had to move to solidify his grip on power. The war with the Romans begun by his father he brought to an immediate end. Khusrow and the Romans agreed to parley. After difficult negotiations, the two sides exchanged the territorial advances they had gained in the other's country. In an eerie distant ancestor to "the war to end all wars" of 1914, the Romans and Persians, like two smiling wolves biding their time, concluded the so-called "Eternal Peace." The Romans agreed to pay a lump sum of 11,000 lb. (3,617 kg) of gold, which Khusrow's representatives emphasized to the Romans was to be used to maintain the region of the Caspian Gates (the Dariel and Darband Passes).

Quiet settled over the western frontiers with Rome. This calm prevailed until, in 539/40, the shahanshah, his grasp on royal authority firmer, received an embassy from the Goths of distant Italy. These Germanic speakers, who had been settled in the peninsula by right of conquest since 488, had been attacked by the Romans under Justinian and were losing the war. Their ambassadors told their woeful tale to the great king and informed him that the Roman east was stripped of its soldiers, occupied as the state was with the reconquest of the birthplace of the empire. It is unlikely that Khusrow needed hairy barbarians, even sophisticated hairy barbarians like the Goths, to tell him the shape of the Roman's eastern frontier. After all, Khusrow maintained a legion of informants, spies, and military scouts.

In 539, the Ghassanid king al-Harith (529–569), whom Justinian had established as supreme leader of Roman-allied Arabs along the frontier, attacked his Lakhmid rival al-Mundhir. Mundhir's men were surprised and defeated in detail, his goods plundered and many of his people taken captive. Khusrow sent numerous appeals on behalf of Mundhir, seeking redress for the violation of the truce; the Persians sought restitution for their client's losses. Justinian ignored these missives until late in the year, when warned that the shahanshah was calling his men to muster, the emperor dispatched messengers in an attempt to forestall war. Roman troops were bogged down

An iron and bronze Sasanian helmet from the 5th century AD. Examples of Sasanian armor are rare. (*Metropolitan Museum of Art*)

in the Italian campaign, and the emperor realized too late that the Sasanians were bent on renewing the war.

As winter was already reaching its close, and the thirteenth year of the reign of the emperor Justinian (540 AD) was ending, Khusrow, son of Kavad, invaded the land of the Romans at the opening of spring with a mighty army and openly broke the so-called eternal peace.[5]

The "Eternal Peace" had endured all of eight years.

Khusrow Anushirwan marched up the Euphrates, bypassed the newly renovated Roman frontier fortress of Circesium, at the confluence of the Khabur and Euphrates. Either at Circesium or just to the north of it, Anushirwan crossed the river and came upon the city of Zenobia where another strong set of walls confronted him, but the great king skirted these as well and sighted the fortress on the lofty banks of the river, with almost no agricultural land nearby and thus no easy source of supplies. A few days later brought the Persians to the city of Sura, a city of some size and importance.

The Sasanian troopers assaulted the settlement, but the Roman garrison, led by an Armenian named Arshak, defended the fortifications vigorously and resisted until the Persians retired. In the scrum for the walls, the Roman leader fell dead from an arrow wound, and the spirit of the citizens, robbed of their spirited commander, ebbed. The next morning, as Khusrow prepared to storm the town, the Surene bishop emerged to beg on behalf of his sheep. The shah received the cleric, bade him rise, and cheerfully promised that his prayers were heard. He gladly received the gifts from the bishop's hand and then sent an escort to accompany the pastor home. When he reached the walls, the jubilant townspeople clapped and shouted for joy as they flung open the gate. Only too late did they notice that the Persian escort had thrown down a great rock at the base of the portal and jammed it. As the melee thickened and the desperate Romans clawed and struggled to close the great door, Khusrow arrived with the vanguard of his army and smashed his way into the city, slaughtering and burning until the city was razed and the townsfolk dead or in chains. Among the enslaved was a Roman of exceptional beauty, Euphemia, who had caught the king's eye. He married her on the spot, and she persuaded him to ransom the captives to the bishop of the nearby city of Sergiopolis. Despite their ransom assured by the bishop there, most of the Surenes died of hunger and exposure.

The great king found the Roman defenses a dog's breakfast. Bouzes, the Roman commander in the absence of Belisarius, fighting in Italy, had dispersed his men into the hills near his headquarters at Hierapolis and consequently lost contact with the city. Farther west, at Antioch, when the emperor's nephew Germanus arrived at the great city with a token force of close retainers, he found the city walls too weak to endure a siege. There was no unified resistance—the leadership of each city was left to cut its own deal with the enemy while the westerners floundered, caught flat-footed by the great king's advance. Considering the muddle in which the enemy found themselves, they dispatched the bishop Megas to seek terms. The great king received the supplicant and marched him to the walls of Hierapolis, which he found strong. But the inhabitants, despite the strength of the troops bivouacked among them, had no confidence in their ability to resist. They offered two thousand pounds of silver, and to this offer Megas agreed that the emperor would pay another thousand pounds of gold if Khusrow would agree to depart. To this, Anushirwan agreed in principle, but without a formal treaty, he pressed onward, coming next to the city of Beroea (today Aleppo in northern Syria).

At Beroea the community leaders agreed to hand over more loot: two thousand pounds of silver. The next day, when the Iranians arrived to collect the ransom, they found the gates barred and the walls empty. The inhabitants had fled to the citadel and hid there. Throwing ladders against the walls, the Persians entered the city, flung open the gates, and the great king trooped in, enraged at the breach of the deal. He fired the city and waited.

Megas, the bishop of the city, returned empty-handed from his mission to have the emperor ratify the agreement he had made with Khusrow: Justinian's new ambassadors had strict instructions not to hand over any money or cities to the enemy. The great king upbraided the bishop for the duplicity of his fellow citizens and allowed him access to his countrymen trapped in the powerful citadel of the city where, despite the stoutness of their position, the Romans were in grave danger, since their water supplies were nearly exhausted. Again, Khusrow received Megas amicably and granted the bishop's request to allow the surrender of his congregants. Many in the soldier's garrison went over to the great king, and most of the population was marched to Persia.

Khusrow paraded his army west and traversed the 100 kilometers (62 miles) between Beroea and Antioch. Refugees streamed from the city and fear gripped the population. The recent arrival of six thousand reinforcements from the south, however, had given them some reason to hope. When the great king arrived, he sent a herald to the walls to remind the citizens of the agreement: he wanted his thousand pounds of gold but could be persuaded to withdraw for less. The negotiations came to nothing, and the next day the boisterous citizens catcalled and rained abuse on the Persian emissary, nearly killing him in the process. Enraged at this turn, Anushirwan readied to storm the walls. Having reconnoitered the defenses, the Iranians concentrated on the high ground where a rock shelf left intact by the negligence of the defenders rendered an already weak stretch of the curtain especially vulnerable. When a makeshift parapet the defenders had built collapsed beneath the weight of the soldiers, the Romans panicked and chaos gripped the city. What had begun as an isolated setback soon became a general rout as the Roman cavalry, in their haste to save their skins, ran down helpless citizens. Khusrow observed the unfolding scene with cautious satisfaction; he held his soldiers back to allow the enemy the opportunity to flee. Cornering them at this crucial time could have led to a desperate fight. Only some of the young men of the city remained to resist and, on these, the king turned his elite savarans, who broke and slaughtered them.

Amidst the unfolding butchery, Khusrow summoned the Roman ambassadors and reminded them of their share of the blame for what had transpired, then descended to the city and watched as his soldiers plundered freely and enslaved the population. Once the looters had picked the city clean, he ordered the city to be fired.

The shahanshah decamped and marched to Seleucia, the port of Antioch. There he bathed in the Mediterranean but left the terrified inhabitants unmolested. He then announced to the Roman ambassadors, who were now like helpless lapdogs of the great king, that he wished to see the famous city of Apamea, south of Antioch. The enemy negotiated the safety of the city in exchange for one thousand pounds of silver, but without force to back their agreement, they were at the mercy of a man who was disinclined to fritter away the strategic advantage he had won. He found the gates of the city open wide to receive the royal train. Once established inside the walls, Anushirwan demanded not a thousand pounds of silver but all of the wealth of the city. With the city's coffers and households emptied and treasure heaped to the sky, the great king took in a chariot race and then marched his army to the next city along his itinerary of unopposed plundering.

Chalcis stands in the middle of a plain and its citadel stood on a high tell, an artificial mound built up from the Bronze Age by successive building and rebuilding over many generations. The city dominated the dusty plain around and fronted the Syrian Desert, gateway to the lands of the Arabs who moved along the corridor of the frontier from the Euphrates to the Red Sea. At Chalcis, the mortified citizenry collected the extraordinary sum of two hundred pounds of gold and thereby bought their own skins, whereupon the triumphal Iranian shakedown continued. Khusrow's men, so loaded down with plunder by now they would have been easy pickings for a Roman force worth any salt, struck north and threw a bridge over the Euphrates near the fortress city of Barbalissos (today Meskene). His next intended victim was none other than the God-guarded city of Edessa, which had defied his father.

Outside the city, Khusrow fell ill: the historian Procopius said the king suffered from swelling in his face and jaw. After receiving two hundred pounds of gold from Edessa, the king apparently had no intention to avenge his father's embarrassment, but instead prepared to fry bigger fish. Justinian's ambassadors arrived and agreed to pay tribute to the shah, who then offered to ransom his prisoners. When the negotiations floundered, the captives were marched off to Persia and the Iranian army filed north against the vexation of Dara, the great fortress city that gaped across the plain of Nisibis. If the march of the great king had, to this point, seemed like a holiday hike mostly spent collecting valuable souvenirs, at Dara the Persians got down to business.

The Sasanians were heavyweights of siege warfare, and Dara was every inch a worthy pugilist. Surrounded by two great curtain walls built in great blocks of ashlar, the inner wall rose to sixty feet and was studded with towers to a hundred feet. To the west the Persians invested the outer wall, setting fire to the gate there, but though the portal was damaged, his troops could not force an entry. On the eastern side of Dara, Persian sappers began to undermine the outer perimeter, but their works were betrayed by a soldier within their own ranks, probably a Roman deserter who suffered a pang of conscience. Thus informed, the Romans dug a trench perpendicular to the Sasanians' works, and when Iranian soldiers broke into daylight, they killed the first through the breach and the rest fled back to camp. When his initial efforts failed, the great king accepted a thousand pounds of silver and withdrew to Persia.

Justinian learned of the successful defense of the bastion at Dara and decided to renege on his proposal to pay tribute, and the war thus continued. When Anushirwan returned to Persia, he built a new city, modeled on Antioch, including a hippodrome and bathhouses, staffed with Roman captives from the cities they had captured from throughout Syria. Among these were musicians, charioteers, and skilled craftsmen. The town, about a day's journey from the capital of Ctesiphon, he named Weh Antiok Khusrow ("better than Antioch, Khusrow built it"). Fed at the expense of the royal treasury, the citizens were subjects of the king and enjoyed his protection.

In the spring of 541, Khusrow attacked in the northern front of the theater of war, in Lazica. The Lazic king, Gubazes II (541–555), whose people suffered unbearable Roman corruption, sent emissaries to the great king, seeking his intervention on their behalf. Assured of Laz guides and local support, Anushirwan mustered his forces and launched his campaign. In order to screen his true intentions, he spread word that his target was Iberia, Persian territory which was being attacked by Huns. When he arrived at the city of Petra in what is today western Georgia, the great king found the recent Roman fortifications to be stout but apparently abandoned. No sign of any enemy could be spotted on the ramparts, not a whisp of smoke or noise to tell of their presence. Khusrow ordered his general Aniabedes to throw ladders against the walls and press forward with a battering ram to hammer down the gate. Amid their preparations, the Romans threw open the gates and made a strong sally, taking the Iranians completely by surprise and killing many.

The next day Khusrow inspected the defenses of Petra and knew that the place would be unlikely to survive a determined attack. He ordered his men to take the walls. As the Persians fired volley after volley and attempted to scale the ramparts, near nightfall a Sasanian archer struck the Roman commander, John, in the neck. With the death of their commander, Roman morale and organization suffered, but coming darkness spared the defenders.

Thwarted in their initial efforts to go over the top, the Persians turned to mining, and chose as their target the great pair of flanking towers that covered the approach to the seaside city. Persian sappers undermined one of the towers, removed the stones, and replaced these with timbers which they fired. The tower collapse left the city open to easy ingress, and the defenders surrendered. While at Petra, Anushirwan learned of an attack in Persian Mesopotamia by the old Sasanian nemesis, Belisarius, who had briefly laid siege to Nisibis and captured the important fortress of Sisauranon. The great king established a garrison at Petra, collected his spoils, and returned home to fight the Roman invasion. By the time he reached his home territory, the Romans had withdrawn, and the king returned to quarters, only to renew the campaign the following spring.

In early 542, Khusrow attacked through Syria at the head of an army said to number sixty thousand. The Persians moved up the Euphrates and blitzed through the desert to invest the city of Sergiopolis where a paltry two hundred soldiers manned the walls. Due to the desolate situation of the place, the Iranians quickly ran out of water and broke off their operations, turning instead to the north where he learned Belisarius had once more arrived. Through emissaries, Khusrow agreed not to plunder any further but to return home, a decision likely influenced in no small part by the outbreak of bubonic plague that raged through the eastern provinces at the time. Breaking his oath to do no further damage, Khusrow found easy pickings at the Roman city of Callinicum (modern Raqqa) at the crossing point of the Euphrates. There the Romans were remodeling the defenses, and entire sections of the curtain had been demolished. Such an inviting target was easily seized. Carrying off the population captive and with their chattel in his hands, Khusrow marched back to his territory. Before doing so, he dispatched part of his forces under Mihr Mihroe, who made no progress against Dara.

The following year, Anushirwan again took the field, visiting first the great Zoroastrian fire temple at Adur Gushnasp in Azerbaijan. There, events turned against the great king. The deadly pandemic, the bubonic plague that had ravaged Roman territory throughout 542, struck Persia. This, the first global pandemic in recorded history, burned its way through the Sasanian soldiery. At the same time, Khusrow faced the rebellion of his son, Kavad. When the Romans learned of the discomfiture of the king, Justinian ordered an invasion through Armenia. Thirty thousand Romans under three generals descended upon the Iranian empire around the Armenian city of Dvin. Opposing them was the Persian commander Nabedes who, along with his four thousand men, had taken up positions in the high ground by the nearby village of Anglon. There his troops ambushed the disorganized Romans and inflicted bloody defeat on them, capturing large numbers of men and horses and a tremendous stock of enemy war materiel.

By 544, his internal troubles dispatched, the great king invaded Mesopotamia and again invested Edessa. On the first morning of the fight, a force of Persian Huns attempted to collect the flocks kept behind a palisade. The shepherds who tended the flocks, however, and the townspeople resisted, once again employing slings to great effect and wounding one of the Hun leaders. From inside, the Roman troops, alerted to the scuffle, rushed forward and the melee became a nasty hand-to-hand confrontation in which neither side would give quarter until midday, when the brawl ended in a stalemate.

Khusrow received a delegation from the town and demanded money—far more, he insisted, than the sum that had delivered them during his previous campaign. The Edessenes, confronted with the demand to hand over everything of value, elected to fight. In response, the Sasanians began their works, throwing up a ramp with which they would overtop the walls. While the Romans poured arrows and sling bullets on their heads, the Persian cordon progressed. The Iranian soldiers worked under the protection of heavy goat-hair nets that proved impervious to the enemy barrage. As the Sasanian ramp advanced, like a noose around the neck of the city, the Romans sent a doctor named Stephen to negotiate with the great king who received him and offered steep terms: five hundred pounds of gold and the surrender of everything in their homes or the forfeit of their city and their lives.

As the Iranian siege ramp rose, the Romans tried to build an opposite mound to counter the growing height and secure the line of the wall where the ramp would soon overtop the fortifications. They had begun this work too late, however, and abandoned it. Instead, they began to dig a tunnel under the Persian hill, hollowing out a chamber and filling it with sulphur, bitumen, and other flammable materials. As these works continued, both sides stalled for time, the Persians pretending to negotiate but confident their strident efforts would deliver the city into their hands. The Romans fired the timbers below and, to camouflage their actions, fired a hail of flaming arrows and other burning projectiles into the midst of the Sasanians. The fires below smoldered throughout the night and into the next day, even as both sides joined at the crest of the hill in vicious hand-to-hand fighting. His tower ruined, Anushirwan nonetheless tightened his grip.

Six days later, in the gloom of the early morning, Persian troops stealthily crept forward and noiselessly hoisted their ladders to the wall. Their spot was well chosen—inside, the Roman defenders slept. But luck would not favor Khusrow on this occasion. A Syrian farmer saw the Persians ascending the ladders and cried out, rousing the garrison to their posts. Driven from the walls, the Persians had even to abandon their ladders. At midday, though,

Khusrow renewed the onslaught against the so-called Great Gate on the eastern side of the city. There, too, the Persians found themselves staunchly opposed and forced to retreat. It was likely during this all-out attack that the following comedic scene unfolded:

> . . . one of the elephants, mounted by a great number of the most warlike men among the Persians, came close to the circuit-wall and made it seem that in a short space he would overpower the men defending the tower at that point . . . for it seems that this was, in fact, an engine for the capture of cities. The Romans, however, by suspending a pig from the tower escaped this peril. For as the pig was hanging there, he very naturally gave vent to sundry squeals, and this angered the elephant so that he got out of control . . . .[6]

Against the Romans and their porcine secret weapon, the king soon launched a third assault, hurling his entire force against every side of the city simultaneously, as related by the Roman historian Procopius:

> And the fighting began early in the morning, and at first the Persians had the advantage. For they were in great numbers and fighting against a very small force, since the most of the Romans had not heard what was going on and were utterly unprepared. But as the conflict advanced the city became full of confusion and tumult, and the whole population, men women and little children, were going up on the wall. Now those who were of military age together with the soldiers were repelling the enemy most vigorously, and many of the rustics made a remarkable show of valorous deeds against the barbarians [the Persians]. Meanwhile the women and children, and the aged also, were gathering stones for the fighters and assisting them in other ways.[7]

Against this desperate defense, most of the attack faltered, but Anushirwan urged his men back to the fight. One Persian group breached the outer wall and forced the defenders back to inner defenses, but a strong Roman sally parried this thrust as well. By midday, the general assault, begun before dawn, had foundered and the two armies separated. Two days later, a small Persian attack was defeated by another Roman counterattack, and the two sides agreed to negotiate. The Edessenes agreed to pay five hundred pounds of gold. The great king accepted their offer and withdrew.

In 545, the Sasanians agreed to a five-year truce, in exchange for the handsome payment of two thousand pounds of gold—a princely sum, to be certain. But Justinian, desperate to conclude his campaigns in the west before he had to deal with his eastern nemesis, likely saw the treasure as worth the time it purchased.

Three years later, in the kingdom of Lazica on the eastern shores of the Black Sea, Khusrow made another push. His plan was to establish Persian dominance over the Laz, who had abandoned the Sasanians and again sought protection from the Romans. A strong Iranian force under the general Mihr Mihroe, some thirty thousand strong, marched to push the boundaries of the Sasanian Empire to the coast of the Black Sea where, it is said, Khusrow intended to build a naval base from which he could contest control of the water and menace the capital of Constantinople itself. Mihr Mirhoe relieved the starving garrison at Petra that had suffered within a cordon of enemy troops. The Sasanian commander strengthened the garrison and fought off a Roman and Laz ambush but soon had to withdraw in the face of a supply shortage.

The following year, the shahanshah sent a mixed Persian and Alan force under the generalship of Khorianes. The Laz under King Gubazes II and the Gothic Roman general Dagisthaeus opposed the Persian attack. Along the narrow valley of the Hippis River (today the Tskhenistsqali in northern Georgia) the Laz cavalry vanguard, confronted by a thousand Sasanian cataphracts, turned tail and became jumbled up with their infantry that followed. One of the best fighters among the Sasanian cavalry fell at the hands of an Armenian deserter to the Romans and, with this, the skirmishing came to an end and the Persians withdrew to their own lines. As the bulk of the Roman forces arrived, the Iranians and Alans watched as the Roman and Laz cavalry dismounted and formed a tight, deep phalanx. Against this deadly hedge of spears the Iranians dared not press their luck, and so Khorianes and his men instead showered the enemy lines with continuous volleys of missiles, hoping to inflict enough casualties to open a gap that they could exploit. The Romans and Laz returned fire with their own bows; an unlucky shot struck down Khorianes, and the Persians fled to their fortified camp, where, bottled up, they were slaughtered.

By 551 the armistice had expired, and the two great powers were once again officially at war. The 2,600-man Sasanian garrison at Petra faced 6,000 Romans and their Sabir Hun allies. After failing in their efforts to undermine the walls, the Romans employed a new kind of composite battering ram of lesser weight and requiring fewer men. These were covered with wood and hides they brought to bear against the fortress of Petra. Against them the defenders hurled petroleum-filled clay grenades. The day grew hotter, and sensing the danger of being trapped there, the Roman general Bessas, now an old man, tried to spur his men over the top of the wall by leading the way. The defenders hurled him from the top of the ladder where he was surrounded by his bodyguards who covered their immobilized commander with their shields while the defenders peppered them with missiles. At last fortune turned against the Persians, as the enemy scaled a lightly defended portion of the wall and the two forces brawled at an opening forced in the circuit by the Roman undermining. Only five hundred Sasanians survived to withdraw to the citadel where the next day they were burned to death.

Mihr Mirhoe led a force of Sasanian cavalry and Daylami infantry accompanied by eight war elephants and four thousand Sabir Hun mercenaries with the intent of relieving Petra. When he learned, however, of the fall of the fortress, he turned instead to seize strongholds that guarded the passes from Georgia into Persian Iberia. Learning that the enemy forces were divided, Mir Mirhoe advanced against the garrison at the mouth of the Phasis River, which the Romans fearfully abandoned. The Sasanians then turned north to attack the key city of Archaeopolis (today Nokalakevi), manned by three thousand Roman defenders. Mihr Mirhoe employed his Daylami mountain troops against the town, where they inflicted numerous casualties. While a traitor inside the city had set fire to the grain stores, the Sasanians tried to breach the walls, but they were driven off by a strong counterattack. During the melee one of the Persian elephants was wounded and went mad, breaking up the Iranian lines. As mayhem spread, the Iranians and their allies panicked and began to flee, and as the fear raced through their ranks the rout became complete. Mihr Mirhoe was defeated and took heavy losses—more than four thousand men fell at Archaeopolis, and the Persians moreover lost upward of twenty thousand horses, many of which had arrived at the battle half-starved.

The general marched to Cotaeum (modern Kutaisi) in modern western Georgia, where he refortified an old stronghold at Mocheresis and cut off the nearby enemy garrison at Onoguris (today Khuntsistsikhe).

In the summer of 554, the Persians suffered a serious blow when the Lakhmid chief Mundhir, the faithful and long-serving vassal of the king of kings, fell in battle at the hands of the Roman Arab warlord, the Ghassanid Harith ibn Jabala. While the Syrian and Armenian fronts remained free of regular forces, the battle in the north raged on. Sasanian operations in the Caucasus continued, with Iranians gaining several successes under Mihr Mirhoe, who captured Laz and Roman strong points but succumbed to illness in 555. By then the war was draining Sasanian resources and wearing thin Anushirwan's patience. The Persian base at Mocheresis placed the Persians at a strategic advantage against the Romans and Laz, but positions so far distant from the Sasanian heartlands were difficult to victual; the forces of the great king were stretched to the limit.

Sasanian war elephants depicted in the Battle of Avarayr (451), Sharaknots, 1482, Akants Desert, MS 1620, 295b-296a. (*National Library of Spain*)

Nonetheless, in 556, determined to strike a decisive blow, Khusrow equipped a powerful army which he dispatched under the command of the *nakhveragan*, a Sasanian governor whose name the sources do not preserve. The Iranian army supposedly numbered some sixty thousand men but, given the lack of supplies in Lazica and the limits of Persian logistics, such a number seems fanciful. Among the Iranian forces were once again a strong contingent of Daylami infantry who, along their line of march to the city of Phasis (probably modern Poti on the coast of western Georgia), thwarted a Roman ambush. Despite their superior numbers, the Persians were defeated at the siege of Phasis and fled eastward, ending their major threat in the north. By the end of the campaigning season, the Persian troops in the Caucasus had suffered tactical setbacks that weakened their strategic position there, leading to the execution of the *nakhveragan* at the hand of Khusrow.

Bogged down in the Caucasus and unable to land a blow that would turn the war in his favor, the shahanshah decided to negotiate once more. Khusrow made extravagant demands, trying to pry from his western foe thirty of forty years' tribute payments in advance, something on which the enemy refused to budge. In the end, the Romans once more bent the knee, agreeing to pay annually thirty thousand gold *solidi* to the shahanshah for ten years. They would pay seven years in advance, thus providing Anushirwan desperately needed cash, a portion of which he likely used to pay tribute to the Hepthalites in the east. All told, the Roman handover amounted to nearly 4,200 Roman pounds (1,370 kg) of gold. In addition to the payments, the full text of the treaty survives and details grievances the Persians viewed as root causes of the war, namely the threat that Dara and its strong Roman garrison posed to the cities of the Persian western front. As part of the agreement, the Romans pledged to station their eastern marshal at a different city and to maintain a garrison at Dara sufficient only for the city's defense. In exchange the Sasanians agreed to drop their objections to the existence of the city, but the place, strong as it was and thrust up against the throat of the empire, would of course never cease to rile the kings of kings and occupy their attention. Both sides opted for harmonious relations for fifty years, certainly a less ambitious timespan for harmonious relations than the Eternal Peace of 532. With the treaty finalized in 562 the long reign of Justinian would end in peace in the east.

Having secured a satisfactory peace along his western borders, Khusrow looked east. There, the Hephthalite menace remained. Obviously, relations between the Persians and these Huns were complicated. The Hephthalites both gave and took away: they had slain Khusrow's grandfather Peroz, whose attempts to halt the advance of the Huns into Khurasan had been in vain. The Hephtalites had played kingmaker and placed Anushirwan's father, Kavad, on the throne following the coup that had likely been spawned in large part by nobles resistant to Hunnic dominance over the empire. Nonetheless, the great kings—in no small part using Roman money—had found themselves tributaries to the Hepthalites for half a century or more. As successful as recent events had seen them in the west, the Hun menace clung to the House of Sasan like the smell of rot.

In 561, a singular opportunity presented itself. Underway across the Oxus was another great migration which characterized the Central Asian steppes since time immemorial. This time, the main actors were a great confederation of Turkic peoples recently removed from the Mongolian steppe lands and the northern borders of China. In fact, the leader of the western branch of the great Turk confederation, Sinjibu Khan (or Istämi, as he is known in the Chinese sources), was the son-in-law of the emperor in China, Wen of Sui (541–604). Sinjibu Khan was the lieutenant of the senior ruler of his people, his brother the *Khagan* (khan) Bumin (d. 552). The name "Gök" or "Kök Turks" ascribed to these new migrants means "celestial Turks" and indicates their royal descent from the sky which Altaic peoples considered the source of the divine. Most historians refer to them as the "Western Turks" to differentiate them from their fellows who remained on the borderlands of China. The Western Turkic appearance on the flanks of the Hepthlalites provided an opportunity for Anushirwan. The ancient eastern maxim, "the enemy of my enemy is my friend," was certainly not lost on Khusrow, who knew full well the risks of replacing a known enemy with a new, uncertain quantity. Nonetheless, around 560, the Persians established friendly relations with the Turks encamped north of the Oxus. The stage was set for the Sasanians to rid themselves of their troublesome eastern neighbors.

The later poet Ferdowsi catalogues the Hephthalite vassals who marched under king Ghadfar.[8] Cities and principalities astride the northern and southern banks of the Oxus form the bulk of these and, since Balkh was one of the Hephthalite power centers from the early days of their empire, it is unsurprising to see its men listed among those who mustered in the Hun army. However, that Ghadfar enrolled troops from the city of Amol far to the west, near the southern shores of the Caspian, indicates that the Hephthalites still lorded over much of Khurasan.

In 563, the troops of the Hephthalites and the Western Turks clashed north of the Oxus. Almost nothing is known of the Battle of Gol-Zarriun except that the result was a decisive Turk victory, which led to the rapid dissolution of the Hephthalite kingdom. The new Hephthalite king, Faghanish, ruled as vassal under Turk overlordship. The Sasanians arrived well after the party had started, just in time to impose hegemony on the remaining Hephthalites south of the Oxus. Khusrow cemented his alliance with the Western Turks through marriage alliances between the two royal families; the daughter of Sinjibu Khan married Khusrow and gave birth to Hormozd IV, who would rule the Sasanian Empire for eleven years. The great victory of the Turks over the Hephthalites left the Sasanians in control of the whole of Khursasan up to the Oxus—a brilliant restoration of Iranian fortunes. In an astonishingly swift stroke of one or two years, the Persians had cut down their old nemesis and erased decades of defeat and humiliation. That much of the triumph was due to Turkic arms could not have been lost among the great families who partnered in the rule of the empire.

When, in 565, the Roman emperor Justinian breathed his last and reposed in a splendid mausoleum awash in porphyry and gold next to the Church of the Holy Apostles, Khusrow was far from hearty and hale himself. In 565, the great king had seen the passing of more than fifty winters. By the time this Persian lion entered his autumn, the crown weighed heavily on his head. Over the years, Khusrow had wrestled with several bouts of serious illness that had kept him from the field. He had faced down unrest among the no-bility whose blood and treasure adorned the fields of battle from Syria to the Caucasus. He had weathered at least two serious challenges to his rule by his own sons. Despite all he had overcome, great obstacles towered before him. The Hephthalites still manned and menaced the northern and eastern bounds of his kingdom, he had to deal with a new, mentally shaky Roman emperor, and before him loomed the question of his own successor.

Threats to the young peace abounded. In 568–69 a delegation from the Western Turk Empire arrived in Constantinople. Through their contacts, the Sasanians became aware of the Gök Turk embassy and the prospect of an un-holy alliance between their new eastern foes and their ancient nemesis in Constantinople the shahanshah rightly viewed as an existential threat. These dalliances of the Romans and Turks eroded whatever hope the Sasanians cherished for lasting peace in the west.

A continual source of friction were the spirited Arab vassals of each em-pire. In 570, the Lakhmid ruler Qabus invaded Roman territory but suffered a serious defeat at the hands of the Ghassanid *phylarch*, leader of the Christian Arabs allied with Rome. By now the Ghassanids had made themselves in-dispensable march wardens along the huge corridor from the Red Sea to the Euphrates. In 571, Qabus again raided Roman territory, but his Lakhmid soldiers again found themselves beaten by the bellicose Arabs hirelings of Constantinople. Quite naturally, the Ghassanid king Mundhir apprised Con-stantinople of his resounding triumphs. No doubt he expected to hear news of celebration of his victories and perhaps even some token of gratitude. In-stead, the emperor Justin ordered Mundhir to be assassinated, an inexplicable act except that the ruler of New Rome had taken leave of his senses. In a Monty Python-esque scene, the letter ordering the Roman general Marcian to murder Mundhir was mistakenly delivered to its intended victim. Mundhir, in a rage, led his confederates into the desert, leaving Roman service and Justin to fend for himself along the fringe of his empire.

Elsewhere, the great game between the two superpowers of late antiquity continued. Khusrow proved himself two steps ahead of his Roman rivals. Around 570, in a tiny hamlet amidst the scorched barrens of the vast Arabian Peninsula, a child was born who would give rise to one of the most momen-tous religious awakenings in world history. His name was Muhammad. Late Islamic tradition records that on the night of the Prophet's birth, the vast palace of Khusrow at Ctesiphon was shaken, as by an earthquake, and four-teen of its pillars toppled and the sacred fires of the Sasanian kings in Fars were mysteriously snuffed out.

Khusrow showed no signs of being spooked by these allegedly portentous events. In the same year, he sent Persian troops to South Arabia and Yemen, where his men drove out the Aksumite Ethiopians, allies of Rome, and established Sasanian hegemony from the Bab al Mandeb to the Persian Gulf. In the process, he threw a noose over the maritime trade the Romans conducted with Ceylon and to the east the seaborne extension of the Silk Road.

The peace frayed completely when the Persians faced Roman interference in Persian Armenia, where a revolt erupted in 571 as the local elites protested corruption by the Sasanian governor, a member of the Suren family, whose abuses included taking advantage of the wives of his Armenian subjects and forcing the Christian Armenians to convert to Zoroastrianism. As the fires of rebellion flared, Khusrow sent a marzban to Persian Armenia with a troop of two thousand cavalry, eventually reinforced with fifteen thousand men, whose objective was to bring the Armenians to heel and impose Zoroastrianism upon them. The Iranian force fell in defeat to a larger Armenian host, and its leading men perished. Khusrow dispatched a Christian named Sebokht at the head of an embassy to the Romans to protest their intervention and receive the peace payments as well as Roman assurances that the emperor would abide by the terms of the treaty. Sebokht found the emperor Justin bellicose; the ten years' peace, he asserted, had expired, and the Romans would continue to support the Christians of Armenia against Khusrow's men. For their part, the emperor insisted, the Persians could pay back the money they had already received and hand over the city of Nisibis. When the Persian emissaries returned home, Ctesiphon prepared for war.

While Justin humiliated the envoys, the Romans were in no sense prepared for war. Khusrow, however, took no offensive action after his failure in Armenia in 571–72. The Persians, too, were unprepared for war in the west, faced with the crisis of the Armenian and Iberian defection in the north, where troubles for the Persians deepened in the winter of 572.

Only in the spring of 573 did either side take strenuous action, and the campaign opened with an attack by the Roman general Marcian, who launched raids across the frontier before he moved to throttle Nisibis. The siege unfolded as a farce, the ill-trained small attacking force the Persians found beneath their contempt—so confident were the Sasanians inside the great city that they left the gates open, inviting the pathetic western force to try their luck. After weeks of ineffectiveness, the attacking army dissolved as its soldiers retreated.

Khusrow marched from Ctesiphon at the head of a great host. Sharing the burden of command was the general Adarmahan, governor in Kerman

Province and founder of the important fortress city of Mahan.[9] At the Roman frontier fortress of Circesium the great king split his forces. Khusrow led an army north, across the Tigris, to reinforce Nisibis. Before the king of kings had even arrived, the Roman general Marcian abandoned much of his war materiel before the walls of Nisibis. The capture of these engines the great king would turn to his profit, as one contemporary Roman source attests:

> For no sooner had the Persian king heard of Marcian's fall and the breaking up of the armies before Nisibis, than he determined to take full advantage of the mismanagement of his enemies, and assembling a powerful force, arrived rapidly at that town, and found the engines and machines which Marcian had erected still standing before it. And with these he forthwith commenced the siege of Dara, having removed thither all Marcian's engines of war, and applied them to his own use, for which purpose he had brought all kinds of artificers with him.[10]

To the south, Adarmahan led six thousand Persian and Arab auxiliaries across the Euphrates, where he scored a path in iron and blood, looted and burned scores of villages, and plundered the cities of Barbalissos and Chalcis while the enemy froze. The Persian general ordered a flying column to strike against Antioch, where the inhabitants, in the throes of terror, abandoned the city and fled headlong, with no thoughts of organized resistance. As the Persian and Arab cavalry scorched the fruitful lands around the city, Adarmahan thrust south against the city of Apamea, which thirty years before had proved such a hospitable host to Khusrow during his victorious tour of the Roman east. This time the Apamenes also expected the clemency they had found at the hands of the great king. Upon learning of their foolish trust in him, Adarmahan bid them open their gates and await the arrival of his force. The Romans did so, credulous to the end. As the marzban paraded into the city, those gathered watched in thunderstruck horror as Iranian troopers seized control of the gates. The rest of the army poured in, flowing over the defenseless town like the waters of a river in flood. Thousands had ropes thrown about their necks, were made captive, and prepared for the long march back to Iran. They watched as smoke from their burning homes boiled into the air and as the hot sun glittered off the heaps of their looted treasures. His mission a stupendous success, Adarmahan marched north to link his army with that of the king of kings.

At Dara, Khusrow assembled a mighty siege force to match the strength of the Roman bulwark. The Persian army counted twenty-three thousand cavalry and forty thousand infantry. Beside them toiled tens of thousands of laborers, set to sapping and mining operations and in building a brick curtain wall around the entire perimeter of the city. Iranian engineers cut the aqueducts to the city and diverted the nearby Cordes River from its bed, so it no longer flowed to the city. Soon, reasoned Khusrow, the city would perish from thirst. As he cut the water supply, Khusrow ordered the construction of two huge earthen siege ramps. Over six months the Sasanians invested Dara and could not force the city. Two Roman siege towers captured at Nisibis were employed in an assault on the walls, but the Romans burned them to the ground.

Sasanian engineers focused their energies against the most powerful bastion at Dara, the massive stronghold called the tower of Hercules. There the great king directed gargantuan efforts in the construction of three new earthen platforms. Once the earthen ramps had reached sufficient height, Khusrow employed the captured Roman artillery seized at Nisibis; again the massive weight of the projectiles cast by these engines implies that they were not fired from ballista but from much more capable artillery pieces. The Roman garrison, despite its losses, grew overconfident, trusting that they had repulsed the worst of the Iranian offensives and, unknown to most of them, the great king had offered to depart on payment of a relatively modest sum of gold, but the Roman emissaries, confident of victory, did not even bother to relay the offer to the city elders and high command.

By now it was November 573 and the frigid rains and snows of winter had come to the highlands of the Tur 'Abdin in which the great fortress city lay. The Persians were expected to suffer from the cold and soon give up. In fact, despite the stalemate which stalled his mighty army and the onset of another bout of serious illness from which the king thought he might die, he ordered another great push against the fortifications. As Roman troops warmed themselves at home and ate and drank the Sasanians dropped planks from the ramps onto the city walls and entered the city in force. The Iranians poured in in such numbers that the shocked Romans were surrounded and fought like the trapped men they were.

After seven days of combat that left the city filled with the bloated corpses of the dead, the Iranians could not gain the city. The two sides agreed to a truce, likely a move planned by the cavalry commander, Bahram, a margrave of the Mihran family from Rayy, whose tall, upright bearing had earned him the nickname "the Javelin," Persian, "Chobin." After the two sides agreed upon a truce, the Persians broke their pledge, stripped the remaining garrison of its arms, enslaved the remaining troops and civilians, and plundered the town. Since Bahram would gain command of the armies of the northern quarter of the empire following the victory at Dara, it stands to reason that he and his troops played a key role in the final capture of the enemy castle. The city fell on November 11, and Khusrow marched home in triumph, having dealt the Romans a defeat the likes of which they had not suffered in decades.

When news of the fall of the great Roman bulwark in Upper Mesopotamia reached Justin in his palace on the Bosporus in Constantinople, so great was the shock that the emperor fell into madness, visited only occasionally by moments of lucidity. During one of these he appointed his faithful guardsman Tiberius, who would rule alongside Justin's wife, the empress Sophia, as emperor. Sophia immediately sent a delegation to the east, carrying 45,000 gold coins weighing some 625 Roman pounds (205 kg) with which to purchase truce for a year. The Roman ambassador promised a full-fledged embassy to discuss further terms for a lasting peace. For the moment, the truce did not include Armenia, where the Persian losses were too great to bear: Roman gains through the defections of the Persian Armenians and Iberians placed them within striking distance of Azerbaijan and the heartland of Iran itself. Matters there, the old king knew, could not stand.

When negotiations opened in the autumn of 574, Khusrow rejected Roman demands for a three-year peace. Instead, the Persians wished for a five-year treaty which would allow them to gain maximum benefit of Rome's tributary status in propaganda, as well as milk the Romans of more gold. Matters reached a stalemate, and the Sasanian commander at Dara raided the surrounding countryside in force, but the Romans had their own successes. The enemy commanders Theodorus and Coursos, the Hun, invaded the rich Sasanian lands in Albania and wintered there in 574 and then returned in 575 when the Persians could offer no effective resistance.

After these mutual retaliations, the two sides struck a deal for a three-year truce. The Romans agreed to pay thirty thousand gold *nomismata* annually for the years 575–577. As the Persians well knew, Roman objectives were twofold: first, to keep the Sasanians out of Mesopotamia, where Dara, the keystone of Roman defenses, was now within the Persian grasp; second, the truce was intended to buy time for the Romans to recruit, train, and deploy their army. Following the overreach of Justinian, the emperor Justin had been forced to economize and drastically cut the army.

While negotiations, whose objective was to forge a permanent peace from the truce, dragged on, the fighting thickened in Armenia. Khusrow himself took the field and led a surprise attack against Theodosiopolis, second only to Dara in its strategic importance to the Romans in the east. Seeing that the city was well prepared for a siege, and shadowed by a Roman force to the south, the king hurried west, bypassing the Roman stronghold at Theodosiopolis and intending to advance to Caesarea, the greatest Roman city on the Anatolian plateau.

Along his line of advance the great king was confronted by Roman forces, and the two sides clashed in repeated skirmishes. The outcome of these encounters bolstered the morale of the untried Romans. The danger grew for Khusrow, whose health had been poor since his probing of the defenses at Theodosiopolis and who faced an incipient mutiny among his troops, who cursed the old monarch for leading them to their deaths in the mountains of Rome. Between Sebastea (modern Sivas) and Caesarea, the Romans drew up the forces. The commander of the Roman right, the Hun Coursos, drove back and then outflanked the Sasanian left and got to the rear of Khusrow's army, pillaging the royal baggage train. The Sasanians narrowly extracted themselves from the cordon of Roman troops who fell on the abandoned camp and plundered the royal treasures. Amid this critical danger, suffering from the castigations of his fractious nobles and in ill health, Khusrow regrouped his men and retreated southwest. It was near Melitene that Anushirwan and his troops effected a breakout.

The Romans had camped apart from one another, apparently too distant to easily support one another. Khusrow selected the enemy's northern camp for his breakout where the general Justinian commanded. In the dead of night, the Persians launched a sudden onslaught and smashed their way through the Roman lines; in the confusion of the Sasanian attack, the Romans panicked and fled. Ahead of the Sasanians lay the city of Melitene (Malatya), some four hundred kilometers (248 miles) southwest of Theodosiopolis, where their incursion into Roman territory had begun. The spoils the Iranians found in Melitene could hardly have compensated them for their suffering, since the city was uninhabited; the citizens had fled far and wide when they had learned of the approaching Persians. The retreating Sasanians, strung out over miles and harassed by continuous Roman attacks, perished in large numbers as they attempted to cross the waters of the mighty Euphrates. Anushirwan only escaped by crossing the river on the back of one of his war elephants. Most of the great beasts did not make their getaway; some two dozen were captured, along with thousands of Persian prisoners, and auctioned in the markets of Constantinople.

Once across the Euphrates, the king pillaged the lands of Roman Armenia and returned home, humbled by his failure in dealing a decisive blow along his western frontier. Matters for the Sasanians worsened as the Romans, led by their general Justinian, invaded Azerbaijan and wintered in Persian lands south of the Caspian, plundering over huge distances and taking numerous prisoners, including the allied king of Suania and his entire family.

As the war dragged on, both sides returned to the peace table. The Persians wanted the Romans out of Persian Armenia and Iberia, whose loss they could not tolerate. On the other side, the Romans wanted the return of Dara. In the summer or autumn of 577, Persian troops under the command of Tamkhusro scored a major victory over the Romans under Justinian, whose troops were surprised along the Araxes and fled like miserable dogs before their outnumbered attackers.

> ... shame and an ill name fastened upon all the Roman armies, with their commanders; for the Persians did not so much as draw sword against them, nor bend the bow, nor shoot a single arrow, but gathered up the arms and coats of mail, which they had scattered in their flight, and their breastplates and shields, and helmets and spears and swords, and lances and bows and quivers full of arrows, beyond numbering. And the cause of their defeat, as all men said, was, that the Romans had made God angry.[11]

Bouyed by God's unexpected intervention on his behalf, Khusrow decided to press on in the conflict. Both sides exchanged large-scale raids intended to inflict pain, but the Persians suffered the most, with an enemy army ravaging close to where the great king summered, in the mountains north of Nisibis.

Cracks in the Persian edifice widened; already, during the negotiations of 577, a Roman captive in Persian hands had tried to convey to the western negotiators that the Sasanians were under duress. The most plausible source of the sudden reversal of Iranian fortunes was the outbreak of hostilities in the east, where the honeymoon with their former Kök Turk allies had ended.

Hostilities between the Western Turks and the Iranians likely began in 570/571, the moment the Armenians and Iberians chose to revolt. After all, the Armenians had long demonstrated that they were well apprised of the internal situation inside the kingdom to which they paid tribute. They no doubt chose a moment when the great king's hands were tied by strong cords. Anushirwan could most probably be put in that kind of bind by the Turks, whose empire was steadily bleeding across boundaries in all directions. Kök Turk riders had made forays across the Oxus, in clear violation of the agreement between the two nations, and their attitude told the Iranians that, like the Hepthalites before them, they intended to stay. To buy peace in the east, Khusrow had to pay annual tribute to the nomadic great power to the tune of forty thousand gold coins.[12] The great king likely divined that full-scale war between his kingdom and that of the western half of the great Turk khanate was inevitable.

Since the end of the 560s the Kök Turks had been in diplomatic contact with the Romans, and the Sasanians could not have remained ignorant of the fact that, in 576, a Roman embassy had journeyed across the Caspian steppe to attempt to strike a pact with the Turks and persuade them to attack the Persians on their northern and eastern flanks. The Roman dalliance with the Turks, posing as it did the threat of an unholy alliance of western and eastern foes, was flame to an already simmering pot. His troubles heated the water by degrees—suitable for boiling frogs; the shah would have to find a way to leap free or be cooked along with his kingdom.

In 578, the Sasanians launched a two-pronged campaign in Mesopotamia. Mahbod marched at the head of around twenty thousand troops, eight thousand of whom were Arab auxiliaries, against Constantia and Theodosiopolis. Meanwhile, another wing of the army, led by Tamkhosrow, struck across Persian Arzanene into Roman lands lying between Amida and Martyropolis but suffered defeat in an ambush laid by the Roman Hun commander, Coursos.

In the end, time spared the aged king the trouble. In February or March 579, as the war that smoldered between the two great powers burned for its eighth year, Roman diplomats braved the winter weather to descend into the warmth of Persia to the court of the great king at Ctesiphon, where they no doubt hoped for a warm welcome from Khusrow and an end to hostilities. But the body of Anushirwan, he of the Immortal Soul, had breathed its last. Less than two years after the hoary old monarch had watched as the Romans plundered his treasures in Cappadocia, the great king had told his men not to be troubled; he would ride, he said, alongside them in the front lines, like a common cavalryman, sharing in their dangers. As the shahanshah expired, around him crowded his many sons, nobles, and courtiers, who would watch his passage into the beyond. The age of Khusrow I had ended. Despite all he had accomplished—or perhaps because of it—his kingdom of Persia was about to spark as bright and fiery as a star, glowing white in brilliance before its fire sputtered and burned to ash.

Hormozd IV (579–590) was the young son of Khusrow Anushirwan, daughter of Sinjibu Khan, former leader of the Kök Turk dynasty. As Khusrow's other male offspring were allegedly birthed by low-born mothers (a distinct possibility if Anushirwan wished to attempt to reduce the influence of the great families) then his selection of Hormozd as heir is brought into even greater clarity.

Unlike his father, Hormozd apparently tried to break the ancient wheel on which the state turned. He is believed to have curried favor among the non-elite castes of Iranian society, a sure sign that the old political highwire act continued, as the kings of kings balanced their interests against those of the powerful Zoroastrian priestly families and the seven great clans of the warlords. While remembered for his incorruptible sense of justice and as zealous champion of the poor, Hormozd dallied in the same forbidden garden as many of his predecessors. Men like the two Yazdegerds (I and II) had vainly sought to refashion royal power and failed, while his grandfather and father had managed only through painstaking effort to alter by degrees the underpinnings of their society through reforms of the imperial bureaucracy and thereby shift some power to themselves. Even Anushirwan, whose reign is considered among the most successful in Sasanian history, faced down a mutinous army during his last campaign—and this after he had won numerous victories over the Romans and engineered the demolition of the ancient Hepthalite enemy in the east. If the Parthian and other Iranian nobility could not be tamed, their defiance would tear the empire apart.

Hormozd's predecessors had often played this great chess match in any number of ways, sometimes relying on the Zoroastrian magi to offset the nobles, sometimes on the nobles to attempt to check the power of the religious elites, but since there was probably great overlap in the two castes anyway, we cannot put too fine a point on these maneuvers. Given, though, the fragility of the coalition of elites on which Sasanian royal authority rested, it is somewhat surprising to witness how Hormozd greeted the Roman ambassadors. The westerners had arrived with the expectation of dealing with the aged but agreeable and tired Anushirwan, only to find his son on the throne and clearly bent on making an impression. After abusing the diplomats and making clear there would be no peace deal, Hormozd kept the ambassadors under house arrest for a long time, ensuring the Romans would make no move against him while they awaited news of their negotiations.

If Hormozd got off to such a start with his enemies, his friends fared worse. A later Arabic author leaves a vivid sketch:

> He was, moreover, well educated, skillful, and shrewd, but bad intentioned, a defect he inherited from his maternal relations, the Turks. He removed the nobles [from his court and entourage] and killed 13,600 men from the religious classes and from those of good family and noble birth.[13]

One can put no faith in the numbers, but the spirit of the autocrat certainly thrived in the person of Hormozd, who was either ill informed or unconcerned about how his ancestors' similar blood-soaked efforts to extend royal power had ended.

While from his father the shah inherited a war along the western frontier, the great king at first prioritized returning to his wing the rebel elements in his domain. To restore the disaffected Armenians and Iberians, in 580 Hormozd sent his son Khusrow to the north. The young Sasanian prince, a boy of but ten, established himself and his Persian guardsmen in Albania. Through a combination of inducements and violence, over the course of the year the country was subdued.

As the Persian prince firmed up Iranian affairs in Armenia, in the south the Ghassanid phylarch Mundhir III (569–581) had returned to enemy service and had beaten the Persian Lakhmids in battle. Later in the campaign season the Roman general Maurice divided his forces into three. He unleashed them in a great chevauchee on the lands east of the Tigris where they met little opposition and spent the whole summer in Media (northern Iran), wreaking havoc.

The following year, in 581, Maurice and his Romans returned. This time the Romans were not content with nibbling around the edges of the kingdom but aimed for a headshot as they marched down the Euphrates with the intention of crossing to the Tigris and striking at Ctesiphon. The Persians broke the bridge at Anatha on the Middle Euphrates and repelled an attempted Roman crossing, inflicting heavy losses. As the Roman offensive had left their frontier poorly guarded, Adarmahan, marzban at Nisibis, crossed the borderlands and ruined large tracts of enemy country. In Iberia, too, the Persians defeated another prong of the Roman offensive. The Romans had to console themselves with another successful Ghassanid raid on the Lakhmid town of Hira in Mesopotamia. In the aftermath of the bungled invasion of Persia, Mundir III fell under suspicion and was arrested, leaving his furious followers to ravage Roman territory south of the Euphrates.

Faced with the unraveling of his plans and under pressure on every front, the emperor Tiberius once more turned to diplomacy. The parties met near Dara where the Persian chief negotiator Andigan informed the Romans that the Persians were at a distinct advantage, having only to fight the Romans, while the westerners faced difficulties everywhere in their realm. This much was true; the Romans faced serious incursions along the Danube by the Avars, who had been driven westward following their defeat at the hands of the Western Turk khanate. In Italy, too, the Germanic Lombards had wrested most of the peninsula from the hands of the Romans, whose coffers were depleted and whose manpower was running short. From this position of strength, the Iranians decided to add to their hand, breaking off negotiations. Hormoz ordered Tamkhusro at the head of a mostly cavalry army into the Roman countryside around Constantia where Maurice opposed him. Adarmahan and his forces from Nisibis reinforced the Iranian troops committed to the offensive. In June 582, the Persians marched on Constantia and cordoned the city, but during a battle outside the walls, Tamkhusro fell, struck by an enemy lance. Alongside the Sasanian commander fell three other Iranian leaders, and the army retreated. The defeat at Constantia was not serious, however, since the Iranian army remained intact, harassing the Romans and raiding into September.

In 582, Hormozd sent his lieutenant the Kardarigan (a title that means "Black Hawk")[14] to oppose a Roman invasion. By now the former general Maurice (582–602) had risen to the imperial throne, and he was determined to once more press affairs in the east. The Kardarigan met the army of the new Roman eastern commander, John Mystacon, in battle on the river Nymphius, not far from Nisibis, and the Sasanians proved victorious. Over the next four years, this circle of raid and counterraid continued annually, with little change of momentum on either side. In the spring of 586, the Persians offered peace in exchange for money—an almost certain sign that the Sasanians were experiencing rising tensions in the east, where full-scale war would soon break out. The Romans rebuffed these overtures and instead offered battle to the forces led by Kardarigan on the plain of Solachon, east of Dara in northern Mesopotamia.

At the start of the battle, the Persian left wing was beaten and retreated, allowing the Romans to flank the Iranians and plunder the baggage train. At the end of a slaughterous battle, in which both enemy centers were said to have stood on the corpses of the slain, the Iranian right was defeated and the Kardarigan's remaining men were forced to retreat. One portion of the army, probably the newly routed right wing, fled as far as Dara, pursued by the Romans over the twelve miles that lay between the battlefield and that city. After being hemmed in on top of a hill for several days, the Sasanians broke through the Roman lines but not before some miserable souls had perished from thirst. In the chaos that erupted in the wake of their defeat at Solachon, the Persians were in no position to oppose the Roman invasion of Arzanene, north of Nisibis, that followed. Upon the Kardarigan's return to Dara, the garrison and colonists there refused to open the gates to one who, through his loss, had brought infamy upon himself. Thus humiliated, the general was forced aside.

When he learned of the enemy general Philippicus's advance into the hinterlands north of Nisibis and siege of the Persian city of Chlomaron, Kardarigan rallied the survivors of the Battle of Solachon and a militia of farmers. Alongside the city garrison, his men forced the attacking force to retreat. During the following campaign season, in 587, the Persians did little to oppose a Roman raid into the region northeast of Dara, probably because hostilities with the western half of the great Turk khanate had already erupted, and Hormozd had to pour men and resources into the east. Despite this, the great king continued the war in the west, a move which was likely deeply unpopular. When full-scale war against the Turk broke out in 588, Hormozd appointed to supreme leadership the hero of the Battle of Dara a decade and a half prior, Bahram Chobin. Bahram was scion of the Mihr family, direct descendants of the ancient princely house of the Parthian Arsacids, who had ruled the Middle East until their overthrow at the hands of the Sasanian Ardashir.

Fortunately for the king of kings, his enemies along his western frontier were paralyzed, as Roman troops there mutinied with the news that the emperor had drastically reduced their pay, crippling their efforts and buying Hormizd precious space in which he could pivot to confront his enemies in the east. In the summer of 588, Bahram Chobin marched east from Ctesiphon to counter Western Turk aggression, whose northern Hephthalite proxies had entered Sasanian Khurasan. Bahram's forces likely numbered closer to twenty thousand rather than the twelve thousand men traditionally assigned him.[15] In wind-scored hills of Badghis north of Herat, in the scorching heat of July, Bahram's outnumbered Persians ambushed the Hephthalites and cut them to pieces.

On the heels of their shocking victory in the east, the Sasanians seized the initiative in the west: between April 4–7, 589, their army captured the important Roman city of Martyropolis, the fall of which dealt a serious blow to Roman morale and the integrity of the frontier, which was already reeling from the loss of Dara. By July, though, a Roman army had arrived at Martyropolis. In a sharp engagement that followed, Mahbod was killed, but the Persian marzban of Armenia, Farhad, reinforced the Iranian garrison and saved it from being overrun.

In the same year, Bahram's eastern army marched to the banks of the Oxus. The Sasanian host forded the great river near Tirmid and boldly engaged the thirty-thousand-man Western Turk army led by Bagha Khan, and this force, too, Bahram's men dealt a heavy defeat.[16] As the battle turned against him, the Kök Turk leader Bagha Khan took refuge on a hilltop where tradition holds that Bahram Chobin felled the great Turk with an arrow loosed from his bow; among the Persian people, the shot would be remembered forever.

The great king did not long savor his victory. On the western front, not far from Nisibis, the Romans handed a defeat to the shah's armies. Among the slain was Farhad, Iranian commander in Armenia. Those Iranian soldiers who escaped to their bivouac near Nisibis became mutinous, likely due to the economizing measures of Hormozd. These included cutting army pay by a tenth and disbanding several regiments of cavalry—another blow leveled against the aristocratic classes who staffed the horse.

As the most outstanding member of the greatest of the seven noble houses, the Mihranid family, Bahram offered a vessel into which flowed the streams of disaffection that gathered over the empire. Something strange and new swirled in the winds that roared against the foundations of the empire: thousands of Zoroastrians whispered or felt their hearts beating as they heard of the ancient prophecy. The calculations of the magi were clear enough; they were living in the end of the age, the last days when out of the darkness a prince would arise, an apocalyptic lord of the end times known as Kay Bahram Varjavand. His shoulders heavy with the woes of his fellow nobles, the kingdom in the grip of a deranged monarch, and the great families of the realm clamoring for a new order, Bahram raised the flag of revolt and marched on Ctesiphon.

Hormozd soon learned of his subordinate's treachery and sent an army to block Bahram's path and shield the capital. Support, though, for the tyrannical Hormozd vanished like a block of ice under a July sun. Among the host sent to oppose the rebels, treacherous soldiers murdered their general. Inside the capital, the young Sasanian prince Khusrow, Hormizd's son and former viceroy in Azerbaijan, joined his maternal uncles, Bestam and Bendoy, in fomenting a palace coup. The cabal cast the great king Hormizd into prison and seized power.

As the armies of Bahram bore down on the royal capital, the trio of Khusrow and his handlers, Bestam and Bendoy, rallied to their side faithful remnants of the western armies. Amidst the searing heat of the dying summer of 589 and into the winter of 590, Khusrow's authority slid through his grasp like so much sand. To put paid to one threat, the new king executed his father Hormozd. All around the plotters were signs of treachery and men of uncertain loyalties.

Bahram's victorious army encamped near the capital, waxing in power daily as defectors came over to the Arsacid prince. Inside the royal city, cut off from any hopes of support by Bahram's blockade, the air hung thick with mistrust and fear, made more stifling by the certain knowledge that Khusrow's ad hoc army could not withstand Bahram's eastern veterans. A series of skirmishes flared along the great royal canal that ran outside the city along the Tigris, and Sasanian resistance flagged. Khusrow's men vanished into the gloom as they sought to save themselves by treachery or flight. With a handful of trusted familiars, under the cloak of darkness Khusrow skulked out of the city and took the only route that remained open to him, the road to the west and to the Roman border at Circesium. There his party received a hospitable welcome from the local military commander, who forwarded news of his distinguished visitor to the emperor.

At the start of spring 591, Bahram was crowned Bahram VI, king of kings, during the traditional festivities of Nowruz, the Zoroastrian New Year. In distant Constantinople, the emperor Maurice heard sympathetically the appeal of the deposed Sasanian prince and weighed his offers alongside those of Bahram, who urged the emperor's neutrality. Despite their source, a parricide and regicide, the emperor struck a bargain with the Sasanian. Although Maurice is remembered as a cautious, conservative emperor, few would have assumed the risks he bore.

The emperor took the extraordinary step to equip a Roman army to aid the deposed prince's bid for the throne. Khusrow swiftly moved to Constantia and his agents crossed into Persian territory where they drew men to his side with notable success. This was true not only in Persian Armenia and Albania, where Khusrow was known among the warrior elite and apparently liked, but also at Martyropolis, where the Persian garrison surrendered. Ctesiphon's greatest failure came at Nisibis, where the garrison transferred its allegiance to his opponent, a defection that cut to the quick. Clearly, despite his illustrious pedigree, Bahram Chobin faced strong headwinds in consolidating his power.

Inside Persia, bitter division rent the great ruling families. The Mihrans, descended from the Parthians who had governed Iran for five centuries before the meteoric rise of Ardashir I, now sought to break three and a half centuries of Sasanian rule. Against the recent tumultuous reign of Hormozd, whose grave missteps and overreach tallied in Bahram's favor, the usurper had nonetheless to contend with the ogre of ideology: generations of Iranians had grown up in a world ruled by a Sasanian king; his divine right to rule had been their bread, and the heights to which the empire had risen, the butter. Had Iran not weathered great tempests before and had there not been, through many a deadly passage, a Sasanian at the helm? The return of the Arsacids, Bahram VI promised, would usher in the millennial empire and the eternal glory of Iran. For his revolution to succeed, Bahram would need not only great skill and courage but extraordinary luck.

As the snows melted and the rivers became passable through the summer of 591, an army of forty thousand Romans led by Narses and John Mystacon pressed south from Armenia into Sasanian Azerbaijan. A separate force of Bahram VI and his army of eastern cavalry, infantry, and elephants hastened to confront the enemy alliance. The Arsacid king found himself heavily outnumbered by the great coalition of Romans, Sasanians, Armenians, and Spahbad household cavalry. The encounter left many dead on both sides, but Bahram's forces were shattered, and he was forced to flee to the far east of the realm to Balkh, not far from his heroic triumph over the Turkish khan only a few years before. Khusrow's assassins caught him there and dispatched the Mihranid, whose heroic life and tragic end would be sung by the lips of poets and bards for centuries to come.

Khusrow, likely officially crowned Khusrow II in the New Year celebrations of 592, dated his reign from the previous year, when Roman arms and the Spahbad family of his uncles, Bestam and Bendoy, had placed him on the throne. The Spahbad brothers, whose Parthian origin perhaps made them natural rivals to the Mihranids, were given plum positions within the empire; Bendoy became the Sasanian vizier at the heart of royal power in Ctesiphon, while his brother replaced Bahram Chobin as commander of the northern armies. Over the five years following his restoration, Khusrow proved himself both a strategic thinker and a clever opponent; in partnership with Maurice he defused tensions in Armenia through hostage taking and siphoning off others to staff distant military posts. Despite his favoring the Christians, most publicly by the promotion of his leading wife, Shirin, the great king managed to tamp down whatever resistance emerged during the early days of his rule.

By his fifth year, however, the young king strained at the bridle. Disgusted by the muzzle he wore, thanks to his uncles, the monarch, likely now around twenty-five years of age, ordered Bestam to the capital. While en route in obedience to the royal summons, Bestam learned of the murder of his brother Bendoy and raised a rebellion that would take Khusrow some eight years to crush.

Despite his rocky start and time as an ornament of power, Khusrow would take his place as the last great ruler of his line and pass into legend as one of the most extraordinary kings of the age. Centuries later the splendor of his court, the radiance of his power, and the image of the realm he governed remained proverbial, the settings of scenes of wonder that adorned the lips of poets and bards from the borders of China to the dunes of Arabia.

> [He] was one of the outstanding kings of the dynasty in regard to bravery, one of them with the most incisive judgment, and one with the most far-sighted perceptions. . . . His strength in battle, valor, success, victo-

riousness, gathering of wealth and treasure, his good fate and fortune, reached a zenith never revealed to any king more exalted. Hence he was called Parviz "the Victorious One."[17]

Khusrow II embodied audacity matched only by plumbless ambition. On his wing his empire was destined to soar to the loftiest of heights, carried by the great king's vanity into the crested towers of oblivion, where at the end of days, lighting the world on fire, Parviz perched to watch it all burn. He earned, rightly, a reputation for cruelty and ferocity, described by a later historian as, "the terrible hunter, the lion of the east, at whose very roar distant peoples trembled and nearby peoples melted like wax."[18]

Around the corpses of his rivals, exposed to the wind and the solitude as his faith demanded, quiet ruled. In the east the great Turk khanate had been caught in the whirlwind of civil war, a throat-slitting saga that would occupy the great hordes for many years. In the west, his Roman benefactors slumbered, sated with the immense plunder their support of Khusrow's enthronement had earned them: Dara and the western Armenian marches of some two hundred kilometers' breadth, including Iberia. Along the old borderlands, only the fastnesses of Nisibis and Dvin remained in Persian hands.

Ancient people had many ideas about cyclical time. The Greek goddess Tyche, whom the Romans called Fortuna (hence the English word, fortune), was a fickle mistress. So great was the hold of Fortune and her wheel, on which one was raised, only to find ruin as the great ring descended, hurling its miserable passengers into the lowest pit of misery, that the great sixth-century philosopher Boethius, writing from a cell where he awaited execution, asked: "Do you esteem that precious happiness that you are to lose? And is this present fortune dear to thee, of whose stay you are not sure, and whose departure will breed your grief?"[19]

In 602, the great king found the irresistible wheel turning, bearing him effortlessly upward. For more than ten long years he had bided his time, tightening the noose around his enemies' necks while peace reigned. Then news arrived in his magnificent halls on the banks of the Tigris. Maurice, Khusrow's adoptive father, was undone by fate and forced parsimony; to spare the citizens of Constantinople their predations and the Roman exchequer the burden of provisioning them, his soldiers on campaign against the Slavs to the north had been ordered to winter in the frozen fields beyond the Danube.

The ringleader of their furious mutiny, a common soldier of the line named Phocas, led the blind mob into the imperial city and there gave vent to unbridled bloodlust as the head of the church and the other great men of the realm lifted not a finger. On the contrary, tired of twenty years of war and meanness, they welcomed the frothing rabble and averted their eyes in the cold night of November 23 as the soldiers killed the emperor's male children one by one, before stringing up like a common thief the leader who had seen the Romans through some of the greatest troubles of the epoch. As the lifeless corpse of Maurice swung, friendless and unaided at the last, the news of his death flew like the wind to the carpeted halls of the great king, whose magnificent palace still towers today not far from the thrumming metropolis of Baghdad.

Khusrow was alone in his grieving as he rent his garments at the news and swore awful vows of vengeance. At last the chance to free himself of the stink of his elevation, of the cloud of foreigners to whom he owed his throne, had arrived. The great king donned black robes of mourning, as did the soldiers of the royal armies. As he dressed for mourning, Khusrow also clad himself in clothes of the righteous avenger as he moved with the swiftness of a thunderbolt.[20] The criminals who slew his benefactor would be punished, and Ahura Mazda had chosen as his instrument the king of kings himself. Soon Persian messengers arrived on the Golden Horn where they sized up the pig-eyed Phocas and delivered their lord's thunderous words: the blood on his hands could be washed only by the sacrifice of men, rivers of which would flow to atone. Across Iran the summons flew, calling the men to muster from Armenia to Khurasan, from the heat of the Euphrates to the Oxus. The last great war of antiquity had begun.

CHAPTER EIGHT

The Last Great War of Antiquity

A s the year 603 opened on an icy January in Constantinople, Phocas knew his enemy would be on the march as soon as the thaws allowed them to cross the snowy mountains into Armenia. Persian armies had not taken the field in anger for more than a decade. In an era where the average male lifespan hovered around forty years, the passage of ten winters changed the face of the court and the complexion of conflict. For the great king, all omens were auspicious. All was quiet on the eastern front: Khurasan slept peacefully, safe from the Kök Turks who tore at each other's eyes in the sanguinary civil war that had raged for nearly twenty years.

A later account describes in (theatrical) detail the moment Khusrow, sensing the opportunity presented by his benefactor Maurice's murder, called for his commanders to test their mettle regarding the upcoming war with Rome:

> And after the time of mourning (Maurice), Khusrow again gathered his army, gave them gifts, and said: I prepare to take vengeance on the Romans. Which of you, most illustrious captains of the Persian host, is ready to enact my will?
>
> Then Farrukhan, an energetic man, one skilled in war, replied: I am ready to fulfill your will and able to carry the war to Rome. Nothing will deter me, nothing will move me to pity, neither respect for old age, nor tenderness of youth.

Hearing this, Khusrow was well-pleased and said to him. Henceforth you shall not be called Rumiazan, but Shahrbaraz, that is the Wild Boar [also Hero of the Realm] of the Empire.[1]

Like Bahram, the great rebel and opponent of Khusrow, whose name had passed into legend, Shahrbaraz was born into the great house of Mihran. His career would prove meteoric, blazing at the greatest of heights, only to flare out in the gathering darkness that would engulf his people.

In the west, fortune favored the Persian cause. Among the enemy, chaos reigned. The Roman commander in chief in the east, Narses, rebelled against Phocas and seized the God-guarded city of Edessa from which he approached Khusrow to aid him in seizing the throne. As the emergency unfolded, the emperor was forced to increase his tribute to the Avars, who menaced the Danube frontier from which the Romans stripped troops to rush to the east. Phocas ordered Germanus, his new magister militum of the east, to oppose Khusrow's forces. The emperor sent another army, under the eunuch Leontius, against Narses in Edessa. The rebel general fled to Hierapolis, and Leontius claimed Edessa for the emperor and then rushed east to reinforce Germanus who now faced the expeditionary force led by the great king.

At the start of the campaigning season of 603, Khusrow unleashed the weight of his Persian army along a broad front from the Caucasus to Mesopotamia, determined first to recover the territory he had surrendered for Roman assistance to regain his throne, a humiliation that the Sasanian monarch wished to wash clean with the blood of his enemies. From the sweep of the green mountains of Iberia, Sasanian troops swung into action, as Khusrow led another prong of the Persian pincer. The great king marched his forces across the Tigris and moved to strike Dara. In the summer of 603, the troops of the great king encountered the Romans under Germanus and Leontius near the river Arzamon in the Mesopotamian plain south of Mardin.[2]

Khusrow rode at the head of this wing of the Sasanian army in person and had in his train a strong unit of battle elephants. These he assembled into a fort-like formation. An obscure description, but one that we can gain insight about from the writings of the Armenian historian Ełishe, who described what appears to be a similar formation employed at the Sasanian victory at the Battle of Avarayr in 451 where the Persian leader:

> ... summoned many generals under his authority and ordered them to bring forward the companies of elephants. These he divided into various groups and assigned to each elephant three thousand armed men in ad-

dition to all the other troops. . . . He set in order the whole army and extended the battle line all the way across the great plain. He disposed the three thousand armed men to the right and left of each elephant, and surrounded himself with the elite of his warriors. In this fashion he strengthened the center like a powerful tower or an impregnable castle.[3]

This "tower" formation is reminiscent of the deployment of elephants in a later battle against the Arabs in 636 at the Battle of Qadisiyyah in Mesopotamia, where the Muslim historian Tabari describes Sasanian elephant troops deploying on the third day of the battle:

> The elephants moved forward, accompanied by infantrymen, who protected them. . . . The infantrymen were, in turn, accompanied by horsemen, who protected them. When the Persians wanted to attack a military unit, they moved toward it with an elephant and its escort in order to scare the horses . . . .[4]

At Arzamon the Sasanians employed this tactic of mixing elephants amidst a strong screen of infantry. They faced Roman troops inexperienced in facing elephants, and the advance of the great beasts spooked the Roman cavalry. Like ink spilled across paper, panic seeped through the enemy ranks. The terrified Romans broke and fled. Among the enemy losses in the battle was the marshal of the east Germanus, who suffered a grave wound. His bodyguards spirited him from the battlefield to the nearby city of Constantia, where he died from his injuries. After the victory Khusrow marched westward and, despite the lateness of the season, began the siege of the fortress city of Dara, probably in October or November. No Roman army mounted any serious opposition; Germanus's troops had scattered and were slow to regroup at Constantia; they could only helplessly watch from afar.

Streams of Roman refugees poured westward from the Euphrates frontier, choking the roads and spreading panic as the Persian advance unfurled. Dara, put to Persian siege, resisted stubbornly. It took the shahanshah some nine months to undermine the walls and thus reduce the Roman bulwark of the east, but the city fell to him in the summer of 604. The seizure of Dara punched a critical hole in enemy defenses, which the Persians were quick to exploit. While Khusrow returned to Persia, his general Shahrbaraz remained in the field. Shahrbaraz spent the following two campaign seasons reducing the heavy belt of strongholds around the Tur 'Abdin, capturing the castle of Rhabdion among others in the approaches to Dara and Edessa. Sasanian movements were largely unhindered, as only in 604/605 were the Romans able to defeat the insurrection of the former magister Narses. In the meantime, the Persians pressed their attack against the chain of forts along the frontier. In 606, the fortress of Cephas (Hasankeyf) in the salient that followed the bulge of the Tigris fell to Sasanian forces.

On the northern front, the Sasanians lashed enemy defenses. There, in the spring of 604, the general Dzuan Veh marched from Dvin in Armenia to the vicinity of Theodosiopolis where he encountered a Roman force at a walled village named Elevard. In the fighting, Dzuan Veh fell, and his force was heavily defeated. In 605, the new general in command, Datoyean, advanced into northwestern Armenia to the district of Shirak where they defeated a Roman contingent at Getik. Following the battle, the Persians massacred the Armenian troops who had fought on the Roman side. The following campaign season the Persians returned, this time led by a general named Senitam-Khusrow, who confronted a combined troop of Armenians and Romans on the banks of the Arsanias (Murat) River near the fortress of Angeł whose commander, the Armenian nakharar Theodosius Khorkhurni, had failed to negotiate a truce:

> The next day the Persian army attacked them. Not a single one of them
> [the Romans and their Armenian allies] had put on his arms or saddled
> his horse. . . . The Persian army came up and formed their opposing line
> near to them on the side of the plain. The multitude of their force
> archers drew [their bows] and emptied their quivers on them, piercing
> with their arrows all the men and horses alike. . . . The enemy [the Per-
> sians] pierced the fortifications and poured into the camp; there was a
> terrible slaughter.[5]

Theodosius negotiated the surrender of the fortress, which allowed for the evacuation of the surviving Roman troops. The Armenian commander handed over the castle and was sent to the Persian capital.

In 607–08 the Sasanians again punched at the defenses around Theodosiopolis where the new northern general, Ashtat Yestayar, defeated a Roman force in the district of Basean and received the surrender of Theodosiopolis and then advanced west to Satala in the Roman province of Armenia Prima. With this offensive, the Persians had achieved a decisive breakthrough in the north; the cities of the Anatolian plateau lay open to them.

Despite the magnitude of the struggle, we possess scant details of Persian action in Mesopotamia. There, for the Romans, years of rebellion and defeat had germinated into a thicket of woe. The enemy now confronted deeper internal troubles as a new revolution broke out—the governor of distant Roman

North Africa had equipped two forces in an attempt to topple Phocas. In 608, one group of rebels under Niketas struck overland to Egypt while the governor's son, Heraclius, prepared a flotilla against Constantinople. In Antioch, a mass uprising among the popular crowds of the chariot racing clubs and their supporters forced Phocas to send in the troops under his general Bonosus. Antioch boiled over in sectarian and political anarchy. After years of repression and tension with the Christian authorities, some Jews in the city apparently formed a fifth column in support of the Sasanians. In the infighting that erupted, the Christian patriarch Anastasius was murdered in the mob violence. To staunch the empire's internal bleeding and stop the infection of sedition from spreading, Phocas prioritized the internal threat to his power and sent his general Bonosus east where he drew off whatever Roman forces remained in the east in an attempt to reform an effective field army.

Shahrbaraz and an officer known from the Roman sources by his title, the Kardarigan, maneuvered together in the west, methodically reducing the hedge of enemy defenses along the length of the Euphrates. Not since the reign of Shapur I had there been such a methodical, multipronged Sasanian attack against the age-old western enemy. But this time the flavor of the Persian attack had a decidedly different taste: the Sasanians had come not as pillagers but as conquerors and colonizers. From Armenia down to the Tigris *limes* and south to the Euphrates, the Persians signaled their intention to stay. Tribute and taxes were levied and Persian garrisons and commanders installed. Over the course of the war, the Persians deported large numbers of Armenians and Romans and funneled them east into the imperial heartland. There the deportees would both add to the economic prosperity of the realm and find it more difficult to rebel. Local populations found new Christian bishops installed in their cities. At times these were members of the anti-Chalcedonian creed that prevailed over most of Syria, or another Christian sect referred to as Nestorians; both were considered heretical by the imperial authorities in Constantinople, and the buttressing of the local Christian creeds indicates Khusrow cleverly exploited religious divisions to further alienate the subject population from their former Roman masters.[6]

As the rebellion of Heraclius and Niketas siphoned off the remaining enemy defenders, Sharhbaraz and his fellow general the Kardarigan systematically reduced their defenses. The great prizes awaited them as the Sasanians made a victorious march into the eastern Roman provinces. In 606/7, the key city of Mardin (Izala) fell in the north; the latter had been abandoned by the enemy when they had learned of the fall of Cephas six months prior. The famous redoubt of Amida soon followed and accepted a Persian garrison. In 607 or 609, Resaina (Theodosiopolis) fell into Sasanian hands and Edessa surrendered to the Persians.

In 609, at Callinicum, Shahrbaraz continued the Persian offensive in the south, capturing the fortress city at the confluence of the Khabur and Euphrates Rivers. With these cities in their grip, Khusrow's forces had crushed the last impediments to his progress in Syria; they could turn into central Anatolia or move south into the rich lands of Syria and Palestine as they wished.

In 610, matters for the enemy turned even more grave—the rebel Heraclius had defeated Phocas's forces under Bonosus in Egypt and were consolidating their hold there. Throughout the east, the civilian population quavered in fear, their loyalties to the government in Constantinople tested beyond breaking as the Persians threatened to sweep aside the last vestiges of imperial resistance. As Heraclius seized power in Constantinople in October 610, the general Comentiolus and his fighters declared their hostility and holed up in Ancyra (Ankara) in central Anatolia. Along the Euphrates, by no later than 610, Shahrbaraz reduced one by one the garland of enemy fortress cities along the great river, including Zenobia, which fell in August 610. The nearby cities of Sura, Sergiopolis, and Barbalissos (Meskene) and others on the west bank of the river likely capitulated around the same time. Shahrbaraz therefore consolidated the gains made in the prior year, and by the end of the season the entire course of the Middle Euphrates had fallen into Persian hands. This provided the forces of the shahanshah command of the major routes into Syria and Arabia, as well as bases of supply and administrative centers. Once bulwarks of the powerful Roman defenses, the captured burgs were now sources of vexation for the Romans and their new emperor, Heraclius.

Upon acceding to the throne, Heraclius forwarded lavish gifts to Khusrow along with pleas for peace. The great king cheerlessly refused to hear their calls for parley and had the unfortunate messengers decapitated. The Roman Empire, he informed Heraclius and his men, by right belonged to the great king, avenger of Maurice. To underscore his point, as the campaign season of 611 dawned, the king unbridled two potent forces to make deep cuts into the ailing body of the foe to the north and south. After centuries of coexistence, with a grudging respect and mutual understanding of the opponent empire as an uncomfortable fact of life, Khusrow had decided to break the wheel of history. No longer would the fight be between those cast as equals, as brothers who might disagree and brawl and then patch up their differences through an exchange of gifts and money. Henceforth the "twin eyes of the world," as the warring states had portrayed themselves, would lock in a decisive struggle which would leave only one hegemon. One of the eyes must be blinded.

If the opening act of the war can be likened to a chess match—a favorite game of the kings of kings—with probes and thrusts to test the foe and movements that showed a deep understanding for the enemy and his castles, his roads, his bridges, and his great, wealthy cities that the web of Roman defenses protected, then the second act of the war resembled a horse race, as Sasanian armies rushed through the gaps that their methodical preparations in the first decade of the seventh century had opened to them.

Khusrow opened this round of the clash of imperial behemoths by sending Shahin against the northern front in Armenia. Shahin moved swiftly beyond the former boundaries between the states and massed his troops against the metropolis of Caesarea in Cappadocia. This city, today cool in the summer with pleasant, shady boulevards, lies at the foot of Mount Argaeus (Erciyes), a dormant volcano that juts nearly four thousand meters (12,851 feet) into the sky. The mountain looms over the black walled city, whose fortifications Justinian had renovated. Roman engineers had shortened and strengthened the defensive perimeter into a stout refuge. On the approach of the troops of the great king, the citizens of this agreeable, well-watered city had no stomach to defend their homes, and the Christian population scattered in all directions. As elsewhere throughout the Roman east, the Jewish population of Caesarea welcomed Shahin and his men as liberators from Roman Christian oppression.[7] By the end of the summer, the Persians had garrisoned the city, which offered them command over key routes over the Anatolian plateau and opened the weakly defended interior of Asia Minor to conquest.

Shahrbaraz and his troops formed the tip of the spear in the south. Moving with speed, the Sasanian lord prized Antioch, the crown jewel of Syria, from the Roman diadem. The famous metropolis, renowned for its riches and high culture, had been in turmoil since its rough handling two years prior by the troops of Phocas under Bonosus, whose bloodletting had earned the enduring hostility of the population. From Antioch, Shahrbaraz turned south and marched down the highway, burning and pillaging as he went. As they rolled on in their summer offensive the Sasanians captured the capital of the province of Syria Secunda, the unfortunate metropolis of Apamea, which the Persians visited and seized for the third time in less than a century. Shahrbaraz also pried from the enemy the important Roman garrison town of Chalcis, a key point fronting the vast Syrian steppe, and the city Emesa (Homs) on the Orontes River. In the same expedition, Persian soldiers also seized the ancient, strategic cities of Beroea (Aleppo) and Hierapolis (Manbij). The road to Palestine, one of the richest regions of the empire long untouched by war, lay open. The enemy, riven as they were by internal conflict and ground down by constant defeat, were in no position to oppose them.

Only late in 611, when Heraclius had eliminated the threat from Comentiolus at Ancyra, were the Romans able to take the field. The old general Priscus, whose previous command in the east had been more than two decades prior, was called upon to lead. At Caesarea, Shahin and his Persian troops prepared the defenses and brought in supplies to endure a siege. By autumn the enemy surrounded the city. Shahin successfully defended the city throughout the winter and spring, and in the summer of 612 the canny Sasanian shrugged off the Roman cordon and moved into Armenia to pass the winter. The following spring, Shahin thrust his troops against Roman units holed up in the strong legionary base at Melitene. Persian forces broke the defenses, captured the city, and then maneuvered to link up with Shahrbaraz and the southern expeditionary force to face an impending Roman counterattack.

Heraclius found the imperial high command bereft of experienced, talented commanders on whose loyalty he could count. Priscus was cashiered on charges of disloyalty, and the emperor turned to another old war dog from his father's years of service in the east during the time of Maurice—Philippicus, last seen in the Roman east more than two decades prior. Called from retirement, Philippicus would lead the northern arm of the Roman counterstrike. In an exceptional turn, the emperor himself took the field at the head of the southern command. For nearly two and a half centuries, no emperor had led imperial troops in person. The last to do so was the star-crossed soldier-emperor Valens, who lost his life in the Gothic War on the field at Adrianople in 378. Heraclius cobbled together a scratch force comprised of his original rebels and Roman units from the eastern army, called the Anatolics, and remaining units of the imperial campaign army, the so-called praesental forces. Berber tribesmen from North Africa had provided a significant portion of the manpower during his rebellion, and these men likely rode alongside their master.

As the elderly Philippicus traversed the dusty plateau of Anatolia at the head of a mixed force of Romans collected from remnants of the broken army of Armenia, it was soon joined by whatever nakharars from the mountains who remained loyal to the Roman cause. As the enemy drew near, Khusrow rushed troops from Iran to counter the threat to the recently reclaimed lands in Armenia. After a series of forced marches into the rugged uplands, the Persians were too exhausted to offer battle, but their presence forced the Romans away. The feint of Philippicus had accomplished its objective to draw away troops from the main fight, which was to unfold farther south on the plains in northern Syria.

In the summer of 613, the Persians met the Roman counterstroke near Antioch and, after a hard-fought, sanguineous engagement, routed them. After the Sasanian vanguard suffered heavy losses, the main army engaged and turned the battle. The shah's men pursued the retreating Romans into the sweep of fertile lands that curves from the hills of Antioch to the ancient pass over the Taurus Mountains at the Cilician Gates. There the Persian vanguard locked in a sharp struggle and were beaten, but the arrival of the main line of Persian forces turned the battle and the enemy broke and fled. Roman casualties were high, up to eight thousand men killed. With the victories at Antioch and in Cilicia, the Persians severed the land routes from Asia Minor to the prosperous provinces of Syria and Palestine, making Roman aid to these exposed regions possible only by sea. It also gave the Sasanians access to the eastern Mediterranean seaboard, with its host of maritime cities filled with merchants, mariners, and shipbuilders. The king would waste little time taking to the sea—the first return of the Iranians to the Mediterranean in force since the days of the great Greek and Persian wars a thousand years prior.

During the same campaign, Shahrbaraz descended on the route from Homs to Damascus, where he received the famous garden city's surrender. The king's men rode on, subjugating Caesarea, the capital of Roman Palestine. His soldiers then fanned out to seize the region of Galilee with its many holy places tied to the earliest days of Christianity. Early in 614, the "Wild Boar" of Persia unleashed his troops along the uplands of the Golan and occupied the Jordan Valley, which offered paltry resistance, as Palestine had been largely stripped of its troops during the rebellion of Heraclius. With enemy arms shattered and the Sasanians occupying the approaches to the south, a glorious prize now lay within reach of the Persians—the most sacred Christian spot in the world, the holy city of Jerusalem.

In early 614, Shahrbaraz stood outside the walls of the City of David. Like those in a litany of cities to have capitulated to Iranian arms without struggle, the citizens of Jerusalem surrendered and accepted Persian officials. Days later, an insurgent group inside the walls murdered the newly installed Sasanian governor, closed the gates, and braced for war. A Roman relief force hastily collected from among nearby frontier soldiers at Jericho and led by a local monk hurried to the city. On sight of the Persian forces encamped at the walls they ran away.

A contemporary writer described the siege and the ad hoc citizen army defending their homes:

Possessed of a steadfast mind, they kept the approaching Persian from the strong walls by showers of missiles and rocks. Then indeed, with raging spirits, the Persian, barbarian that he was, after thousands of clashes, employed siege engines. Having set fires everywhere beneath the wall, (as well as) an army of siege engines, he destroyed the strong wall and came to be inside the city. Equipped with bloody sword, he cut down the people . . . .[8]

After a nineteen-day siege Shahrbaraz's artillery smashed a stretch of the city walls and his men poured through the fractured defenses. The city was put to the sword. Iranian troops unleashed their fury on the inhabitants of (as they saw it) a turncoat city—a deception paid for in heaps of treasure and rivers of blood. The loss of life was great, and alongside the dead, the entire empire wept at the news that the Persians had seized one of the greatest of all holy relics, the True Cross, on which Christ was believed to have been crucified. The holy tree was loaded onto a cart and hauled, along with thousands of captives, back to Iran. As Persian soldiers ranged throughout the countryside and chaos gripped the land, thousands of Romans fled south to Egypt, the last territory in Roman hands in the eastern Mediterranean.

Buoyed by his success in the Levant, Khusrow set his eyes on the ultimate prize—the capture of Constantinople. With Heraclius's men reeling in defeat and the frontier defenses smashed, the road to the capital lay open. Khusrow could scarcely believe his fortune. In ten years' time his armies had achieved the likes of which his predecessors could only distantly dream; the great king stood at the threshold of conquering the age-old western foe. Aiming another critical blow at the reeling body of the enemy, in 615 the shahanshah ordered Shahin westward at the head of a force that plunged a sword through the belly of the Roman heartland in Asia Minor. Shahin's victorious march culminated in his arrival on the Bosporus shores opposite the imperial capital. Persian arms now stood at Chacledon (today the suburb of Kadıköy, Istanbul), 1,635 kilometers (1,016 miles) from the capital of Ctesiphon. Heraclius came aboard the royal yacht to meet Shahin. The Sasanian general received his rival warmly and welcomed the discussions that followed. The emperor lavished gifts on the general and dispatched other treasures to Khusrow, along with an urgent renewal of his pleas for peace. Khusrow accepted the gifts but refused to respond to the peace feelers.

War raged on in the following year, which Persian forces under Shahin spent targeting enemy cities holding out in the interior of Asia Minor. Rich pickings were to be found in the renowned cities of western Asia Minor, famous from the time of the era of Greek colonization of the land a millennium prior: Sardis, birthplace of King Midas; Ephesus, the city of the goddess Artemis, whose temple had been one of the ancient wonders of the world, now a famous Christian center after the death of the old pantheon of gods; Miletus; Pergamum; and Smyrna. These are but a few of the cities that the troops of the great king seized in the years 616–18. Like shining coins from a rent purse, they dropped one by one into Sasanian hands. The flood of captives and cartloads of treasure poured east like the monsoon rains that scoured the eastern reaches of his empire.

Then, while the wheel of fortune carried Khusrow higher and higher along its sweep, an old foe seized the spokes. In 614 or 615, sensing the moment ripe to shake off the yoke of Khusrow, the empire's Hephthalite subjects south of the Oxus rose in rebellion, led by a king holding sway over Balkh. Since the lands south of the Oxus had been ceded to the Sasanians following their joint defeat with Turkish help in the war of Bahram Chobin, the war on the eastern front was more an uprising against Iranian rule than simply a foreign invasion. Supported by the khagan of the Western Turks, the Hepthalites thundered across the frontier into Khurasan.

To meet the barbarian storm, the Sasanian king summoned from retirement a feisty old hand of many wars, the Armenian marzban of Persian Armenia, Smbat Bagratuni (607–616/7). Smbat had won fame over decades spent fighting for both the Romans and the Persians. The salty veteran led two thousand Armenian and Persian heavy cavalry and horse archers from their headquarters in Hyrcania south of the Caspian. Near Nishapur, the Armenian and Persian troop snared a raiding force of Kushan cavalry and trounced them. Soon after, Smbat and his followers found themselves facing down rebel reinforcements, strengthened by Turks from Transoxiana. Surrounded in a fortified village near Nishapur, Smbat sent urgent pleas for aid to Ctesiphon. The new Persian arrivals were severely defeated and driven back, but the Armenian commander took advantage of the battlefield confusion to make his escape to Khusrow, who exonerated the prince from the debacle and renewed his command.

In 615, Smbat led a large Sasanian-Armenian troop to the northeast frontier where he encountered a force comprised mainly of insurgent Hepthalites but backed too by Western Turk warriors. To decide the affair, one of the Kushan kings challenged Smbat to hand-to-hand combat:

> Coming out from either side [of the armies], they rapidly confronted each other. Between the two battle-lines they fought with each other.

They were not able immediately to overcome the other, because they were both men of gigantic strength and fully covered in armor. But help came from on high: the armor of the Kushan king, chain-mail from Balkh and a solid cuirass, was split by Smbat's lance, and he powerfully struck him as a corpse to the ground and slew him. When his army saw their king [killed], they were terrified and turned to flight. The others [the Armenians] pursued them with cavalry attacks as far as Balkh, the capital of the Kushans, and they plundered the whole country.[9]

The war in the east ended with the death of the Kökturk khagan in 614. Upon the accession of his son the Kökturks pivoted their ambitions to the east, where the Chinese Sui dynasty was crumbling and where the Turks sought opportunity for conquest and plunder amidst the wealth and splendor of the east. With the threat in the east temporarily squelched, Khusrow renewed his western offensive. The Persians launched a battle fleet in the Mediterranean and invaded Cyprus, where they attacked the rich city of Salamis. Although part of the island apparently fell into their hands, the Sasanians diverted their forces to a richer prize to the south.

By 618 Sasanian forces had made a strategic pivot, redeploying forces to their imperial juggernaut to face south even as they consolidated their administration and logistical organization in preparation for the next phase of their grand offensive. That year, Sharhbaraz and Shahin combined their armies for a push into the ancient land of Egypt. The rich lands on the Nile, which had known no foreign invader since the days of Julius Caesar, now tasted Persian steel. Alexandria, the most populous and vibrant city of the Levant, was betrayed to the army of the Wild Boar. In June 619, Persian soldiers paraded in triumph into the metropolis, home to upward of a half million souls. The city was the gateway to the whole of Egypt, and its surrender meant the end of organized Roman resistance. Persian forces methodically advanced south. By 621 Shahrbaraz's men had mopped up the remaining holdouts and captured the vast countryside to the First Cataract of the Nile and the Nubian frontier at Aswan, a journey of more than two thousand kilometers (1,242 miles) from the imperial capital at Ctesiphon.

Khusrow's empire now embraced a huge sweep of Asia and Africa, from the Hindu Kush to the shores of the Sea of Marmara and from the Oxus to the Nile. His troops swept unhindered to surround the last islands of resistance in Asia Minor. There the city of Nicomedia had somehow avoided prior Sasanian capture but fell to the forces of Shahin around the time of Alexandria's seizure. As the great king pondered his long reign, now amidst its thirtieth year, he could be content with how well earned was his epithet, Parviz, "the Victorious." From his overthrow in 590 and desperate hours in flight to the Romans, to the humiliation of begging for crumbs from the enemy table and his risky scrabbling back to power, Khusrow can be forgiven for viewing himself as an anointed figure. By 622 it appeared to the Iranian world, at least, that the great king enjoyed the special anointing of Ahura Mazda, called on to carry Persian greatness to lofty new pinnacles, and to thereby restore order to the universe. Blessed with such good fortune, few men could maintain a steady disposition, and it seems that the great king indulged the worst of his nature, becoming even more despotic and domineering. His men fanned out through the new conquests and plundered the churches, hauling the gold and silver liturgical vessels and even the rich marble cladding of the Christian temples back to Ctesiphon. The farmers and townsfolk of his new conquests, their taxes poured in streams into the imperial coffers where the mints spit out coins that depicted the Sasanian king of kings on both sides as world conqueror with the inscription "Khusrow, King of Kings, has increased royal glory, has increased Iran, [he is] well-omened."[10]

Hostile to the king as the surviving sources are, there is little doubt that the captured former Roman provinces found the Persian boot to their neck and suffered as the Iranians took what they viewed as theirs by right of conquest:

> They pillaged and took innumerable captives. They brought into Persia riches, prisoners and all manner of things. They even brought there a good many marble columns and altar tables from Asia Minor, Syria and the other western lands. Khosrow acted harshly towards the people in his realm. The power of speech is not capable of recounting the oppression, the exaction of taxes and tribute, the enslavement and slaughter that went on at that time, as Khosrow behaved arrogantly due to the victory of the Persians.[11]

In 622 the Persians pressed their advance to the west, where they captured the strategic central Anatolian city of Ancyra. Despite their successes in the region, the Persian presence in Asia Minor remains foggy; while the Sasanians installed administrators and moved colonists into Palestine and Syria along with garrisons, they preferred to despoil the cities of Asia Minor. At sea, a Sasanian fleet operated in the Aegean and the Mediterranean, taking the island of Rhodes and other islands. A millennium of Greek civilization, a light that burned long before the arrival of the great god-king Alexander in the fourth century BC, sputtered and burned down. The light which would illumine western Eurasia belonged to the sacred fires of Zoroastrianism. In the coming years the Sasanians foresaw the hour when the eternal flame of Ahura Mazda blazed in sanctuaries from Thrace to the Indus and Persian replaced Greek in the streets of Antioch, Alexandria, and Constantinople. Their ascendancy was so swift, so decisive, that a contemporary could but gape in wonder at the fickle turn of fortune that carried the great king to ever greater heights.

The Roman enemy, prone under the weight of repeated disasters, faced the deepest crisis of their long history.[12] Foes beset them on all sides. The Persian lion prowled across the east. In Italy, Germanic Lombard invaders made a mockery of attempts to halt their inexorable advance. In the Balkans, the nomadic Avars had conquered the Slavic peoples north of the Danube and exerted their will on the empire, destroying and plundering as their strength revived in the wake of the chaos gripping Constantinople in the wake of Maurice's death. Heraclius's own record was wobbly at best; his decision to confront the Persians in the decisive battle outside Antioch had broken the last of his armies and opened the riches of Egypt to Khusrow's men. Bankrupt and laid low, the emperor turned to the churches remaining within his territories and obtained a loan of their remaining plate, which he melted down to revive the corpse of his bludgeoned army. With fresh forces levied and drilled, the Roman emperor struck out into Anatolia to staunch the bleeding there.

In the summer the Romans advanced east where Shahrbaraz moved to intercept them as they made for Caesarea in Cappadocia. Heraclius outmaneuvered the Persians and skirted northward by another way. Clearly the army led by Heraclius was formidable, comprised not only of native Romans but mercenaries recruited around Europe, and had to be dealt with cautiously. Shahrbaraz now hesitated—he considered different stratagems with which to deal with this sudden resurgence of Roman arms. He considered moving into Cilicia and then to Persia where his army could expect reinforcements. A second option was to attack the Romans directly along their route to the east. The Persians feared an invasion of this magnitude approaching from the north. Awaiting reinforcements, Shahrbaraz kept his forces in close contact with the enemy as they marched eastward. Skirmishes and probing of the enemy told him that this was a well-trained, well-equipped force, and subsequent actions would prove his suspicions correct. The emperor could only apply a tourniquet to the regions where such heavy losses had been suffered. Soon Heraclius had to scurry back west to meet a new crisis that flared in the Balkans, where the Avars and their Slav subjects pressed their attacks.

Along the Long Wall, the defensive perimeter west of Constantinople that braced the peninsula on which the capital perched, the Roman emperor parleyed with his Avar adversaries on June 5, 623. The foes' duplicity was revealed when they sprung from ambush and tried to grab the person of Caesar and haul him into captivity. Thanks to a disguise and the fleetness of a thoroughbred Roman horse, Heraclius made his escape by a hair's breadth as the Avars tore through the suburbs of the capital, seizing captives and rich plunder, including priceless holy relics, among them the robe of the Virgin Mary held in one of the suburban churches. After this debacle, the emperor's men restored order only with difficulty. Faced with no choice, the Romans accepted humbling terms from the barbarian Avars.

Whether distracted elsewhere or determined not to anchor their forces so far from the richest territories of Syria, Palestine, and Egypt, the Persians did not post a heavy guard in Asia Minor. Thus, when Heraclius ferried his troops across the Bosporus and began the long march up country, no serious Iranian force barred his progress. Ancyra fell into Roman hands, and the enemy was able, by the summer of 624, to ensconce themselves in the vital city of Caesarea in Cappadocia where Roman arms had last been seen a dozen years prior. By now the great king had been roused to action and marched west to meet the latest challenge from the crippled empire. Khusrow marshaled his forces southeast of Lake Urmia at Ganzak (near modern Laylan), scene of his final triumph over Bahram Chobin decades prior. There, forty thousand soldiers at his train, the king of kings prepared for the final confrontation. As intelligence flowed into his encampment, Khusrow made a critical error, concluding that the enemy would, as he had done in 613, cross the Taurus Mountains via the Cilician Gates south of Caesarea in a thrust intended to oust the Iranians from Antioch and thereby open the path to the lands of Syria.

Instead, Heraclius marched his troops along the northern Roman trunk road, past Silvan, and into Persian Armenia where his army cut a broad swathe of devastation by fire and sword. Moving down the Araxes River valley, no opposing forces barred the way, and the westerners' march continued toward the Shahanshah's base at Ganzak. One author claims that, on hearing the news of the emperor's temerity, the great king exclaimed, "Is this not he who was plunged into an abyss of fear for me? But now, what is this?"[13]

Suddenly and inexplicably, the Persians scattered like driven sand, as if by the breath of God to whom the English and Dutch ascribed their miracle victory centuries later over the Spanish Armada: "By the blast of God they perish, and by the breath of his nostrils they are they consumed," the Persians panicked.[14] Following the inexplicably poor showing, Khusrow managed to scrape together a force to shadow the enemy, who wintered in the Kura valley in Caucasian Albania.

As the Persian force under the general Shahrplakan surveilled throughout the winter months, the Roman host swelled with allied contingents recruited by Heraclius among the Albanians, Iberians, and Armenians. At the same time, the emperor sent an embassy to the khagan of the Western Turks, seeking their intervention on his side in the titanic struggle.

Khusrow managed to seize the initiative as the campaign season of 625 began. Three Persian hosts, one led by Shahrplakan, barred the way to the Persian lands southwest of the Caspian, which the enemy threatened. Shahrbaraz moved with his forces from his base in Nisibis to maneuver behind the Romans in Persian Armenia. Finally, thirty thousand troops under Shahin stationed themselves in the south of Armenia, in the high country southwest of Lake Van astride the Bitlis Pass. With these three forces, numbering at least seventy thousand and perhaps as many as ninety thousand, the Persians pinned the enemy in Albania. Slowly they would tighten the noose around the neck of the emperor until he was forced to turn and fight at the time and place of the great king's choosing. These bold maneuvers were not without risk—to supply and synchronize large armies scattered across a triangle of land from near the shores of the Caspian into the Armenian highlands. To close the envelopment, the Sasanians would need flawless communications and command.

In the spring of 625, Heraclius assumed a position near the great inland sea with Shahrplakan and his levies close behind. Alerted to the great maws of the Persian trap sent to snap on him, the emperor launched relentless attacking swarms against Shahrplakan, who retreated to link up with Shahrbaraz. By the time his exhausted and demoralized forces joined, led by the Wild Boar, they were hardly fit for scratch. Hearing from Roman deserters that the emperor was fleeing in fear, Shahrbaraz marched in pursuit. The report of the headlong flight of the Romans was likely a ruse. When Shahrbaraz caught up with the enemy army, he planned a surprise dawn attack, only to find that the Romans had stolen a march on him. Shahrbaraz lost control of his men, who surged south after the enemy whom they believed were panicked and collapsing into disorder. As the Sasanian vanguard caught sight of the opposing force, it was not a terrified rabble but a carefully drawn up formation packed on a hill, their flanks screened by a dense forest. The Roman counterattack against the ramshackle Persian onslaught ended in a rout, culminating in the wounding of Shahrplakan, who was run through the back with a sword.

The arrival of Shahin's third force should have reversed Sasanian fortunes, but he too found his troops defeated. The camp and baggage were captured as the Iranian soldiery and their general dashed to save their skins. As the two surviving generals recovered and collected their scattered troops, the Romans dogged their trek up the Araxes River valley past Nakhchivan. In a running battle, Sasanian cavalry units constantly challenged the Roman line of march, but Heraclius refused battle, maintained discipline, and took up winter quarters near the shores of Lake Van. As the winter snows clad the mountains, the Armenians in Persian service dispersed for the season, while Shahrbaraz settled in to wait out the cold at Archesh (Erci , eastern Turkey). With his scouts reporting that the bulk of the Persian force had departed, Heraclius launched a surprise attack on Shahrbaraz's headquarters, and though the incident is much exaggerated in the sources, the Romans plundered a great deal of loot and the Wild Boar barely escaped with his life, further damaging Persian prestige and adding substantially to Heraclius's growing reputation.

In 626, the Persians maintained tremendous advantages over the foe. They outnumbered them in the field, had far greater material resources, and despite their recent setbacks, had two seasoned, capable generals who had proven successful over multiple campaigns. The scales balanced as they were, the great king ripped a page from his enemy's book and took the fight once more to the Roman heartlands. Khusrow thereby shielded his own territories from devastation and trained a blow against Constantinople. In preparation for the summer offensive, Persian emissaries arrived in the court of the Avar khagan on the Hungarian Plain north of the Danube and sealed an alliance. Aided by a Persian thrust into Anatolia, which would defeat or draw away Roman forces, the Avars would attack the capital. After the Avars claimed the capital, they would rule over the European portion of the former empire while the Persians would control Asia. The twin strokes, if brought home, would end the war and with it the long history of Rome.[15]

Shahin had made good his losses, reinforced with a bevy of new recruits stiffened by veterans of the triumphant blitz of the east. His troops ground westward through Roman Armenia, past Theodosiopolis, and along the ancient Persian Royal Road from Achaemenid times. Once their threat to the capital became clear, the Persians anticipated that Heraclius would abandon his offensive through Armenia into the heartland of Iran. The Wild Boar and Shahin would then harry the imperial forces across Anatolia and destroy them and thus free the path to the capital.

Once more, Heraclius caught the Persians unawares. Before the end of winter, on March 1, the emperor departed his seasonal quarters and, in another turn, opted against the direct march through the north country. Instead, the enemy host passed through the warmer and well-stocked lands of Cilicia and thence through the Taurus Mountains via the Cilician Gates. Behind, Shahrbaraz collected his forces and set out in pursuit. His army caught the Romans along the Euphrates and unmoored the pontoon bridge where the enemy sought to cross. Undaunted, and to the consternation of the Persians, Heraclius found a spot along the river whose furious currents, swollen by snowmelt, would make any crossing hazardous to the point of suicidal. Probably because of the delay of warmer weather in the northlands, the Romans were able to ford the Euphrates and continue their march, Shahrbaraz in pursuit. The general harried the Romans across Syria and into the heart of the Cilician Plain, but the pesky emperor stubbornly held a key bridge on the Sarus River (Seyhan) at Adana as Sharhbaraz moved to attack.

> Finding the bridge and its forward bastions occupied by the Romans, he [Shahrbaraz] encamped. Now many of the Romans made disorderly sorties across the bridge and attacked the Persians, among whom they caused much slaughter. The emperor forbade them to sally forth indiscriminately in case a way might open for the enemy to enter the bridge and cross it at the same time they did, but the army did not obey the emperor. Shahrbaraz set up ambuscades and, feigning flight, drew many of the Romans to cross over in pursuit of him against the emperor's wish. He turned round and routed them, and killed as many as he overtook outside the bridge. . . . When the emperor saw that the barbarians had broken ranks in pursuit and that many of the Romans who were standing upon the bastions were being slain, he moved against them. A giant of a man confronted the emperor in the middle of the bridge and attacked him, but the emperor struck him and threw him into the river.[16]

Shahrbaraz withdrew and allowed the enemy to pass into Anatolia. With the capital under direct threat, the emperor would have to move westward to defend Constantinople, and in the great expanse of the Anatolian plateau the Wild Boar and Shahin could catch him and bring him to battle. Shahrbaraz did not pursue Heraclius—his objective was to press on to the Bosporus. Given the enemy's line of march, Shahrbaraz prioritized his support of the coming attack on Constantinople and left the Romans to Shahin. The odds seemed favorable that the emperor would relent and attempt to return to shield his capital, and when he did, Shahrbaraz would be waiting for him, the hammer to Shahin's anvil.

Once again, the emperor surprised his rivals. Instead of flying west to protect the approaches to Constantinople, Heraclius plunged northward. He peeled off troops to reinforce the capital and then moved with the bulk of his forces to intercept the slower-moving column of Shahin. The two armies clashed near the town of Euchaita. The emperor himself led a small vanguard against the Persian camp. While the melee thickened, the main Roman force maneuvered behind the Sasanian host and blocked their retreat to Persia. While the initial engagement ended in only minor losses, the two armies locked horns in a running battle that unfolded over the next fifteen days, only ending when the Persians were broken near Mount Ophlimos, ninety kilometers (fifty-six miles) east of Euchaita. The Sasanians fell back thirty kilometers (eighteen miles) east to the river Lycus where more of them perished. The defeat was so severe that Shahin was cashiered and never heard from again.

Shahrbaraz, meanwhile, had marched to the shores of Bosporus where he took up position and awaited the arrival of his Avar allies. On June 29, the Avar vanguard, numbering some thirty thousand men marched into sight of the walls of Constantinople. They found the city well prepared, defended by more than ten thousand Romans. For years, the emperor and his ministers had prepared the city for an expected attack. The capital was well provisioned with stockpiles of food. A fleet of small, nimble craft and manned by sailors expert in navigating the swirling currents of the straits and the Sea of Marmara had been readied to safeguard the weaker sea walls of the city and thwart enemy naval action. The walls bristled with Roman artillery, defensive screens, and anti-siege equipment.

On July 31, the Avar host, numbering eighty thousand nomads and their Slav auxiliaries, launched a tremendous assault on the land walls. Along the entire six-kilometer (3.7-mile) length of the massive triple line of defenses that barred the European side of the city, the khagan's troops employed dozens of war machines, including heavy traction trebuchets and huge mobile assault towers. Like waves on a breakwater, the barbarian tide washed against the fortifications and broke. Undaunted, the Avars intensified their pressure, constructing more artillery and towers. On August 1, the Avars launched an armada of small craft, manned by Slavs, to ferry three to four thousand Persians across the straits to join the attack. As Shahrbaraz could only spectate, the Roman navy swept the assaulting host from the seas. Five days later, on August 6, the Avars launched another general assault, throwing the great weight of their host against the land defenses. By brute force they pounded against the powerful curtain of stone that barred their way into the streets of the richest city in Europe. Through the day and night, wave after wave of nomad troops carried forward their towers and threw their ladders against the walls. In the dawning hours of August 7, the attackers launched a full naval assault. Hundreds of small boats thronged the Golden Horn, the deep-water inlet north of the city where the walls facing the sea were weaker and less heavily defended. As the Slav mariners pressed toward the walls, Roman skiffs and fast fleet ships swept them from the straits. The savage fighting left the waters choked with the broken bodies and boats of the attackers. On the land side, the Avar battering of the walls brought only death and destruction on the khagan's army and, in the face of terrible losses and with no prospects for a breakthrough, fissures opened within the nomad confederation. As the Avars quietly retreated, the walls of Constantinople flickered with the dancing shadows and orange glow of the siege machines and towers that the attackers torched as they melted into the dark.

One cannot be sure whether the Persians sensed that the war, waged for more than fifteen years in their favor, had turned. Likewise, there is no knowing when Shahrbaraz learned of the destruction of the army of his colleague Shahin, the latest in a string of heavy blows which the Iranians had to absorb. Shahrbaraz moved his troops east and south—through Syria and Palestine and into Egypt where he would wait out events that unfolded in the campaign of 627 that would prove decisive. As he had broken with his powerful family of Mihran during the rebellion of Bahram Chobin nearly thirty years prior, so now the hero of the realm would abandon his loyalty to Khusrow and the House of Sasan. After the defeats of 626, the general could have expected nothing from the great king but disgrace and, at best, being consigned to spend the last of his days pent up in the prison of the Castle of Oblivion.

At the start of the marching season of 627 things turned even more grim for the Persians. An alliance, forged with ample bullion provided by the Romans, was forged between the two most powerful foes of Iran. The Western Turks entered the war, descending through the Caucasus passes and smashing to pieces the Sasanian defenses of the mountain passes; these were sorely depleted, as more soldiers were required in the campaign armies in the west. At the head of the Turk army, numbering about sixty thousand troops, rode Sipi Khan, the chief deputy and likely the brother of the great khan Tong Yabghu (618–28). The unification of the great steppe nomad power of the east, whose scepter shaded the lands from beyond the Oxus to the sea of grass north of the Caspian, posed the gravest of threats to the Sasanian Empire. Such an unholy alliance, feared for some fifty years, since the first contacts between

The Siege of Constantinople (626) by the Avars on a mural at the Moldovi a Monastery, Romania. Althought the mural is titled as such, the presence of cannon are anachronisitic and probably reflect the later capture of Constantinople by the Ottomans. (*Public Domain*)

Roman and Turk, had finally come to fruition. The great king and his lands were in mortal danger.

Why did Shahrbaraz not move with all speed to intercept the Romans, who operated at Tiflis in Georgia alongside the Kök Turk chief lieutenant of the great khan? The costs of the war in lives and years of hard marching and combat led to ill feelings and rebellion. Sedition seeped through the rank and file of Persian fighters and infected even the high-ranking officers. Though doubtless only a sketch, the Shakespearean words of the Moses Daschurants'i certainly capture the sentiment that prevailed among the eastern troops:

> How long shall streams of the blood of our Aryan countrymen flow on all these battlefields? they asked. How long shall we fear and tremble before this bloody king? How long shall our goods and chattels, our gold and silver be gathered into the royal treasury? How long shall our roads be shut off and blocked to the detriment of the prosperity of many kingdoms and countries? How long shall the souls quake in our bodies and be repressed by his terrible command? Did he not destroy and swallow up like the sea the very best of our comrades, the country's leaders? . . . Did he not take men from their wives and fathers from their sons and

send them to distant peoples as slaves and bondmen and conscripts among cruel foes?[17]

At the start of 627, a combined Roman-Turk army, said by one later source to have numbered ninety thousand, entered and thoroughly ravaged the northern lands of the empire.[18] Along the route of march, which was slow and deliberate, Sipi Khan sent a sternly worded missive to the great king informing him that, if Khusrow refused to negotiate a peace that restored the former territories to Rome, their combined armies were coming to meet him at Ctesiphon. Abandoned by his chief general, Shahrbaraz, who ignored the summons from the king of kings and remained fixed in Alexandria, Khusrow levied two small armies in a desperate attempt to retrieve the situation. The first, led by Shahrplakan, who had apparently recovered from the wounds he suffered in battle against Heraclius in 625, had at its core a thousand elite guard cavalry. This force hurried north to relieve the siege of Tiflis but apparently accomplished nothing. In Mesopotamia, the great king levied a scratch force from local troops from around the capital. This army, led by Razadh, one of the last commanders loyal to the crown, tried to stem the Roman-Turk advance. Heraclius again made a surprise maneuver and turned farther east, marching into Sasanian Atropatene in September where he threatened the heartland of the empire.

As winter approached, the Kök Turks departed for the north, leaving the emperor to conduct operations with his Roman forces. On October 9, the emperor halted to rest his men before their next great push. Razadh failed to anticipate the next thrust of the enemy, which pushed through the foothills of the Zagros Mountains. To overtake the enemy, the outnumbered and beleaguered Sasanians resorted to a series of forced marches that finally brought them in striking distance. On December 1, with Heraclius driving south along the banks of the Greater Zab River, the Iranians were forced back from the crossings and allowed the enemy to enter the plain of Nineveh in what is today northern Iraq. With three thousand Persian reinforcements on their way north, about which Heraclius was apprised by his spies, the Romans went on the attack. The Battle of Nineveh, fought on December 12, began as the land was covered in the haze of an early morning fog that concealed enemy movements. In the clash that followed, the Sasanians were decisively defeated, "scattered like dust in a hurricane."[19] The Persians lost many men and suffered four thousand captured. No battle-worthy Persian force remained in the land capable of halting the westerners' advance. The Romans marched farther east, into the rich, irrigated plains behind Ctesiphon, and there, along the Diyala River, Heraclius and his troops sacked the great royal center and fire temple complex at Dastagerd and pillaged the summer palace of the great king who, at the news of the enemy approach, had fled south to Ctesiphon. The blow undermined the already waning prestige of Khusrow, whose support quickly ebbed. Despite this, Heraclius sought a political settlement and withdrew to Ganzak, there to await news from the interior of the Persian Empire, which he knew to be rending at the seams.

The court at Ctesiphon was in turmoil. As no sources survive save from the last fateful days of his reign, the actions of Khusrow II Parvez, who had fallen ill, can only be conjectured. With the war now lost, it is almost incomprehensible that the great king remained committed to conflict, especially since the Roman emperor had repeatedly made clear his desire for a negotiated settlement that would restore the boundaries of the empires to their former position. Even if Khusrow rejected the notion of making peace with a man he considered a usurper and one who stood in the way of his rightful domination of the Roman Empire, the apparent military inaction of the great king is mind boggling. Despite the loss of Egypt, and likely portions of Palestine and Syria to the influence of the turncoat Shahrbaraz, the great king still commanded vast resources. Only the withdrawal of the great backers of the House of Sasan, especially the Mirhan family, can explain the paralysis of the king of kings and the lack of further recruitment among the Persians. But this fracturing of Iranian elites can only offer a partial answer to Khusrow's impotence in the face of impending disaster.

Some faint whisper of diplomatic effort finds echo in the report of the great king's reception of the emissaries of Sipi Khan in 628, when Khusrow reminded the Turks of their old alliance and of their kinship through intermarriage.[20] Possibly the great king counted on these traditional ties to draw away the Kök Turks from their dalliance with the Romans, but this remains purely speculative.

Beyond the withdrawal of the support of the great families from their loyalty of Khusrow, there were other recruiting grounds available. Certainly the Sasanians could not have turned to the conquered Roman provinces whence to draw troops, yet it remains unexplained why the great king did not use the massive sums he had collected in his decades of conquest and taxation to recruit mercenaries with which to oppose the Romans. Large numbers of Arabs, who raided the empire following Khusrow's dissolution of the Lakhmid kingdom along the southern fringes of the empire, could have been brought into Persian service during the years of great emergency from 626–28. The same is true of Hephthalite remnants both inside and outside of the empire.

As Khusrow tried in vain to secure the succession of his son by his favorite wife Shirin, events overtook him. His son, Kawad II Shiroe, hatched a plot against the great king and secretly apprised Heraclius of his intentions. Aided by the cavalry commander, Gushnasp, and Mehr Hormozd, prominent man of the Suren clan, the rebel forces seized control of Ctesiphon. These clandestine maneuvers explain the withdrawal of the emperor to the north following the Battle of Nineveh. At the end of February 628, the aged great king, abandoned by his courtiers, was hunted down in his palace outside of Ctesiphon and beheaded. Kawad II's men then butchered all eighteen of his brothers in a vain effort to maintain the unity of his rule.

Kawad II Shiroe immediately dispatched ambassadors to Ganzak to treat with Heraclius. The terms of an armistice were quickly agreed and fighting halted while the two imperial powers settled into negotiations. While the Sasanians were humbled, Heraclius was careful not to put the new shahanshah in an untenable situation. A restoration of the 591 borders ceded by the king's father to Maurice in exchange for military aid against Bahram Chobin had the very real potential to rally the Persians to renewal of the war, as the near two decades of blood and toil would have amounted to nothing. Instead, the great powers settled on the pre-591 frontiers and the return of the True Cross to Jerusalem as the major components of the agreement. Likely, too, was an exchange of prisoners and the return of Roman deportees from Iran to the eastern lands of the Romans. The peace was not secured when, after a reign of a mere eight months, en route to one of his palaces in Media, Kawad II Shiroe died in Dastagerd, probably from the plague. His young son was crowned Ardashir III.

A serious impediment to the implementation of the peace deal was the continued presence of Sharhbaraz, who remained entrenched in Alexandria and thus commanded the vast resources of Egypt to back his troops there and in Syria. Heraclius treated with the Wild Boar on separate terms. The bargain that the Sasanian generalissimo pushed was far harder than that of Kawad Shiroe. Shahrbaraz insisted on keeping the lands up to the Euphrates as his new frontier, thus forcing Heraclius to abandon the old Roman line of forward posts in Mesopotamia, including Dara. That the emperor agreed to such extraordinary concessions indicates just how war weary were the exhausted emperor, his troops, and his exchequer. The Persians agreed to pay an indemnity to the Romans and withdraw behind the Euphrates. High in the mountains of eastern Cappadocia, at the town of Arabissos, Heraclius and Shahrbaraz met in person. During the formalities, Theodore, the emperor's son, married Shahrbaraz's daughter. The Wild Boar and his men then marched off to Ctesiphon at the head of six thousand men. As Persian troops slowly withdrew from the cities of the Romans they had occupied, Shahrbaraz entered the capital in the spring of 630, overthrew Ardashir III, had the boy killed, and seized power. The unpopular general would only hold power for two months from April until June 9, 630, when he, too, was murdered. As peace took hold between the Romans and Sasanians and as the curtain closed on the Last Great War of Antiquity, the Sasanian Empire tottered under the weight of defeat as the families that had glued the state together found their allegiance to the House of Sasan strained to breaking. The coming years would be filled with tribulations, and the emergence of a new threat that would tear the empire to its foundations. To the south, the armies of the prophet had consolidated their hold on the Arabian Peninsula and set the wheels in motion for the establishment of a great new world empire.

CHAPTER NINE

The Muslim Conquest

I n the wake of the halcyon days of Khusrow II's glory, in which the world trembled at his name and in which the wealth and sophistication of the court at Ctesiphon was proverbial, the Sasanian Empire was bent to breaking. As the internal unity of the kingdom began to crack, the edifice of Sasanian power fractured, the foundations of the kingdom would crumble to dust, scattered into the winds of history. Successive kings would stand in quicksand, mired in vicious civil wars that would lead to the ruin of the empire. In 629, a force of Turks invaded the empire from the Caucasus—the great system of frontier defenses had been ruined since the invasions of Heraclius and his Turk allies. Shahrbaraz sent a Sasanian army of ten thousand cavalry to oppose these invaders from the north, but the Turkish forces ambushed and annihilated them.

As the Turks advanced, they ravaged widely throughout Georgia and into Albania. The Albanian historian, Moses Daschurants'i, evoked the pall cast by their approach:

> . . . a dark fog suddenly enveloped the face of our country, plains and mountain-tops, hills and deep valleys, and not a yard of earth remained untouched in the whole of our land, in town or country, in house or road. Every mouth cried "Woe! Woe!" . . . For they had planned it all in advance and had allotted to the several bands the various cantons and villages, ravines and rivers, springs and marshes, mountains and plains, and

all attacked as one man and swallowed up our country. . . . Our land shook from border to border, and the words of the prophet were fulfilled: "As if a man should flee from the face of a lion and a bear should meet him; and escaping from him should go to his house and lean his hand on the wall, and a serpent should bite him." [Amos 5.19][1]

As the new decade of the 630s dawned, none could have foreseen the momentous upheaval and trauma of the coming years. Sasanian defeats and internal strife exposed the frontiers. In the south, Persian defenses crumbled in the face of inroads by marauding Arabs. Few would have understood that these tribesmen followed a new religion, soon to be called Islam.

Historians have long pondered the astonishing fact of the Arab conquests. Seemingly out of nowhere, the tribesmen of the Arabian Peninsula, inspired by the message of their prophet, Muhammad, and galvanized by the new religion of Islam, erupted and, in a few short decades, founded the largest empire the likes of which, to that point in time, the world had never seen. While the Roman Empire would suffer tremendously under hoof and heel of the invading Arab armies, losing their most populous and richest provinces, the Sasanians would not survive the crisis and vanished from history. How had an obscure Arabian preacher changed the course of world history? How did his followers, seemingly untutored in the ways of the neighboring great powers, outmaneuver and defeat the two superpowers of the day?

Inside the Sasanian Empire, chaos prevailed, as an obscure parade of claimants representing rival power bases tried to cling to power. After the death of Khusrow II, the kingdom had been riven by internal strife and rival warlords with their armies vied to be king or queen-makers, two of whom ruled for brief stints during this period. Kavad II (628) was succeeded by the usurper Shahrbaraz (629), who lasted a mere forty days in power. Succeeding the generalissimo were Queen Boran (629–30 or 632?) and Azarmidokht (630–631), both daughters of Khusrow II. The reigns of these women, noted the Persian epic poet Firdawsi, proved "the world had had its fill of kings." The presence of women on the throne of the shahanshah, the great dais of the mighty Sasanian Khusrow whose deeds had shaken the world to its foundations, emboldened the Arabs—"the Persians no longer have a king, they have sought refuge in a woman"—whose raiders fanned out over the fringes of Mesopotamia.[2] The lack of male candidates was due in large part to Kavad's massacre of his brothers and half-brothers. The death of the king thus created a crisis that polygamy was supposed to solve, namely the production of suitable candidates to rule. Queen Boran reigned in fits and starts from 630 to 632, and other claimants include Khusrow III (630–632), Khusrow IV (630–636) and Peroz II (631–632). These rulers do not exhaust the list of those vying for power, as in the provinces others who would be king minted coins and contested central authority. In 632, the magnates of the empire crowned Khusrow II's grandson, and he would rule as Yazdegerd III (632–651). He was eight years old.

The story of Islam's rise, as is conventionally told and generally agreed upon, is not without many unanswered questions. What concerns us here, though, are the course of the Muslim thrusts—first into the fertile heartland and vulnerable underbelly of the rich granary and most populous part of the empire, Mesopotamia, and then, like a millstone grinding grain, the inexorable advance of these great conquerors, ambitious and hungry for more. This story began upon the death of the prophet in 632. Muhammad, through force and skilled diplomacy, had welded the loose tribes of the vast Arabian Peninsula into a loose confederation, a coalition dedicated to service to Allah, the supreme deity. Like Jews and Christians, Muhammad claimed the patriarch Abraham as a common ancestor, but unlike the Christians in particular, Islam was a religion of the strictest monotheism. In a famous riposte to the Christian communities around his people, Muhammad delivered the message in the Qur'an, "He begets not, nor is he begotten," a clear rebuttal to the notion that Christ was God incarnate of the Virgin Mary.[3]

After the death of the prophet, who had managed to bring many of the tribesmen of western Arabia under his banner, some of those who formerly swore allegiance to his cause hived off and resisted incorporation into the new super-tribe of Islam. Others were to be brought in as well, as the new community aimed to bring all Arabic speakers under their tent. The carrot they held forth was conquest. The stick they held was violent confrontation. Noncooperative groups were coerced to join the growing Arab armies. After ca. 630, resistant groups were defeated in detail. In 632 and 633, the great tribal confederacy grew during the so-called "Wars of Apostasy" or Ridda Wars. These skirmishes were fought by men loyal to the caliph Abu Bakr (whose title means "successor" to the prophet, a title that did not imply any special divine or charismatic religious aura). One of the chief lieutenants of the caliph, Khalid b. al-Walid, a prominent Meccan, fought in northeastern Arabia in the Ridda Wars.

Among the first targets of the skillful Meccan commander was Hira, the Arab town that lay not far from the west bank of the Euphrates and where once the Lakhmid tribal confederation under the Nasrid dynasty had maintained its seat of power. Despite their record of loyal service to the Sasanians, which included the support of the Nasrid king, al-Nu'man III (582–602) to Khusrow II when he faced the rebellion of Bahram Chobin, the Lakhmids had fallen out of favor. Nu'man shared the fate of so many of Khusrow's men. In 602, Arab tradition relates that the great king had the Lakhmid lord poisoned, and consequently the great pre-Islamic Arab confederation gradually faded. Khusrow dispatched a Sasanian governor and elevated a local chieftain at Hira named Iyas ibn Qabisah al-Ta'i. Unlike his predecessor, Iyas could not maintain order over the tribes along the borderland, and prior to the Muslim attacks on the region, he led his Arabs in a joint Arab-Sasanian force that fell in defeat against Arab tribesmen in the little Battle of Dhi Qar in southern Mesopotamia—an ominous sign of the days to come.

Hira hosted a Sasanian garrison under a Persian commander who, along with Arab auxiliary troops, defended the elaborate linear systems of defense that the Sasanians had erected fronting northern Arabia. After skirmishes between the Muslims and Persian-Arab coalition, the leaders of the town soon came to terms with the invaders. Khalid led his troops on a successful lightning campaign and subdued lands along the Middle Euphrates. These battles were small-scale and involved no large forces from the professional Persian ranks. Khalid defeated local Arab and Persian troops at a place called Ain al-Tamr, an oasis west of the great river, and collected tribute. This phase of the war would have looked little different than the endemic Arab raiding that had plagued much of Mesopotamia and Syria during the chaotic decades of the Roman-Persian wars. Pressed for coin like their Persian rivals, the Romans had ended their subsidies to the Ghassanids, whose star subsequently waned and would, like their Lakhmid enemies, flare out under the bright dawning of Islam. Both great powers would, no doubt, have gladly traded heaps of treasure to avoid what came after. Of all the many, complex, tangled reasons for the Arab conquests, the demise of the sixth-century Arab client states numbers among the most salient. Before Khalid could test his mettle against the Sasanians, in 634 he was withdrawn and ordered to Syria. In that theater of war Khalid would win everlasting glory as one of the leaders of the great army of conquest that decisively defeated the Romans.

The new caliph Umar ordered one of the early followers of Muhammad, Abu Ubayd al-Thaqafi, to Iraq. With the arrival of the new Muslim force, the next phase of the conquest of Iraq began. After a series of minor encounters, the Arabs met a major Sasanian force at the Battle of the Bridge, fought in 634 on a bend of the Euphrates not far from Hira. The Sasanians that day were reinforced with troops from the capital and comprised a large number of mailed cavalry and several elephants, whose presence frightened the Arabs.

After a hard-fought engagement, Abu Ubayd fell, and the Muslim lines broke. Up to three thousand of them perished, many by drowning as they attempted to cross the river. Arab historians recount Persian losses twice as high as Muslim casualties, which seems unlikely. The Battle of the Bridge would be the only major Persian victory of the war. In the Armenian tradition it is possible to reconstruct two sieges of Ctesiphon, one which dated before the Battle of the Bridge that pushed the Arabs from across the Tigris and back to near their original invasion points around Hira. Whatever the case, Rustam and his Persians could not hold the line.[4]

Both sides regrouped, with the caliph Umar (634–644) determined to continue the fight for the prize of Iraq. The great king, Yazdegerd III, having managed to shore up his powerbase, readied his kingdom for a major push against the Arabs. Traditionally the Battle of Qadisiya, the decisive battle of the Arab conquest of Iraq, is placed in the year 636.[5] Yazdegerd sent the noble-born Persian Rustam, the kingmaker and commander in chief of the army, with a strong Sasanian force, perhaps numbering up to twenty thousand men—not the much higher numbers usually claimed. This army marched across the Euphrates, and the Sasanians established their heavily fortified marching camp not far from Hira. The Muslim forces, led by Sa'd b. Abi Waqqas was the smaller of the two, although the Arabs received two reinforcing contingents from Syria on the eve of the battle, but even with these additional troops it is likely that the invaders were outnumbered, with about twelve thousand men in the field. The two armies clashed at the village of Qadisiya. The surviving accounts are verbose but provide extraordinarily little in the way of reconstructing the tactical movements of the armies. Despite claims to the contrary, Qadisiya was unlikely the battle of massive armies. The Sasanian elephants are depicted as playing a great role in the battle, especially on the first day, and archers on both sides inflicted numerous casualties. After a battle said to have stretched over four days, the Muslim armies won a decisive victory. Rustam fell, and with the loss of their commander, the Persians were routed.

Before the defeat, Rustam is said to have seen the signs of the ruin of his homeland written in the stars and exclaimed:

> But for the Persians I will weep, and for
> The House of Sasan ruined by this war
> Alas for their great crown and throne, for all
> The royal splendor destined now to fall,
> To be fragmented by the Arab's might[6]

The defeat at Qadisiya opened the road to Ctesiphon and exposed the heartland of the empire to conquest. In the wake of the rout, much of the local Persian gentry, the *dehqans* who comprised the main government presence in many rural regions, made terms with the invaders as Sasanian military and political authority disintegrated. Already before Qadisiya, important contingents of Persian troops defected to the Muslims. Among these was a force of four thousand Daylamites whose prominence in the Sasanian army indicates a growing foreign element and reliance on mercenaries who could not be fully integrated into the ethos of the core Persian and Parthian soldiery. They would fight against their former masters at the Battle of Jalula. These Daylamites later established themselves in Kufa, as did another group of defectors, a troop of cavalry.[7] The survivors of Qadisiya tried to organize themselves at the ruins of the great ancient city of Babylon, but the Arabs swept them aside as if swatting a fly. The Persian commanders scattered, with prominent men hurrying home to their provincial power bases to attempt to organize resistance. Only a few went to Ctesiphon to make a stand there.

Ctesiphon was comprised of several discreet settlements that straddled the banks of the Tigris. In March 637, Sa'd led his men against the Persian capital where the boy king Yazdegerd and his courtiers organized the defense. Not long after the arrival of the Arab armies, the Sasanians abandoned the portions of the city lying west of the Tigris and withdrew to the settlement along the eastern banks, taking all the ferry boats with them. Since no bridge linked the two sides of the city, the Arabs made a dramatic crossing, plunging into the swift flowing Tigris with their cavalry mounts and the Persians countered with their own rush into the river. The Sasanians were driven back, and the Arabs gained a foothold on the eastern shore, marking the city's doom. The great king fled the city as did most of the inhabitants. The Arabs entered the great halls of the Sasanian kings and found vast hoards of treasure. Among the finds was a magnificent, massive carpet more than thirty meters on a side. The conquerors seized an abundance of gold and silver objects and royal regalia that had once adorned the bodies of kings. Arab raiders found the last Sasanian war elephant in its stables, and when they tried to move the marvelous beast through the city streets, the ill pachyderm collapsed and died. Thus ended the awe-inspiring elephant troops that the shahanshahs had carefully built up and maintained over many years.

To the east the Persians fled, beyond the Diyala River watering the fertile hinterland of Ctesiphon, the Muslims in pursuit. Yazdegerd established his headquarters in western Iran, at Hulwan in the Zagros Mountains., probably led by Sa'd, though different accounts list different commanders of a troop said to number twelve thousand. Likely in December 637, at a place called Jalula, the Arab conquest army encountered a Persian force that perhaps numbered as many as ten thousand, led by Mirhan Razi. Here we see a Persian army utterly different in complexion from the great forces of conquest of three decades prior. The Persians were dug in, their backs to the Diyala, with ditches on the flanks and wooden stakes in front. While their defensive posture was due likely to their relatively small numbers (and not the hundred thousand or more some Arab accounts relate), the Persians were never a great infantry army, and the narrow confines into which they were restricted blunted whatever edge their savaran cavalry who were present might have held. This unfortunate tactical decision helped to doom the Persians. While they fought bravely and fiercely, the Arab forces overwhelmed them and destroyed the Sasanian force. A Muslim historian remembered the Battle of Jalula:

> The fight that ensued was the fiercest they ever had, in which arrows and lances were used until broken to pieces, and swords were applied until they were bent. Finally, the Muslims altogether made one onslaught and drove the Persians from their position, putting them to flight. The Persians fled away and the Muslims kept pursuing them at their very heels with fearful slaughter until darkness intervened and they had to return to their camp.[8]

Yazdegerd III fled northward toward Hulwan, where the noble Farrukhzad had taken control. Arab forces marched on Hulwan and captured it, probably in 640. The conquest of the city gave the Muslims control of a main pass through the Zagros into the Iranian plateau and thus the key to one of the main routes of travel from the lowlands of Iraq into Iran.

After Jalula, the Muslims established a cantonment along the Euphrates near the Hira. They named their new city Kufa, and it would rise to prominence as one of the most important settlements of the early Islamic period. With the middle Euphrates and Tigris valleys conquered and the Persians driven out of the heart of Mesopotamia, including their great former administrative capital, the Arabs also pressured the Persians to the north and south. At the head of the Persian Gulf just east of modern Basra lay al-Ubulla, "gateway to India," Arab forces defeated the local Persian garrison said to have numbered five hundred strong.

The invaders progressed, heading eastward into the environs of Sasanian Ahvaz, today Khuzestan, a region that comprises a large province on the Iranian border with Iraq. The Arab presence there dates to the seventh-century conquest. The local Persian commander, Hormuzd, was closely related to the great king; following the fall of Hulwan, Hormuzd had asked the king to go to Khuzestan to organize resistance against the Arabs. Hormuzd initially tried to buy time and so treated with the enemy. He agreed to pay the Arabs the required poll tax in exchange for noninterference, but the Persians later reneged, and the Muslims intervened militarily.

The Sasanians had made considerable investments in Khuzestan, where irrigated agriculture was made possible by rivers flowing south from the Zagros Mountains. Sasanian engineers had developed elaborate and impressive hydraulic installations. Royal investment is also seen in the cities like Gundeshapur, founded by Shapur I, with the captives he had deported after his sack of the Roman city of Antioch. Karka, Susa, and Shushtar formed the other important cities of the agriculturally vital area. Gundeshapur, with a population of perhaps a hundred thousand, fell without much resistance. The Arabs sacked Susa and plundered the famous church of the Prophet Daniel, sending its treasures to the caliph.

In 638, Yazdegerd sent an embassy to the Chinese Tang Empire, pleading for military assistance against the ferocious wolves from the desert who rampaged over his once mighty empire. The powerful emperor Taizong (626–649) believed the affair to be too distant in which to take part, and the Persian embassy returned to the Shah empty-handed, as would subsequent diplomatic missions. By 638, Hormuzd had failed to stall the Arab advance deeper into Khuzestan. Hormuzd chose to take his stand at Shushtar, a city built on a rocky bluff with a strong citadel. The interlacing canals and waterways around the city made it a formidable obstacle to the Arab advance. Only after a two-year siege did the city fall into Arab hands and, along with it, Hormuzd, whom they took captive. With the fall of Khuzestan, the Sasanians lost another fertile and wealthy region, and the tide of Islam now washed over the Iranian heartland amidst the high plateau. Around the same time and no later than 640, Arab forces rooted out or came to terms with Persian garrisons all the way up the Euphrates to Tikrit. Mesopotamia was now largely in their hands and, with its conquest, the great king had lost not only his capital but his richest lands.

The numerous folds of the great Zagros Mountains that embraced Iran allowed space for only two major routes of passage. To the north lay the Khurasan Road, and to the south a route led from Basra along the hot lowlands into the north and east. Amidst the rugged peaks of the mountains unfolded valleys used by small farming communities but mostly by transhumant pastoralists. On the plateau proper broad plains, interrupted by desolate lunar salt flats, allowed the movement of people from one staging post to the next and offered no major natural obstacles to the movement of large forces of men. In Iran, as elsewhere among the semi-arid lands of Eurasia, settlement closely embraced the water, and the power that held the waterpoints in their fist held sway over the vast majority of people and the only sites that really mattered. The Arabs comprehended and maneuvered easily in such spaces.

Around 640, an Arab invasion from the coastlands of Oman struck into southern Iran, into the old Sasanian heartlands of Fars, where the invaders defeated and killed the Persian governor. Having established a foothold on the southern coasts and in an island in the gulf, the Arab tribesmen pressured the Persians on all fronts. Led by the Arab general Uthma b. Abi'l-As, the enemy penetrated first to the city of Istakhr, birthplace of the Sasanian dynasty. Yazdegerd's men successfully defended a first attempt on the city made in 644. Bishapur, another lynchpin of Sasanian power, fell in 647 and, following the opening of the main overland route from Iraq, Istakhr and the city of Jur fell, sometime around 650. Both cities held out and offered staunch resistance, for which they were repaid by the great carnage wrought by the Arab armies upon the capture of the two cities.

While the invaders were not content with their conquests, Yazdegerd was not idle. The great king sent messengers throughout the realm, ordering the faithful to gather in the northern reaches of the Zagros at Nihavand, ninety kilometers (fifty miles) south of Hamadan, across the massif of Alvand Kush. Nihavand lay astride an important north-south route from central Iraq to northern Iran. The great heights of the mountain squeezed out plenty of moisture that rendered the lands verdant and prosperous. Nihavand served as the seat of the Karin family, who were likely descendants of the great Parthian clan of the Arsacids of ancient fame.

In 641/42 the caliph Umar ordered the Muslim troops in the region of Kaskar, the region that included the cantonments of Kufa and Basra in southern Iraq, to marshal and advance on the enemy. Under the command of the governor of Kaskar, N'uman b. Muqarrin, thirty thousand Arabs and Persian defectors advanced on Nihavand. There, the Sasanian force led by Perozan that opposed them likely were similar in numbers to the enemy. Among the Persian forces were elements of the heavy savaran cavalry and a troop of soldiers from Isfahan. Other sources mention elements from the east of the empire, from Khurasan and Sijistan. The muster of the army at Nihavand was clearly intended to provide the backbone to absorb a heavy blow from the Arabs.

At the approach of N'uman's forces, the Persians again took a defensive stance. They covered the front of their army with lines of iron caltrops to blunt the force of any cavalry charge. Arab scouts soon discovered the iron spikes and reported to their general. The Persian disposition at Nihavand once again was intended to narrow their exposure on the flanks and rear. The seventh-century Roman military handbook, *Strategikon*, noted that Sasanian armies of the age were vulnerable to flanking and rear attacks. A heavy Persian reliance on archery meant that the gaps between armies had to be closed quickly, and their lack of lancers rendered them vulnerable to hand-to-hand fighting.[9] The Persian choice of the battlefield, on high and rugged ground, surrounded by defiles, was in keeping with what the *Strategikon* states was textbook practice for them, aimed to eliminate any enemy advantage in infantry and cavalry by creating a deeper killing zone, as the enemy approach to the Persian lines would be slowed by the rugged ground and thus exposed to more volleys of archery fire, which could cripple a frontal assault.

Against the advice of his junior commanders, N'uman waited until after the midday prayers to begin his attack and ordered his cavalry to feign a retreat. When the Persians removed the iron spikes that covered their position and ran in pursuit of the enemy, the Muslims wheeled about and charged on them. "They killed so many Persians in this battle that the battlefield was inundated in blood and warriors and animals lost their footing in it."[10] Despite the death of N'uman due to an arrow wound, the Muslims pressed their attack, and as darkness fell, the broken Sasanian troops fled into the night, and many fell from the heights into the broken ravines near the battlefield. Among the dead was the Persian commander Perozan, who was hunted down in the darkness and killed.

As the bulk of the survivors from the shattered Sasanian forces fled to Hamadan, the Arabs pressed them, the "Muslim cavalry hot on their heels," according to Tabari.[11] The city was soon surrendered, along with the nearby city of Dastaba, and thus the Arab tide rolled on. By now the Persians were suffering in multiple dimensions. Psychologically, the dehqans and nobles who formed the backbone of the state bureaucracy and cavalry were demoralized by the string of major defeats that had begun at Qadisiya. Militarily, the Turk invasion of 629 had led to a massacre of veteran Persian troops, which told in subsequent battles against the Arabs. The unrelenting bloodletting of able-bodied and trained men in the shah's army over three decades, beginning with the war against Rome, surely had a pronounced effect on the manpower upon which the Persians could draw. Fiscally, the former wealth of the great king poured into the hands of the enemy in rivers of silver, gold, and precious stones—the legendary wealth of Persia fills the pages of the stories of the Arab conquests. Deprived of his richest provinces and with more cities falling or surrendering with each passing year, the financial resources available to Yazdegerd were dangerously thin.

From the size of the force gathered at Nihavand, the Sasanians aimed to staunch the bleeding there and to turn the tide of the war. Instead, the poor performance of their troops sealed their fate and the Arab juggernaut was destined to roll forward. With the lands of Iraq now secured, Muslim victory at Nihavand opened the whole of Iran to the wild barbarians of the south. For their part, the Arabs tracked the Sasanian king like hunting dogs scenting the stag. The great king's movements during the war are difficult to trace, but he seems to have spent much of his time in Fars after he fled from Hulwan and then moved on to Kirman and Sistan in the deep south of Iran along the Persian Gulf. These were his ancestral homelands and wellspring of the House of Sasan.

After the battle of Nihavand, the Sasanians failed to stay the conquest at Isfahan, in central Iran, some 470 kilometers (292 miles) southeast of Hamadan where, after a short, sharp clash, the Persian defenders fled. From Isfahan, with little resistance, the Muslims pressed along the road to the eastern lands of the empire. At Waj al-Rudh, a village in the region of Hamadan, the twelve thousand Muslims found their progress barred by a Daylamite chieftain named Muta and the commander of the army of Rayy. The fight that ensued, according to Tabari, was "a great battle like Nihavand, not at all inferior. Great, incalculable numbers were killed, and the bloody struggle between them was no less than other great battles."[12]

There the Arab commander, the Yemeni Yazid b. Qays, led his forces to victory, remembered by Nu'aym, the supreme Arab general in the region:

We repelled them at Waj Rudh with our force
On the morning we inflicted upon [the Persians] one of the great calamities
They could not endure for any time at all, as death hovered
Against our sharp spears and cutting swords.
When their forces scattered, they were like
A wall the baked brick of which has crumbled with destroying blows[13]

After the clash at Waj al-Rudh, Muslim forces advanced on the vital city of Rayy (now part of Tehran). The city sits in a large fertile area south of the Elburz Mountains and north of the desert plateau and thus is a key point between the plains of Mesopotamia and the steppe lands of Central Asia. When the Muslims arrived around 643, they would have found a citadel of mud brick in use since ancient times and a lower city surrounded by a large mud-brick curtain wall that spread out to the south of the fortress in a roughly tri-angular shape. Here the Arabs encountered the defenses prepared and led by the head of the Mihranid family, Siyavush, who was grandson of none other than Bahram Chobin. It seems that the one-time Sasanian kingmaker, Far-rukzhad, who had long supported the Sasanian family, betrayed the city to the enemy; in a night attack Muslim troops entered Rayy and put the de-fenders to flight. After this short fight, the city fell and with it an immense amount of booty into the hands of the invaders. The road to Khurasan and the east lay open before the armies of Islam.

The Arab military commander Suwayd b. Muqarrin led his troops toward the Elburz Mountains, which run south-southeast before turning to the northeast around the town of Simnan. The mountains wall off the Iranian plateau from the narrow plains of the Caspian and then merge into the Al-adagh range to the east. From west to east, the regions just south of the Caspian are Daylam (Gilan), Tabaristan, and Gurgan. Along their route the Elburz frame the rolling country and plains of Gurgan. The Aladagh form the southern spine of the eastern region of Khurasan. Because of the moun-tains, the diversity of landscapes and microclimates along their flanks, as well as the difficulty in crossing them, Tabaristan and Gurgan were always more loosely attached to the Sasanians than regions in the imperial core. At the time of the conquests, the ruler of Gurgan held the title of Sul. To Sul Ruzban in Gurgan and the ruler of Tabaristan to the west, the Arabs stipulated pay-ments and general shows of good faith, for example, displays of loyalty and suppression of banditry. Neither Daylam nor Tabaristan, with their little spits of fertile land south of the great inland sea, would host Muslim armies. In-stead, local magnates managed to maintain their largely independent status they had enjoyed under the Sasanians, a situation allowed in no small part by their poverty and isolation.

As Muslim forces thrust east, they also moved northwest, fanning out over the plains and rolling country of Azerbaijan, once a major stronghold of Sasanian power. There, the Muslim leader Bukayr b. 'Abdallah captured Is-fandiyar, a Persian commander from a prominent magnate family who had survived and fled the Battle of Waj al-Rudh. Isfandiyar helped the Muslims to come to terms with most of the elements in the countryside. Some fighters under Bahram, Isfandiyar's brother, clashed with Bukayr's forces and were crushed. Bahram fled into the mountains, and the country fell under Arab rule, probably in 642. At the pass of Darband, the Muslims found the force guarding the fortifications under the command of Shahrbaraz, who, like the earlier general and star-crossed shah, was a scion of the Mihran family. Shahrbaraz promised to incorporate his border troops into the Muslim army in exchange for being freed of paying taxes, and with this the Arabs agreed.

In 643, the Arabs made a massive military push into Armenia, last of the western bastions of former Persian power, and agreed on tribute. The Armenians, related to the Sasanians by culture and language and, in some instances, blood, pledged to pay taxes and to maintain a force of fifteen thousand cavalry at the disposal of the conquerors. Much of the country would only be subjugated ten years later, when the Arabs and their allies renewed their northern drive on a massive scale.

By then, the Sasanian Empire was no more. The last great king, Yazdegerd III, crowned as an eight-year-old child, had known only a life of war and discord that rent the once great empire limb from limb. He had been on the run from the Muslims from the days of the siege of Ctesiphon, first to Istakhr in his family's strongholds, amidst Fars, his ancestral homeland where the enemy could be more easily resisted. After the fall of Istakhr, the great king fled to Kirman, the region east of Fars and then farther east still to the frontier region of Sakastan. With the Arabs in pursuit, and with a cool reception from his deputy in Sakastan, in 651, Yazdegerd decided to move to Khurasan and the great oasis citadel of Merv, ostensibly because he viewed the marzban Mahoe there as his appointee and thus bound to be friendly to his cause. Instead, on his arrival at Merv, Mahoe's men attempted to seize the shah, who ran from the city. Yazdegerd III took refuge in a mill where he was found to be hiding and murdered. Thus, the line of Ardashir, who won glory and founded a new dynasty on the plains of Hormozdgan, some 427 years prior, came to an end. The House of Sasan and its fire of empire, which the line had carried from the frigid mountains of the Hindu Kush to the warm shores of the Mediterranean, sputtered and went out. In the end, the military arms that had birthed them and bore them to such heights could not, while they stood at the pinnacle of their success, save them from the fall.

Epilogue

Though the Sasanian dynasty is thought to have died in 651 with Yazdegerd III, this is not strictly true, as has been observed by a number of historians. Of course the cohesion and power of the dynasty was at an end and had declined precipitously some years before. The battle at Nahavand marked the last united face the Persians were able to present to the enemy. Though we know little about Yazdegerd or his rule, he was clearly not a man who could inspire his people to superhuman feats; he was no Heraclius. However, it could be said that Yazdegerd confronted even greater odds than that emperor because, as an eight-year-old boy, he faced an Arab invasion already underway on the heels of a ruinous war that had left warlords in power over the body of the empire. The loss of the Roman war had shaken state authority root and branch, and the House of Sasan could not offer a suitable candidate who could arrest the body politic from its terminal decline. In part, this was due to the purge of the male children of Khusrow II by Kavad II. From among these men, a man of suitable temperament and energy may have emerged, but of such ifs and buts history is not made.

By the time Yazdergerd III was enthroned, the empire had devolved into competing factions, the leaders of which were unwilling to dance to the great king's tune. Between the death of Buran in 630 and the enthronement of Yazdegerd III, no fewer than six pretenders minted coins in various regions of the empire. These men were most likely the most prominent and ambitious of the *dehqans* of each region in which they operated. Multiple kinglets with their local armies siphoned troops from the forces of the great king and hoovered up taxes normally due his treasury. The situation was not unlike the days of the first Sasanian—a world of kinglets, regional strife, and parochial self-interest—that Ardashir had smashed when he had taken the hammer to the Parthian Empire of his day. The rot had reached the hull of the ship of state in an astonishing swiftness.

Around 690, a Syriac-speaking monk in Mesopotamia wrote a book detailing the history of the world from the creation to his own day. The days of the Arab conquests were fresh in the mind of the writer, John bar Penkaye, who explained the amazing success of the Arabs as part of God's plan:

> God put victory in their hands in such a way that the words written concerning them might be fulfilled, namely, "One man chased a thousand and two men routed ten thousand" (Deuteronomy 32:30). How, otherwise, could naked men, riding without armor or shield, have been able to win, apart from divine aid, God having called them from the ends of the earth so as to destroy . . . a sinful kingdom and to bring low . . . the proud spirit of the Persians.[1]

The question, settled in John's mind nearly 1,500 years ago, has nonetheless continued to perplex historians who have, over the past hundred years, once more looked seriously into the events and causes of the conquest. How did these "naked men, riding without armor or shield" defeat and destroy one of the greatest empires in world history in the Sasanians and very nearly do the same to the East Roman Empire?

At the peril of disagreeing with the sources, like those written by the monk John just quoted, we must dispel the myth of the "naked savage" as the centerpiece of the Arab conquests. To be certain, many of the townsmen and Bedouin who fought in the wars of the conquest were, even by the low material standards of the day, poor. Most Arab soldiers fought as infantry spearmen, and initially only a small percentage would have possessed armor or other weaponry. In material terms, the Arab armies of the day *were* at a disadvantage, but how much of a disadvantage? Not much, it seems, in light of what they were able to accomplish. This is, after all, an era where no army really possessed a significant technical advantage over another—certainly we must expel from our minds anything like the role that technology played in the wars of colonial conquest of the nineteenth century, where troops with repeating rifles and machine guns took on indigenous peoples armed with spears. Nothing of this sort of disparity separated the Arabs from the Persians or the Byzantines. Men fought face to face, hand to hand, and in this kind of deeply personal, bloody tête-à-tête, other factors matter at least as much as the soldier's equipment. After major clashes like Qadisiya and the siege(s) of

Ctesiphon, the disparity in armor, swords, and other equipment would have quickly vanished.

We must also dismiss the claims made in the Arabic sources that the Arab conquest armies were always outnumbered, fighting against tremendous odds and thus witnesses to a series of military miracles. While it may have been the case during the initial thrust into the alluvium of Iraq, the almost unbroken string of successes enjoyed by the Arabs undermines this claim. As the Sasanian Empire had largely fractured into competing factions, it is highly unlikely that the local nodes of resistance had the resources to marshal men and equipment in anything approaching parity with the invaders. Although it would be unorthodox to say so, and we introduce the perils of arguing against the sources, in most engagements the Arabs likely enjoyed numerical superiority, and in many fights their advantage in numbers was likely high. As news of their successes spread, people from all over the Arabian Peninsula rushed to the banners of the conquest armies. As I have noted, swelling the ranks of ethnic Arabs, as we have seen, were large numbers of deserters, both from the ranks of the Romans and the Persians as well. Many of these men brought with them considerable military experience, along with their equipment.

The example of Palmyra in the third century is instructive: in her confrontation with the emperor Aurelian, Zenobia of Palmyra was said to have mustered upward of seventy thousand troops, many of whom would have been drawn from the frontier regions from the Euphrates to the Red Sea. It is not much of a stretch to see in the mobilization of the peoples of the Arabian Peninsula a military potential on par with that which could be accessed by their sedentary rivals.

The Arabs of the seventh century were hardly babes in the woods of military conflict. Certainly, the Sasanians recognized that the tribesmen along their southern frontiers could be dangerous. Since the first days of the empire, the shahs had watched the deserts of Arabia with a wary eye. Shapur I undertook his punitive, murderous wars in the peninsula against the Arabs to cow them into a fear of Persian might, and it is clear that the lesson was not soon forgotten. Later shahs built up a series of linear defenses, manned by Persian frontier troops, to maintain order along this zone of uncertainty, where tribal groups made their homes and where Bedouin groups, fluid and impossible to effectively control, ranged at will. For centuries, then, the Arabs of north Arabia had contacts, through trade, raiding, and other interactions, with the settled empires of Rome and Persia, who, to be certain, stereotyped them as savages beneath contempt. Reality, of course, was vastly different.

When Persia and Rome both sponsored Arab clients along the limits of their empires, they acknowledged that Arabs were better able than they to police other Arabs. They also acknowledged that the settled empires, with their vastly greater wealth and thus much at stake, had to manage the threat of these people as well as exploit their advantages. The sixth-century wars against Rome, in which the Lakhmids of Hira played such a prominent role is the most salient example of this, but the presence of a dominant power to manage the north Arabian Desert goes back much further—to Palmyra in the third century, certainly. Thus, when Khusrow II dissolved the Lakhmid confederation, he did so in the mistaken belief that the Persians had nothing to fear from the tribes, ignoring the fact that history told elsewise. Lulled by the successes of their policies over the past centuries, the Persians came to believe that it was their power, rather than a combination of cooption through economic incentives and social prestige, backed by the reality of military force, which had created the relative equilibrium on the frontier. The instability that followed the dissolution of the great confederations of Ghassan and Lakhm should not be underestimated. Nor should it be forgotten that, like the old days of the Palmyrene kings, the Ghassanids and Lakhmids had occupied many of the fiercest and most capable warriors and managed them on behalf of their imperial masters.

One should recall that these forces were not inconsiderable. The Lakhmids could field five thousand cavalrymen during the wars with Justinian. Probably they also maintained infantry and garrison troops as well. Our scant sources focus on the image of the flying Arabian horsemen whose unpredictability of movement and action fascinated and appalled his settled contemporaries, as it would sedentary folk for centuries to come. More than a few of the Arab soldiers who fought in the wars of conquest had likely served in the imperial armies of their neighbors. As we have seen, even the dissolution of the Lakhmids and Ghassanid confederacies did not end the service of these tribal elements in the armies of the empire. Of those who did not serve in the armies of the empires, there were many who participated in frontier raids and skirmishes during the Roman-Sasanian war of the seventh century, which left the desert fringes easy pickings.

In battle, the Arabs showed sophisticated leadership, and their commanders adapted readily to new situations. They were quick to negotiate and generally avoided the kind of bone-grinding sieges that would have threatened their cohesion and success. While there are plenty of marvels to gape at in the case of the Arab conquests, several myths can be removed from the scene. In the Sasanians, the Arabs never faced a unified empire at anything like the peak of its power. Had the followers of the message of Muhammad entered the arena in the middle of the sixth century, they would likely have been swiftly dealt with. That they did not arise then and were not stopped until they reached the gates of Constantinople three quarters of a century later is one of the many reasons that history continues to hold our attention.

After the death of Yazdegerd III in 651, his sons fled to the eastern lands of the former empire and its periphery. The Turks of Tokharistan held Peroz (c. 677), the eldest son, hostage. After the Chinese army intervened against the Turks in 657, Chinese military power overwhelmed them. The Chinese then established a protectorate over the Turks, which ebbed and flowed in its ability to control these groups along the Silk Road. From 661–64, Peroz sent delegations to the court of the Chinese emperor Gaozong (649–683), direct contact enabled by the establishment of the Tang protectorate over the Kök Turks. In 670–674, during a personal journey to the court of Gaozong, Peroz pleaded for aid against the Muslims. Peroz, who was married to a Christian and apparently one himself, asked the emperor for permission to build a "Persian temple" in China, likely a Christian church. It also seems that Wahram, brother of Peroz, died after trying and failing to reclaim the lost lands of the Sasanians as well. In alliance with the Turks, Khusrow, son of Peroz, took part in a military expedition against the Muslims in Transoxiana, but the Arabs thwarted him as well.

Narseh, another son of Peroz, could not secure meaningful Chinese support in his endeavors against the Arabs. Sometime between 677 and 681, Narseh likely led several thousand of his supporters to the eastern frontiers of the Arab caliphate in a bid to retake his ancestral lands, but this effort came to naught and the Sasanian who would be king spent the next decades in Central Asia, likely among his Persian and Turkish allies who resisted the encroachment of the Arabs. Narseh returned to the Tang capital of Chang'an, where he died at an unknown date while still in the service of the Chinese emperor.

Memories of the splendor of the Sasanians died hard. Among the princely families that maintained a fair degree of autonomy within the Muslim caliphate, especially in the Iranian lands around the Caspian and Khurasan, where Arab influence was limited, stories of the deeds of the great kings circulated with a life of their own. Those loyal to the memories of the greatness of the kings of kings of the House of Sasan would see their stars wax with the arrival of the Abbasid caliphate in the eighth century and the subsequent rise of local dynasties in Iran which, while Muslim in religion, were Persian in language and outlook. In them the memory of the Sasanians lived on.

Notes

INTRODUCTION

1. James Howard-Johnston, "The late Sasanian army," in *Late Antiquity: Eastern Perspectives*, ed. Adam J. Silverstein and Teresa Bernheimer (Warminster, UK: Gibb Memorial Trust, 2012). On the organization and composition of the Sasanian army, see: Kaveh Farrokh, Gholamreza Karamian, and Katarzyna Maksymiuk, *A Synopsis of Sasanian Military Organization and Combat Units* (Publishing House of Siedlce University of Natural Sciences and Humanities, 2018).
2. Maurice, *Maurice's Strategikon: Handbook of Byzantine Military Strategy*, 114.
3. Ibid., emphasis mine.

CHAPTER ONE: THE RISE OF THE SASANIAN EMPIRE

1. Herodotus, 1.135.
2. Edward C. Echols, *Herodian of Antioch's History of the Roman Empire from the Death of Marcus Aurelius to the Accession of Gordian III* (Berkeley: University of California Press, 1961).
3. William Adler and Paul G Tuffin, *The Chronology of George Synkellos* (Oxford University Press, 2002), 547; Zonaras, 41.
4. Herodian, 6.2.5, trans. Echols.
5. David Frendo, "Cassius Dio and Herodian on the First Sasanian Offensive against the Eastern Provinces of the Roman Empire (229–232)," *Bulletin of the Asia Institute* 16 (2002).
6. The fifth-century Armenian source for this calls these nomads "Huns," which is clearly anachronistic, as the Huns did not appear on the scene until the fourth century. Probably he is referring to Sarmatians or Scythians.
7. Dinawari, trans. Bonner: http://www.mrjb.ca/current-projects/abu-hanifah-ahmad-ibn-dawud-al-dinawari.
8. Herodian, 6.5.9-10.
9. Herodian, 6.6.

CHAPTER TWO: THE GREAT KING

1. Richard Nelson Frye, *The History of Ancient Iran* (Munich: CH Beck, 1984), 371.
2. Mas'udi et al., *Les prairies d'or*, 159.
3. David Magie, *The Scriptores Historiae Augustae II* (Cambridge, MA: Harvard University Press, 1921-32), 429.
4. *Historiae Augustae* II, 431.
5. *Historiae Augustae* II, 433.

6. Eutropius, *Breviarium*, ed. H. Bird, (Liverpool: Liverpool University Press), 56.

7. Zosimus, 67.

8. *Encyclopaedia Iranica*, "Shapur I"; Frye, 371.

9. Or so claims Eusebius of Caesarea; the claim is not substantiated by other ancient sources, though Zonaras did seem to have more than one source in mind when he wrote of Philip's Christianity. If the emperor were a Christian, it may explain some of the animosity by contemporary historians, as the cult was considered a bizarre novelty.

10. Zonaras, 47.

11. Zonaras, 46.

12. Moses Khorenatsi, *History of the Armenians*, Michael H. Dodgeon and Samuel N. C. Lieu, eds., *The Roman Eastern Frontier and the Persian Wars A.D. 226–363: A Documentary History* (Abingdon-on-Thames: Routledge, 1994), 269.

13. Frye, 371.

14. The following discussion follows James, 2011.

15. John Malalas, 162.

16. Frye, 372.

17. Ibid.

18. Khorenatsi, *History of the Armenians*, 270.

19. Southern, 43.

20. Southern, 48.

21. R. T. Ridley, *Zosimus: New History*, 12.

22. Encyclopaedia Iranica, "Kushanshah," http://www.iranicaonline.org/articles/kushanshahs-01, accessed August 22, 2020.

23. Ghirshman, 1954, 342–43.

24. Encyclopaedia Iranica, "Kushan Dynasty i. Dynastic History." http://www.iranica online.org/articles/kushan-dynasty-i-history, accessed August 20, 2020.

CHAPTER THREE: THE CHALLENGE TO ROME

1. Mathisen, "DIR Diocletian," https://www.roman-emperors.org/dioclet.htm, accessed August 28, 2020.

2. Khorenatsi, *History of the Armenians*, 271. The Armenian historian mistakenly claims that the victory belonged to Hormozd Ardashir, but he had become the shahanshah after the death of Shapur and himself died in 271. It was likely that, upon the accession of Bahram I in 271, Narseh, as the highest-ranking of Shapur's sons, assumed the viceroyalty of Armenia at that time.

3. Aurelius Victor, *Liber de Caesaribus* 39, 22, Dodgeon and Lieu, 108.

4. Faustus Buzandats'i, *History of the Armenians*, Dodgeon and Lieu, 263.

5. Petrus Patricius, frag. 13, 188, Dodgeon and Lieu, 115.

6. Petrus Patricius, frag. 14, Dodgeon and Lieu, 116.

7. Chronicon a. 354, 145, 26–28, Dodgeon and Lieu, 117.

8. Encyclopaedia Iranica, "Hormozd II," https://iranicaonline.org/articles/hormozd-ii, accessed November 7, 2021.

9. Zotenberg, *Histoire rois*, 513.

10. Hoyland, *Kings of the Persians*, 66.

11. Tabari, V, 52.

12. Tabari, V, 54.

13. Tabari, V, 55.

14. Hoyland, *Kings of the Persians*, 63–64.

15. Frendo, "Constantine's Letter to Shapur II," 57.

16. Frendo, "Constantine's Letter to Shapur II," 59.

17. Libanius, *Orationes LIX*, 63–64, Dodgeon and Lieu, 137–38.

18. Barnes, "Constantine and the Christians of Persia," 132.

19. Barnes, "Constantine and the Christians of Persia," 132.

20. Other historians, I am aware, have very different interpretations of events in Armenia during these decades; the sources are gnarly: Hewsen, 1978-79, 99–108.

21. Marilungo, *Shaping Diyarbakir*, 56.

22. Libanius, *Orationes LIX*, 69-70, Dodgeon and Lieu, 138–39.

23. Ammianus Marcellinus, XXI, 16.19, 185.

24. Ammianus Marcellinus, XXI, 16.11, 180-81.

25. Ammianus Marcellinus, XXI, 16.9, 179.

26. Theodoret, *Historia religiosa* II, 11-12, Dodgeon and Lieu, 146.

27. Julian, Or. I trans. Wright 1, 97.

28. Encyclopaedia Iranica, "Chionites," citing Moses Khorenatsi, 2.89.

29. Moses Khorenatsi, *History of the Armenians*, tr. Thomson, 265.

30. Chronicle of Arbela, §14 translated Kröll, modified by author.

31. Ammianus Marcellinus, XVI, 9.1.

32. Ammianus Marcellinus, XVII, 5.4.

33. Ammianus Marcellinus, XVII, 5.14.

CHAPTER FOUR: CLASH OF EMPIRES

1. Ammianus Marcellinus, XVIII, 6.13–14, 441.

2. Ammianus Marcellinus, XVIII, 6.20, 447.

3. Ammianus Marcellinus, XVIII, 8.8.

4. The famous 115-mile march from Camp Toccoa to Atlanta was accomplished by Colonel Sink's 506th US Parachute Infantrymen in thirty-one hours. There is little reason to doubt that late imperial Roman legionnaires could match such a feat.

5. Ammianus Marcellinus, XIX, 1, 471.

6. Ammianus Marcellinus, XVIII, 6.22, 447–49.

7. Ammianus Marcellinus, XIX, 1.9, 475.

8. Ammianus Marcellinus, XIX, 7.8, 507.

9. Ammianus Marcellinus, XIX, 8.4, 511.

10. Ammianus Marcellinus, XXIII, 5.19, II, 347.

11. Ammianus Marcellinus, XXIV, 6.8, II, 467.

12. John Chrysostom, *de S. Babyla contra Julianum et Gentiles* XXII (122–4), quoted in Dodgeon and Lieu, 219.

13. Khorenatsi, *History of the Armenians*, 3.37, 296, slightly modified.

CHAPTER FIVE: THE FRONTIERS ERUPT

1. By the fifth-century eastern sources, like those in Armenian and Syriac, frequently refer to the Romans of the eastern lands as "Greeks," reflecting their Greek language and the heavy influence of Hellenic culture in those regions. In order to distinguish them from ancient Rome, historians have (improperly in the view of some, including this author), labeled them "Byzan-

tines," a term which I will use alongside "Roman" to denote these East Roman actors.

2. Ammianus Marcellinus, XXXI, 2.

3. Jerome: Thompson, 1996, 31.

4. Payne, "The Reinvention of Iran: The Sasanian Empire and the Huns," 288.

5. Daryaee, "History, Epic, and Numismatics," 91.

6. Asmussen, 1983, 940.

7. Christian views of Yazdegerd are generally favorable. Although his assertion is usually dismissed by scholars, the Christian historian Socrates insisted Yazdegerd did not persecute Christians during his reign, and it is entirely possible, probable even, that later historians, who did not have a firm grasp of the chronology of the last years of the king of kings' life, shifted the persecutions of Bahram onto his father. In this way, "the Sinner" became a convenient scapegoat for the war with the Romans that followed. The Sasanians clearly linked in their minds the treatment of Christians and the dubious loyalty of the latter with the troubles of the war of 421–22 (and later wars for that matter).

8. I have preferred here the idea that Bahram's brother is the Narse mentioned in the Greek sources; other historians follow Tabari and other eastern writers who identify this Narse as Mehr-Narseh, the vizier of Yazdegerd who apparently continued to serve Bahram. Among the fantasies that Tabari spins here is that the vizier, at the head of forty thousand horsemen, entered Constantinople.

9. As we have noted, the course of events of that war would not have permitted Bahram V to invest Theodosiopolis for more than thirty days, as reported by the Christian Theodoret. It could not have happened in 421, when Bahram was dealing with the Kidarites, nor can it be safely attributed to the campaign season of 422, when the king's movements are relatively well known and he was preoccupied with relieving the siege of Nisibis and the subsequent peace negotiations. The confusion is compounded by the existence of two cities bearing the name Theodosiopolis. While scholarly opinion tilts toward Theodosiopolis in Syria (modern Ras al-Ayn), the evidence is slender in support of this identification. The Armenian historian Ełishe (probably sixth century) makes it clear that Yazdegerd attacked the Romans in the second year of his reign, although he, too, is confused as to the geographical scope of the campaign. Moses of Khorene, writing in the fifth century, preserves alleged correspondence during overtures of the Armenian clergy and nobles at the time, and the general Anatolius, who facilitated the diplomatic exchange, was near the city of Melitene, which supports a station at Theodosiopolis or, the other great base of Roman power in the east, Amida, at the time.

10. Thomson, Vardan, 66.

11. Ghazar, tr. Bedrosian, §48; the chronology of the Armenian sources is confused; this episode is sometimes placed much later, at the end of the reign.

12. Priscus, *Exx. De Leg. Rom.* 8 ed. Blockley, 1983, 336–37.

13. Litvinsky, citing Lazar, 139.

14. Livtinsky, 139.

15. Warner and Warner VII, 166; in Firdowsi's medieval Persian, the Hepthalite title Akhshunwar was transformed into Khushnawaz "the beautiful player, musician." See Encyclopaedia Iranica, " UŠNAW R/ UŠNAW Z."

CHAPTER SIX: THE STRUGGLE WITH ROME

1. Zotenberg, 587.

2. The Oracle of Baalbek, ed/tr. Alexander, 118–20.

3. Trombley, ps. Joshua, 52, note 249.
4. Bogdanov, 15–16.
5. Trombley, ps. Joshua, 59-60; translation slightly modified.
6. Rossi et al., 86.
7. Chevedden, et al., *The Traction Trebuchet*, 440.
8. This is ps. Zachariah of Melitene's name for him, elsewhere he is called Adergoudounbades, see Encyclopaedia Iranica, "Adergoudounbades."
9. Greatrex and Lieu, 68.
10. Ibid.
11. Trombley, ps. Joshua, 80.
12. On the effectiveness of slings and slingers and what follows, see C. Harrison's "The Sling in Medieval Europe," *Bulletin of Primitive Technology* 31 (2006): 29–34.
13. Diodorus Siculus XIX, 109, tr. R.M. Geer, slightly modified.
14. Harrison, "The Sling."
15. Kurbanov, *The Hepthalites*, 170.
16. Procopius Wars, 1.xvii, 40–43, translated Dewing, slightly modified.
17. Accepting the argument of K.I. Maksyumiuk that the Romans mistook the name of the Mihr-Mihran family as a title and that one of the Mihr-Mihrans identified in western sources was Shapur of Rayy, who was instrumental in establishing Kavad on the throne at the start of his second reign, we might argue that Procopius was partly right: the *mirranes* at Dara (Mihr-Mihran, that is member of the Mihran clan) was named Firuz. This Firuz was probably the son of Shapur of Rayy, the supreme commander of the Sasanian army at the time, and the Mihr-Mihran who led the Sasanians at Satala later in 530.
18. Procopius Wars I.xiii., 32.
19. Wars, I.xiv., 5.
20. Wars, I.xviii., 39-40.

CHAPTER SEVEN: DEFENDING THE EMPIRE
1. Encyclopaedia Iranica, "Spahbed."
2. Agathias, tr. Frendo 3.17, 6–9, slightly adapted.
3. Bivar, 276, citing Tabari I/2, p. 964, tr., 262–63.
4. The date of the establishment of these works has been dated as early as Alexander the Great in the fourth century BC or as late as the Sasanian period.
5. Procopius, tr. Dewing, II.v1.
6. Procopius, tr. Dewing, VIII.xiv.35-38, 201–3.
7. Procopius, tr. Dewing, II.xvii.31-35, 511.
8. Alongside the Huns came people from Balkh, Shughnan (a region which today straddles the northeastern Afghan-Tajik border), Amol, Zamm (Kerki in Turkmenistan) on the south bank of the Oxus, Khuttal (the region between the Hissar Mountains in the north and the Panj River in the south), Termez (on the north bank of the Oxus), and Washgird (on the Oxus between Zamm and Tirmidh): see UNESCO Civilizations Central Asia III Litvinsky and Zamir Safi, 176.
9. Whether before or after the campaign of 573 is unknown.
10. John of Ephesus, Eccl. Hist. VI.5, tr. Payne Smith, 379.
11. John of Ephesus, Eccl. Hist. VI.10, tr. Payne Smith, 401.
12. Theophylact Simocatta, iii.6.10-11, tr. Whitby and Whitby.

13. Tabari, tr. Bosworth, volume V, *The Sasanids, the Byzantines, the Lakhmids, and Yemen*, 297.

14. An honorific; his real name is unknown.

15. If the Sasanian field army numbered seventy thousand, as Tabari asserts, cf. above, 302.

16. Nihayat al-Arab, 450.

17. Tabari, tr. Bosworth, modified, 305.

18. Moses Daskhurantsi, *History of the Caucasian Albanians*, tr. Dowsett, 90.

19. Boethius, *Consolation of Philosophy* II.40-45, tr. Steward and Rand, modified, 175.

20. The Chronicle of 1234 tells us that, on hearing of Maurice's death, Khusrow dressed in the black of mourning.

CHAPTER EIGHT: THE LAST GREAT WAR OF ANTIQUITY

1. The Syriac sources call him Rumiazan: Chronicle of 1234, ed.tr. Chabot, 174.

2. See Hoyland, Theophilus of Edessa, p. 55 n. 51, for localization of the battle.

3. Rance, "Elephants," 373–74, Ełishe, tr. Thomson, 166–67.

4. Rance, "Elephants," 379–82; Tabari, tr. Blankinship, 109–10.

5. Sebeos, tr. Thomson, 61.

6. Anti-Chalcedonians were so called for their resistance to the creed imposed following the Council of Chalcedon in 451, which declared that Christ had two natures, one human and one divine, according to a formula worked out by Leo, the bishop of Rome (440–61). Nestorians followed the teachings of Nestorius (ca. 386–ca. 450).

7. Many secondary authors place the capture of Caesarea in 610, but the Armenian Sebeos, one of our best sources of the period, places the fall of the city to the Sasanians in 608/09, Sebeos, tr. Thomson, 64. I follow here Howard-Johnston, who places the fall of Caesarea in 611: Sebeos, tr. Thomson, 202.

8. Sophronius, *Anacr.* 14.69.105-6, tr. Greatrex and Lieu, 191, slightly adapted.

9. Sebeos, tr. Thomson, 52, modified.

10. Howard-Johnston, Encyclopaedia Iranica, "Khosrow II," https://iranicaonline.org/articles/khosrow-ii, accessed November 7, 2021.

11. MSyr, tr. Hoyland, *Theophilus of Edessa*, 67, modified.

12. The best reconstruction, followed here, is expertly analyzed by Howard-Johnston, "Heraclius' Persian Campaigns." This author's new book, *The Last Great War of Antiquity*, appeared after the present manuscript went to press and could therefore not be consulted.

13. Doswett, tr., *The History of the Caucasian Albanians*, 79.

14. Job 4:9 (KJV).

15. This is the likely scenario, as argued by Howard-Johnston, "The Siege of Constantinople," 133.

16. Theophanes AM 6116 in Greatrex and Lieu, 206.

17. Doswett, tr., *The History of the Caucasian Albanians*, 89.

18. Tabari, volume 5, tr. Bosworth, 323.

19. Doswett, tr., *The History of the Caucasian Albanians*, 89.

20. Doswett, tr., *The History of the Caucasian Albanians*, 88.

CHAPTER NINE: THE MUSLIM CONQUEST

1. Doswett, tr., *The History of the Caucasian Albanians*, 97. There are disagreements about when to place this incident, which occurred in the time of the Catholicate of Viroy (596–630) when he was restored by the "newly crowned" King Kavad II (r. 628). Viroy, who had been under

arrest in Ctesiphon, returned to Albania probably in the spring of 629 when already Kavad II had perished and Queen Boran ruled.

2. Hoyland, *In God's Path*, 50.

3. Qu'ran 112.3, tr. Shakir. The Arab conquests are the source of endless puzzlement and debate among scholars.

4. Sebeos, *The Armenian History attributed to Sebeos*, 245.

5. 637 or even later is also possible. After the initial advance of Khalid it is possible that the Arabs had advanced as far as the capital of Ctesiphon.

6. Shahnameh, tr. Davis, Vol. III, 492–96.

7. Hugh Kennedy, *The Great Arab Conquests: How the Spread of Islam Changed the World We Live In* (Philadelphia: Da Capo, 2007), 131–32.

8. Baladhuri, *The origins of the Islamic state, being a translation from the Arabic, accompanied with annotations, geographic and historic notes of the Kitâb futûh al-buldân of al-Imâm Abu-l `Abbâs, Ahmad ibn-Jâbir al-Balâdhuri*, 420.

9. Maurice, *Maurice's Strategikon*, 115.

10. Tabari, Juynboll, 208.

11. Tabari, Juynboll, 210.

12. G.R. Smith, Tabari (1994), 22.

13. G.R. Smith, Tabari (1994), 23.

EPILOGUE

1. Sebastian P. Brock, "North Mesopotamia in the Late Seventh Century: Book XV of John Bar Penkaye's Riš Mell '," *Jerusalem Studies in Arabic and Islam* 9 (1987).

Bibliography

Adler, William, and Paul G Tuffin. *The Chronology of George Synkellos*. Oxford University Press, 2002.

Baladhuri, Ahmad ibn Yahyá. *The Origins of the Islamic State, Being a Translation from the Arabic, Accompanied with Annotations, Geographic and Historic Notes of the Kitâb Futûh Al-Buldân of Al-Imâm Abu-L `Abbâs, Ahmad Ibn-Jâbir Al-Balâdhuri*. Translated by Philip K Hitti and Francis Clark Murgotten. New York: Columbia University Press, 1916.

Brock, Sebastian P. "North Mesopotamia in the Late Seventh Century: Book Xv of John Bar Penkaye's Riš Mell '." *Jerusalem Studies in Arabic and Islam* 9 (1987): 51–75.

Echols, Edward C. *Herodian of Antioch's History of the Roman Empire from the Death of Marcus Aurelius to the Accession of Gordian Iii*. Berkeley: University of California Press, 1961.

Farrokh, Kaveh, Gholamreza Karamian, and Katarzyna Maksymiuk. *A Synopsis of Sasanian Military Organization and Combat Units*. Publishing House of Siedlce University of Natural Sciences and Humanities, 2018.

Frendo, David. "Cassius Dio and Herodian on the First Sasanian Offensive against the Eastern Provinces of the Roman Empire (229–232)." *Bulletin of the Asia Institute* 16 (2002): 25–36.

Frye, Richard Nelson. *The History of Ancient Iran*. Munich: CH Beck, 1984.

Howard-Johnston, James. "The Late Sasanian Army." In *Late Antiquity: Eastern Perspectives*, edited by Adam J. Silverstein and Teresa Bernheimer, 87-127. Warminster, UK: Gibb Memorial Trust, 2012.

Kennedy, Hugh. *The Great Arab Conquests: How the Spread of Islam Changed the World We Live In*. Philadelphia: Da Capo, 2007.

Magie, David. *The Scriptores Historiae Augustae Ii.* Cambridge, Mass.: Harvard University Press, 1921–32.

Mas'udi, C. Barbier de Meynard, Abel Pavet de Courteille, and Charles Pellat. *Les Prairies D'or.* Paris: Société asiatique, 1861–1917.

Maurice. *Maurice's Strategikon: Handbook of Byzantine Military Strategy.* Translated by George Dennis. Philadelphia: University of Pennsylvania Press, 1984.

Sebeos. *The Armenian History Attributed to Sebeos.* Translated by R.W. Thomson; historical commentary by James Howard-Johnston; assistance from Tim Greenwood. Translated Texts for Historians. Liverpool: Liverpool University Press, 1998.

Index